Melville Madison Bigelow

Elements of the Law of Bills, Notes and Cheques

And the English Bills of Exchange Act - For Students

Melville Madison Bigelow

Elements of the Law of Bills, Notes and Cheques
And the English Bills of Exchange Act - For Students

ISBN/EAN: 9783337111861

Printed in Europe, USA, Canada, Australia, Japan

Cover: Foto ©Suzi / pixelio.de

More available books at **www.hansebooks.com**

ELEMENTS

OF THE LAW OF

BILLS, NOTES, AND CHEQUES

AND THE

ENGLISH BILLS OF EXCHANGE ACT

For Students

BY

MELVILLE M. BIGELOW, Ph.D. Harvard

BOSTON
LITTLE, BROWN, AND COMPANY
1893

Copyright, 1893,
BY MELVILLE M. BIGELOW.

University Press:
JOHN WILSON AND SON, CAMBRIDGE, U.S.A.

TO

THE RT. HON. SIR EDWARD FRY,

IN WHOSE RETIREMENT FROM THE BENCH
ENGLISH JURISPRUDENCE EVERYWHERE
SUFFERS LOSS.

NOTE.

The English Bills of Exchange Act, 1882, forms the last chapter of this book. For purposes of comparison, and, wherever the American Law is incomplete, uncertain, or unsatisfactory, for purposes of suggestion, the statute will be found helpful.

A Selection of Cases, following the order of the text, will soon be issued as a companion volume.

The reference 'L. C.,' of the notes, signifies Bigelow's Leading Cases on Bills and Notes.

August 15, 1893.

CONTENTS.

		PAGE
CASES CITED	. . . .	ix

CHAPTER		
I.	INTRODUCTION	1
II.	PHYSICAL REQUISITES	10
III.	THE MAKER'S CONTRACT	27
IV.	THE ACCEPTOR'S CONTRACT	36
V.	THE DRAWER'S CONTRACT	47
VI.	THE INDORSER'S CONTRACT	61
VII.	INDORSER'S CONTRACT CONTINUED: PROCEEDINGS BEFORE DISHONOR	81
VIII.	INDORSER'S CONTRACT CONTINUED: PROCEEDINGS UPON DISHONOR	106
IX.	INDORSER'S CONTRACT CONTINUED: EXCUSE OF STEPS	143
X.	ACCOMMODATION CONTRACTS	157
XI.	CONTRACTS OF GUARANTOR AND OF SURETY	161
XII.	HOLDER'S POSITION	170
XIII.	LEGAL OR ABSOLUTE DEFENCES	174
XIV.	EQUITIES	206
XV.	DISCHARGE OF SURETY: DEALINGS WITH PRINCIPAL DEBTOR	231
XVI.	PAYMENT	242
XVII.	CONFLICT OF LAWS	249
XVIII.	ENGLISH BILLS OF EXCHANGE ACT . .	256

INDEX	. . . .	305

CASES CITED.

A.

	PAGE
Abel v. Sutton	65
Adams v. Blethen	69
v. Frye	184
v. King	13
Ætna Ins. Co. v. Winchester	190
Akers v. Demond	252
Aldous v. Cornwell	182
Aldrich v. Smith	181
Alexander v. Burchfield	56
Allaire v. Hartshorne	229, 230
Allen v. Brown	235
v. Kemble	255
v. King	51
v. Merchants' Bank	253
Alvey v. Reed	201
American Bank v. Blanchard	21
Anderson v. Drake	85
Andrew v. Blackly	53
Andrews v. Boyd	147
v. Franklin	23
v. German Nat. Bank	57
Angle v. Northwestern Ins. Co.	227
Armstrong v. Armstrong	27
v. Christiani	114
v. Thruston	118
Arnold v. Cheque Bank	176, 178, 179, 192, 193, 195
v. Dresser	82, 84, 104, 150
v. Kulloch	118
Arnot v. Woodburn	228
Arpin v. Owens	39
Ashcroft v. De Armond	201
Atkinson v. Brooks	219, 220, 236
Attorney-Gen. v. Continental Ins. Co.	20
Attwood v. Rattenbury	65
Auerbach v. Pritchett	15

	PAGE
Austin v. Curtis	218, 220, 237
Ayer v. Tilden	252
Aymar v. Sheldon	252, 253

B.

Backus v. Shipherd	152
Bailey v. Dozier	109
v. Smith	229
Baker v. Stone	201
Ballou v. Talbot	31
Banbury v. Lisset	20
Bange v. Flint	229
Bank of Alexandria v. Swann	110, 138
Bank of America v. Woodworth	195
Bank of Columbia v. Lawrence	142
Bank of Commerce v. Union Bank	188
Bank of England v. Vagliano	178, 186
Bank of Ireland v. Evans Charities	177, 192
Bank of New York v. Vanderhorst	220
Bank of Old Dominion v. McVeigh	110, 138
Bank of Red Oak v. Orvis	86, 104
Bank of Republic v. Carrington	217
Bank of United States v. Bank of Georgia	200
v. Carneal	119
v. Daniel	6, 108
v. Davis	134
v. Dunn	67
Bank of Utica v. Bender	131, 140, 142
v. Phillips	137, 138
Bank of Washington v. Triplett	59

CASES CITED.

	PAGE
Barclay v. Bailey	99
Bardsley v. Delp	215
Barlow v. Bishop	77, 199
v. Congregational Society	32
Barnwell v. Mitchell	141
Barron v. Cady	239
Bartlett v. Wells	201
Barton v. Baker	104, 155
Bassenhorst v. Wilby	91, 92, 134, 152
Bassett v. Avery	228
v. Haines	38
Baxendale v. Bennett	176, 178
Baxter v. Little	228
Bay v. Coddington	215
v. Shrader	195
Bayley v. Taber	203
Beale v. Parrish	142
Beals v. Peck	122
Bean v. Arnold	145
Beard v. Dedolph	26, 62
v. Westerman	147
Belcher v. Smith	70, 167
Belknap v. National Bank	190
Bell v. Alexander	54
Bellamy v. Majoribanks	295
Benedict v. Cowden	195
Benoist v. Creditors	50
Benthall v. Hildreth	195
Berkshire Bank v. Jones	152, 154
Berridge v. Fitzgerald	137
Berry v. Robinson	134
Bertrand v. Barkman	215
Beuerman v. Van Buren	217
Bickford v. First Nat. Bank	57
Bigelow v. Colton	35, 67
Bikerdike v. Bollman	49
Bird v. Le Blanc	145
Bishop v. Dexter	134
Bissenthall v. Williams	12
Black v. Ward	16
Blakely v. Grant	167
Blakey v. Johnson	183, 227
Blanckenhagen v. Blundell	14
Blodgett v. Durgin	88
Bond v. Farnham	147
Born v. First Nat. Bank	56, 57
Bouldin v. Page	122
Boulton v. Walsh	113, 114
Bower v. Hastings	225
Bowling v. Harrison	124, 127

	PAGE
Boyd v. Cummings	220
v. McCann	228
Bradlaugh v. De Rin	250, 251
Bray v. Hadwen	133, 134
Bridges v. Winters	182
Brill v. Crick	195
Britton v. Dierker	183
Brooks v. Allen	183, 190
v. Blaney	86, 88
v. Elkins	12
Brown v. Butchers' Bank	10, 25, 63
v. Donnell	203
v. Leavitt	220
v. McHugh	26, 62
v. Maffey	49
v. Olmsted	221
v. Reed	187, 195
Bryant v. Wilcox	144
Buchanan v. Marshall	152
Buckner v. Finley	107
Burchfield v. Moore	184, 187
Burke v. Allen	201, 202
v. McKay	102, 103
Burkhalter v. Second Nat. Bank	55, 56
Burley v. Russell	201
Burmester v. Barron	141
Burns v. Rowland	219
Burson v. Huntington	176, 178, 227
Butler v. Paine	16
Byrne v. Becker	218

C.

Came v. Brigham	202
Cameron v. Chappell	211
Canal Bank v. Bank of Albany	195, 196
Capital Bank v. Armstrong	192
Capron v. Capron	25
Carew v. Duckworth	52, 53
Carpenter v. Farnsworth	14
v. Reynolds	146
Carr v. Rowland	34
Carrier v. Sears	201
Carroll v. Upton	141, 142
Carter v. Burley	109
v. Union Bank	102
Caruthers v. West	225

CASES CITED.

	PAGE
Case *v.* Spaulding	73
Catlett *v.* Catlett	27
Caulkins *v.* Whistler	180
Central Bank *v.* Hammett	243
Chaddock *v.* Vanness	73
Chadwick *v.* Jeffers	134
Champion *v.* Ulmer	180
Chandler *v.* Drew	228
Chanoine *v.* Fowler	119
Chapman *v.* Keane	120
v. Rose	178
Charles *v.* Denio	67
v. Marden	225
Chatham Bank *v.* Allison	252
Cheshire *v.* Taylor	147
Chester *v.* Dorr	225
Chicopee Bank *v.* Chapin	230
v. Philadelphia Bank	82, 83, 177
Childs *v.* Laflin	88, 89
Chipman *v.* Tucker	176
Chism *v.* Toomer	187
Chouteau *v.* Webster	139
Church *v.* Barlow	134
Citizens Bank *v.* Richmond	187
City Bank *v.* Cutler	102, 108
Clapp *v.* Hanson	80
v. Rice	35
Claridge *v.* Dalton	51
Clark *v.* Eldridge	118
v. Pease	223, 224
v. Whiting	69
Clews *v.* Bank of New York	188
Cline *v.* Guthrie	180
Clonston *v.* Barbiere	33
Clute *v.* Small	182
Cocke *v.* Bank of Tennessee	123
Cockrill *v.* Kirkpatrick	15, 16
Coddington *v.* Davis	146, 147, 154
Coffman *v.* Bank of Kentucky	254
v. Campbell	21
Coggill *v.* American Bank	196
Cohen *v.* Teller	200
Cohns *v.* Bank of Tennessee	109
Collott *v.* Haigh	240
Commercial Bank *v.* Varnum	108
Comstock *v.* Hier	215
Conner *v.* Routh	10
Cony *v.* Wheelock	65
Cook *v.* Baldwin	38

	PAGE
Cook *v.* Lister	247
Coolidge *v.* Payson	44, 45
Cooper *v.* Meyer	196
v. Waldegrave	255
Corbett *v.* Clark	20
Corby *v.* Weddle	178
Cornell *v.* Nebeker	195
Cottrell *v.* Conklin	70
Coulter *v.* Richmond	33
Course *v.* Shackleford	134
Coursin *v.* Ledlie	20
Cowling *v.* Altman	212
Crandell *v.* First Nat. Bank	184
Crawford *v.* Branch Bank	117
Crawshay *v.* Collins	64
Creamer *v.* Perry	148
Crist *v.* Crist	63
Crocker *v.* Getchell	118, 134
Cromer *v.* Platt	118
Cromwell *v.* Sac	228, 229
Crosby *v.* Grant	212
Cummings *v.* Boyd	215
Currie *v.* Nind	213
Currier *v.* Lockwood	11
Curtis *v.* Brown	39
v. Goodenow	182
v. Leavitt	202
v. Mohr	221

D.

	PAGE
Dabney *v.* Stidger	123
Dale *v.* Gear	67, 73
Dana *v.* Sawyer	98
Davis *v.* Brown	67, 80
v. Clarke	37
v. McCready	211
Deblieux *v.* Bullard	133
Denison *v.* Tyson	16
Dennistown *v.* Stewart	109
Develing *v.* Ferris	147
Dewey *v.* Washburn	16
DeWitt *v.* Walton	31
Dewolf *v.* Murray	117
Dickins *v.* Beal	48, 49, 50
Dickinson *v.* Edwards	252, 254
Dietrich *v.* Bayhi	17
Dole *v.* Gold	118
Donegan *v.* Wood	102

Doolittle v. Ferry	67
Douglass v. Wilkeson	66
Downer v. Cheseborough	73
v. Remer	136
Drake v. Henly	80
v. Markle	16
Draper v. Ward	181, 185, 186, 187
Dresser v. Missouri Const. Co.	225
v. Missouri Ry. Co.	229
Dumont v. Williamson	68
Dunavan v. Flynn	40
Dunbar v. Tyler	143
Duncan v. Gilbert	224
v. McCullough	88
Dundas v. Bowler	254
Dunlop v. Silver	4
Dunn v. Adams	253
Durden v. Smith	143
Duvall v. Farmers' Bank	145
Dyer v. Rosenthal	217

E.

Eagle Bank v. Hathaway	125
Eaton v. McMahon	67
Ecfert v. Des Coudres	134
Eckert v. Cameron	243
Edwards v. Jones	229
v. Thomas	139
Eigenbrun v. Smith	218
Eilbert v. Finkbeiner	34
Ellis v. Ohio Ins. Co.	198
Emmons v. Meeker	183
Erwin v. Downs	77, 78, 119
Essex Bank v. Russell	220
Estabrook v. Smith	64
Etheridge v. Ladd	84
Etting v. Schuylkill Bank	118
Evans v. Underwood	28
Everard v. Watson	114
Exchange Bank v. Rice	44, 45

F.

Fairchild v. Ogdensburgh R. R. Co.	52
Fales v. Russell	149
Farmers' Bank v. Allen	107
v. Butchers' Bank	45, 46, 201
v. Gunnell	142, 143
v. Rathbone	30, 240, 247, 248
Farnsworth v. Allen	99
Farrell v. Lovett	212
Farrington v. Sexton	218
Fenouille v. Hamilton	215
Fentum v. Pocock	240
Ferris v. Bond	14
First National Bank v. Gay	18
v. Hall	65
v. Leach	56, 57
v. McAllister	217
v. National Marine Bank	73
v. Ricker	199
v. Whitman	56
Fisher v. Fisher	217
Fletcher v. Blodgett	195
v. Chase	220
Foard v. Womack	49, 51
Folger v. Chase	70
Foltz v. Powrie	65
Foster v. Julien	88, 151, 154
v. Mackinnon	37, 176, 180
v. Parker	149, 155
Fowler v. Strickland	229
Fralick v. Norton	17
Frank v. Wessels	15
Franklin Sav. Inst. v. Reed	195
Frazer v. Jordan	240
Freeman v. Boynton	88
v. Brittin	79
v. O'Brien	145, 146
Fry v. Hill	91
Furze v. Sharwood	113, 114, 119

G.

Gardner v. Walsh	184
Garr v. Louisville Banking Co.	17
Garrard v. Haddan	187
Gates v. Beecher	104, 105
Gawtry v. Doane	137, 140
Geary v. Physic	10, 25
George v. Surrey	26
Gerrish v. Glines	195
Gibbs v. Fremont	254

CASES CITED. xiii

	PAGE
Gibbs v. Linabury	178, 180
Gibson v. Connor	217
v. Tobey	221
Gilbert v. Dennis	116
Gilchrist v. Donnell	139
Gill v. Cubitt	209
Gillispie v. Cammack	51
Gist v. Lybrand	88, 151
Gladwell v. Turner	131, 132
Glover v. Robbins	183
Good v. Martin	34
Goodell v. Bates	200
Goodenow v. Curtis	182
Goodman v. Harvey	209
v. Simonds	210, 212
Goodnow v. Warren	122, 123
Goshen Turnpike v. Hurtin	25
Gough v. Staats	56
Gould v. Robson	236
Goupy v. Harden	91
Gove v. Vining	144
Gowan v. Jackson	122
Gower v. Moore	96, 97, 104, 153
Graham v. Adams	15
Grant v. Ellicott	224, 226
v. Hunt	44
v. Wood	23
Gray v. Bell	134
Greenfield Bank v. Stowell	187, 190, 191, 192, 193, 194, 227
Greenough v. Smead	34, 35, 104
Griffin v. Kemp	54
v. Weatherby	20
Grimshaw v. Bender	6
Grocers' Bank v. Penfield	219
Grosvenor v. Stone	50
Grugeon v. Smith	113

H.

Hagey v. Hill	234, 238
Haines v. Dennett	79
Hale v. Burr	96, 97, 153, 155
Halifax Union v. Wheelwright	193
Hall v. Bradbury	104
v. Fuller	193
v. Newcomb	33, 70, 166
v. Steel	40

	PAGE
Hamilton v. Hooper	184
v. Spottiswoode	13
Hare v. Heaty	101
Harker v. Anderson	91
Harmer v. Steele	243
Harness v. Davies	48, 49
Harris v. Clark	104
v. Memphis Bank	138
Harrison v. Courtauld	240
v. McKim	67
v. Ruscoe	121
Hartley v. Case	113
Hascall v. Whittmore	228
Haskell v. Champion	184
v. Lambert	21
Hatcher v. McMorine	252
Hawkins v. Watkins	15
Hedger v. Steavenson	113, 114
Helmer v. Krolich	18, 24
Henrietta Bank v. State Bank	45
Herbage v. McEntee	34
Hersey v. Elliot	63
Hervey v. Harvey	182
Heywood v. Perrin	195
v. Pickering	6, 54
Hibernia Bank v. Lacombe	252
Hildreth v. Shepard	254
Hill v. Ely	67, 73
Hoffman v. Smith	51
Holcomb v. Wyckoff	230
Holland v. Cruft	218
Holman v. Hobson	230
Holmes v. Kidd	212
v. Trumper	183, 187, 192, 193, 194
v. Williams	205
Hopkins v. Adams	149
Hopkirk v. Page	48, 49
Horne v. Redfearn	11
v. Rouquette	253, 254
Horst v. Wagner	185
Horton v. Buffinton	205
Hortsman v. Henshaw	189, 195, 196
Hough v. Loring	40
House v. Adams	60
Housum v. Rogers	221
Howard v. Ives	128
Hubbard v. Matthews	123
v. Morely	18, 24
Humphreys v. Gwillow	183, 187

CASES CITED.

	PAGE
Humphries v. Chastain	65
Hunt v. Hall	252
v. Maybee	102
v. Standart	253
Husband v. Epling	23
Huse v. Hamblin	253
Hyslop v. Jones	135

I.

Ireland v. Kip	137
Iron Mountain Bank v. Murdock	192
Irvine v. Lowry	15
Iser v. Cohen	67
Isnard v. Torres	192

J.

Jacobs v. Benson	13
Jaffrey v. Cornish	221
James v. Hackley	221
Jefts v. York	34
Jewell v. Parr	225
v. Wright	254
Johnson v. Cleaves	221
v. Frisbie	18
v. Heagan	195
Jones v. Bank of Iowa	44
v. Broadhurst	247
v. Fales	16
v. Gordon	210, 229
v. Heiliger	54
v. Thorn	64
v. Wardell	126
Jordaine v. Lashbrooke	79
Juniata Bank v. Hale	110, 148

K.

Kearsley v. Cole	234, 235
Keene v. Beard	53, 54, 64
Keith v. Goodwin	184
Kelley v. Hemmingway	20
Kelly v. Brooklyn	20
Kellogg v. Barton	225
v. Steiner	176, 178

	PAGE
Kendrick v. Lomax	236
Kennedy v. Lancaster Bank	183
Kilgore v. Jordan	201
Kimball v. Huntington	11
King v. Crowell	84, 86, 128, 150
v. Doolittle	215
v. Hoare	29
v. Holmes	86
Kinsley v. Robinson	51
Kinyon v. Stanton	54
Kirtland v. Wanzer	108, 109
Klauber v. Biggerstaff	12, 15
Knight v. Pugh	224
Konig v. Bayard	42
Koons v. Davis	200
Kountz v. Kennedy	185
Kramer v. Sandford	147, 148
Krause v. Meyer	185

L.

Lafitte v. Slatter	51
Lamar v. Brown	183
Lambert v. Ghiselin	142
Lancaster Bank v. Taylor	26, 62
Landry v. Stansberry	96, 153
Lane v. Bank of West Tennessee	143, 149
v. Steward	152
Langenberger v. Kroeger	190
Langton v. Lazarus	189
Lawrence v. Miller	141
Lawson v. Farmers' Bank	130, 131, 134
Laxton v. Peat	240
Lay v. Wissman	229, 230
Leavitt v. Putnam	67, 68, 92, 225
Lebel v. Tucker	250, 251
LeBreton v. Pierce	217
Ledwick v. McKim	227
Lee v. Smead	215
Leftley v. Mills	102, 109
Leggett v. Raymond	156
Lehman v. Jones	88, 151, 154
Lewis v. Brehme	146
Light v. Kingsbury	91
Linderman v. Guldin	123
Little v. Phenix Bank	15, 54

CASES CITED.

	PAGE
Little v. Slackford	13
Lochnane v. Emmerson	183
Lockwood v. Crawford	118, 134
Logan v. Smith	221
Loos v. Wilkinson	218
Lowe v. Bliss	18
Lowery v. Scott	141
Lunt v. Adams	100
v. Silver	184
Lysaght v. Bryant	121

M.

McDonald v. Bailey	145
McDowell v. Keller	15
McEvers v. Mason	45
McGee v. Prouty	242
McGrath v. Clark	192
McKinney v. Crawford	134
McKleroy v. Southern Bank	198
McLemore v. Powell	237
McRaven v. Crisler	182
McVeigh v. Allen	138
Magoun v. Walker	109
Magruder v. Union Bank	110, 148
Main v. Lynch	218
Maitland v. Citizens' Bank	219
Malden Bank v. Baldwin	86, 87
Manchester Bank v. Fellows	127, 132, 134
Manley v. Geagan	39
Manrow v. Durham	166
Marden v. Babcock	214
Marion v. Clark	228
Marsh v. Burr	137
v. Griffin	183
Marshall v. Mitchell	147
Mason v. Franklin	59, 85
v. Pritchard	141
Mathewson v. Strafford Bank	123
Matthews v. Allen	146, 147
Matthey v. Gally	152
Mattison v. Marks	18, 24
May v. Kelley	37
v. Quimby	215
Mayhew v. Boyd	238
Mechanics' Bank v. Merchants' Bank	83
Mellish v. Rawdon	91

	PAGE
Merchants' Bank v. State Bank	45, 46
Merchants' Ins. Co. v. Abbott	217
Merchants of the Staple v. Bank of England	176, 192
Merriam v. Cunningham	201
Merritt v. Duncan	209
Metropolitan Nat. Bank v. Jones	57
Meyer v. Hibsher	87
Michaud v. Lagarde	154
Michigan Bank v. Leavenworth	219, 220, 236
Middleton Bank v. Morris	91
Miller v. Austin	12
v. Farmers' Bank	140
v. Gilleland	182
v. Thompson	52
Mills v. Bank of United States	110, 115
Minet v. Gibson	196
Minot v. Russ	55, 56
Miser v. Trovinger	122
Mitchell v. Hewitt	16
Mohawk Bank v. Broderick	53, 56
Montelius v. Charles	90
Moore v. Baird	229
v. Ryder	219
Mordecai v. Dawkins	205
Morehead v. Parkersburg Bank	187
Morgan v. Davison	99
Morley v. Culverwell	243
Mornyer v. Cooper	228
Morris v. Bethell	200
Morrison v. McCartney	54
Morse v. Huntington	234
Morton v. Westcott	136
Mott v. Hicks	202
Mullman v. D'Eguino	91
Munn v. Baldwin	126
Mussey v. Eagle Bank	45, 46
Musson v. Lake	82, 107
Mutual Nat. Bank v. Rotge	57
Myer v. Hart	18
Myrick v. Hasey	71, 166

N.

National Bank of N. A. v. Bangs	199
National Com'l Bank v. Miller	56

CASES CITED.

	PAGE
Nave v. Richardson	107
Nazro v. Fuller	184
Nebeker v. Cutsinger	195
Neff v. Horner	187
Nelson v. Fotterall	102
Newcomb v. Raynor	233
Newell v. Holton	80
New York Co. v. Selma Sav. Bank	122
Nutter v. Stover	215, 220
Niagara Bank v. Fairman Manuf. Co.	85
Nichols v. Norris	240
Nicholson v. Gouthit	104
Nickerson v. Sheldon	17
Nicolls v. Webb	108, 109
Northern Bank v. Porter	203
Nunez v. Dautel	23

O.

Oates v. First National Bank	218, 219
Ocean Bank v. Fant	84
v. Williams	102, 107
Okie v. Spencer	236
Ontario Bank v. Petrie	118
Orear v. McDonald	48, 50, 51
Oridge v. Sherborne	66, 94
Oriental Bank v. Blake	96, 97, 153, 155
Orr v. Maginnis	107
Osgood v. Pearsons	14
Otsego Bank v. Warren	107, 148
Overend v. Oriental Corp.	234

P.

Pack v. Thomas	53
Page v. Gilbert	118
v. Wight	31
Palmer v. Thayer	218
Pannell v. McMechen	234
Park Bank v. Watson	230
Partridge v. Davis	71, 166
Paton v. Coit	205, 223, 224
v. Winter	188
Patten v. Gleason	225
Patterson v. Todd	73, 92

	PAGE
Paul v. Joel	114
Peacock v. Purcell	217, 218
Pearson v. Bank of Metropolis	85
Peaslee v. Robbins	201
People's Bank v. Brooke	107
Percival v. Frampton	217
Perry v. Green	147
Peters v. Beverly	221
v. Hobbs	142
Peterson v. Hubbard	38
Pettee v. Prout	171
Phelan v. Moss	187
Phillips v. Cox	34
Pierce v. Cate	88, 152
v. Kittredge	39
v. Struthers	141
v. Whitney	85
Pinnes v. Ely	69
Pitt v. Chappelow	200
Pons v. Kelly	51
Poole v. Tolleson	134
Porter v. Kemball	146
Pownal v. Ferrand	66
Pratt v. Conan	219
Prentice v. Zane	228
Price v. Edmonds	240
v. Neal	198
Prideaux v. Criddle	56, 101, 134
Prince v. Oriental Bank	89
Pring v. Clarkson	236
Pryor v. Bowman	92
Putnam v. Hubbell	218

Q.

Quinby v. Merritt	15

R.

Railroad Co. v. Ashland	252
v. National Bank	217
Randall v. Moon	247
Ransom v. Mack	118
Ray v. Smith	148
Read v. Adams	253
v. Marsh	44
Reddick v. Jones	217

	PAGE		PAGE
Redlich v. Doll	192	Seaton v. Scovill	17
Reed v. Roark	10	Semple v. Turner	34
Reid v. Morrison	151	Seneca Bank v. Neass	109
Requa v. Collins	149	Sessions v. Johnson	29
Rey v. Simpson	34	Seymour v. Leyman	35
Rhett v. Poe	51	v. Mickey	34
Rice v. Raitt	220	v. Wilson	220
Richie v. McCoy	51	Shanklin v. Cooper	253
Ricketts v. Pendleton	108	Shaw v. Croft	121
Ridington v. Woods	192	v. First Methodist Soc.	195
Riggan v. Green	201	v. Knox	70, 71
Rindge v. Kimball	146	v. Mix	125
Robb v. Bailey	64	Shed v. Brett	137
Roberts v. Corbin	6	Shelburne Falls Bank v. Townsley 127, 136	
v. Magrath	176		
v. Taft	135, 136	Shelton v. Carpenter	126
v. Wood	176	v. Gill	18
Robertson v. Kensington	70	Sheridan v. Carpenter	146
Robinson v. Ames	48, 49, 51	Shoe and Leather Bank v. Dix	31
v. Hawksford	54	Shoenberger v. Lancaster Sav.	
v. Reynolds	228	Inst.	123
Rodney v. Wilson	67	Short v. Trabue	253, 254
Rodocanachi v. Buttrick	34	Sigerson v. Mathews	144, 146
Rogers v. Blackwell	201	Simpson v. Pacific Ins. Co.	55, 56
Rosher v. Kiernan	121	v. Turney	121, 128, 130
Ross v. Espy	67	Sipe v. Earman	218
v. Hurd	146	Sittig v. Birkestack	227
Rothchild v. Currie	254	Skilding v. Warren	80
Rounds v. Smith	57	Slocomb v. De Lizardi	123
Rouquette v. Overmann	252, 254, 255	Small v. Smith	226
Routh v. Robertson	118	Smalley v. Wright	123
Roxborough v. Messick	215	Smead v. Indianapolis R. Co.	202
Royer v. Keystone Bank	215	Smith v. Allen	11
Rucker v. Hiller	49, 51	v. Gibbs	102
Rudd v. Matthews	200	v. Kendall	18
Russell v. Whipple	11	v. Mace	187
Ryan v. Chew	220	v. Miller	56, 149, 155
		v. Smith	221
		Sohier v. Loring	234, 235
S.		Solarte v. Palmer	113, 114
		Southwark Bank v. Gross	184
Saco Bank v. Sanborn	136, 137, 140	Spear v. Pratt	37, 38
Sanford v. Mickles	65	Spence v. Crockett	108
Schimmelpennich v. Bayard	42, 44	Spencer v. Bank of Salina	141
Scott v. Greer	145	Sperry v. Horr	17, 18
v. Ocean Bank	221	Spies v. Gilmore	70, 151, 166
Sea v. Glover	19	Sprague v. Tyson	141
Seacord v. Miller	148	Stafford v. Rice	79
Sears v. Lantz	69	Stalker v. McDonald	215

xviii   CASES CITED.

	PAGE		PAGE
Staniback v. Bank of Virginia	107	Tiernan v. Woodruff	238
State Bank v. Fearing	77	Tindal v. Brown	120
v. Hurd	85	Tobey v. Barber	221
v. Slaughter	122	Todd v. Bank of Kentucky	184
v. Thompson	205	Towne v. Rice	205
Stevens v. Beals	63	Townsend v. Bush	79
v. Blanchard	217	v. Lorain Bank	118, 145, 146
Stoddard v. Penniman	183	Treon v. Brown	79
Stoneman v. Pyle	17	Triggs v. Newnham	99
Stotts v. Byers	221	Trimbey v. Vignier	250
Strong v. Wilson	80	Troy Bank v. Lauman	184
Stults v. Silva	18, 24	True v. Thomas	53
Stump v. Napier	79	Tucker Manuf. Co. v. Fairbanks	31, 32
Sturgio v. Metropolitan Bank	209		
Sturtevant v. Forde	225	Tunstall v. Walker	139
Sullivan v. Langley	224	Turner v. Killian	217
Sussex Bank v. Baldwin	85, 86	Tuttle v. Bartholomew	70, 167
Swan v. Crafts	218	v. Standish	149
v. North British Co.	176, 192, 193	Tyler v. Young	91
Swartz v. Redfield	92	Tyson v. Oliver	141
Sweeny v. Easter	68		
Swetland v. Creich	16		
Swift v. Tyson	215, 216	**U.**	
Swope v. Ross	42, 243	Union Bank v. Hyde	59, 102, 108, 145, 154
Sylvester v. Downer	34	v. Roberts	184
		v. Stoker	137
T.		v. Willis	34, 104, 105
		United States v. Hodge	236
Tappen v. Ely	69	Upham v. Prince	167
Tardy v. Boyd	142, 143		
Tarleton v. Shingler	188		
Tarver v. Nance	49	**V.**	
Tassel v. Lewis	109		
Taylor v. Beck	79	Vagliano v. Bank of England	14
v. Blakelock	217	Valette v. Mason	217
v. Curry	21	Valk v. Simmons	51
v. Dobbin	27	Van Brunt v. Vaughn	127
v. Snyder	88, 141, 151	Vance v. Lowther	183
Temple v. Seaver	65	Van Etta v. Evenson	227
Thayer v. Buffum	64	Van Hoesen v. Van Alstyne	134
v. Crossman	80	Voorhies v. Attee	152
v. King	149		
Third Nat. Bank v. Ashworth	146, 147		
Thompson v. Briggs	221	**W.**	
v. Cumming	59		
v. Sloan	15	Wade v. Withington	181
Thornton v. Maynard	247	Walker v. Bank of New York	85
Thorp v. Craig	253	v. Ebert	176

	PAGE		PAGE
Walker v. Rogers	50, 146	Willis v. Green	104, 122
v. Stetson	58, 138, 139, 142	Wilson v. Eitler	218
Wallace v. McConnell	22	Windham Bank v. Norton	95, 143
Walmsley v. Acton	107	Witherspoon v. Musselman	18
Walton v. Shelley	78, 79	Witte v. Williams	243
Wamesit Bank v. Buttrick	127	Wolf v. Burgess	139
Ward v. Allen	189	Wolfe v. Jewett	151
Washington Bank v. Krum	221	Wood v. Draper	191
Washington Ins. Co. v. Miller	25	v. Price	48
Waterbury v. Sinclair	70, 166	v. Steele	183, 191
Watkins v. Cranch	147	Woodhull v. Holmes	80
Watts v. Pub. Admr	27	Woodland v. Fear	89
Way v. Butterworth	34	Woodruff v. Hill	229
v. Lamb	228	v. Plant	56
v. Smith	18, 24	Woods v. North	18
Wayne Bank v. Low	254	Woodworth v. Huntoon	228
Weaver v. Barden	220	Woolfolk v. Bank of America	187
Welch v. Taylor Manuf. Co.	149, 155	Worcester Bank v. Wells	44, 45
Weldon v. Buck	59	Worden v. Dodge	19
West v. Brown	86, 87	Works v. Hershey	24
Westgate v. Healy	14	Worrall v. Gheen	187, 192
Wetherall v. Clagett	109	Wright v. Hart	15
Wheeler v. Field	88, 142, 150	v. Morse	34
v. Guild	244, 245, 246	v. Shawcross	133
Whistler v. Forster	62	Wynn v. Alden	118
White v. North	11		
v. Richmond	15, 16		
v. Smith	25	Y.	
Whitehead v. Walker	228		
Whitesides v. Northern Bank	184		
Whitmore v. Nickerson	227	Yocum v. Smith	227
Wieland v. Kobick	201	Young v. Grote	193, 194
Wilkins v. Jadis	99	Youngs v. Lee	220
Williams v. Bank of United States	140		
v. Brashear	50		
v. Smith	229	Z.	
v. Wade	254		
v. Walbridge	79	Zimmerman v. Rote	195

LAW OF BILLS, NOTES, AND CHEQUES.

CHAPTER I.

INTRODUCTION.

§ 1. CUSTOM OF MERCHANTS : COMMON LAW.

IT is common to say that the law of bills of exchange, promissory notes, and cheques is derived from the custom of merchants. Rightly understood, that is true; it is not quite true in a sense in which the statement might naturally be taken by a person not familiar with the subject. Not all of the law of bills and notes — to use, for the sake of convenience, the shorter and familiar designation — is derived from the custom of merchants; not even the greater part of it, in point of bulk, is derived directly from that custom. Indirectly, most of the law of the subject finds there its source; for it has mainly grown out of elements supplied by the custom of merchants. But the development of the subject has taken the ordinary course in English jurisprudence; it has in the main followed lines of judicial reasoning; the courts have declared the law of the subject, in its growth out of the original material supplied by the custom of merchants, as matter of reasoning, without inquiring of the custom.

It is important rightly to apprehend the meaning of the statement referred to; only what may be called the elements of the law of bills and notes are drawn from the very life of the custom of merchants. In other words, only that which is peculiar to the subject, peculiar not as a special manifestation of fact to which ordinary rules of law might well apply, but peculiar in matter of law, is derived from that custom. What then is peculiar to the subject? That is, excluding growth and mere manifestations of fact, what is essentially peculiar to it, what are its elements?

Before answering that question it will be well to recall the state of things existing in England during, let us say, the later period of the Hanseatic League. London and the other commercial towns of England were full of foreign merchants engaged there in trade. These foreigners not only trained the fine hand of England to its cunning in commerce, but what is more to the present purpose, they brought with them the usages of business on the continent whence they had come. The custom of merchants was a foreign importation into England. That is sufficient to explain its unlikeness to the great domestic product, — the common law.

What these foreign merchants brought to England in the way of peculiar usage, so far as the present subject is concerned, was negotiability and grace; they brought bills of exchange, and with those instruments, as part and parcel of them, the property of circulation and a short extension of time in case of the payor.

Negotiability is the property by which certain choses in action, that is, undertakings to pay, pass from hand to hand like money. The common law knew nothing of that; or rather the common law repudiated entirely the notion that a promise by A to B could be treated as a promise extending also to C. The utmost which the law allowed was assignment; and that only after long debate and serious misgiving. Assignment merely works the appointment of another as beneficiary of the assignor's rights; the assignee 'takes the shoes' of the assignor. That would never have served the purpose of circulating paper; that purpose required a denial of the maxim Nemo dat quod non habet. The new taker of a bill of exchange must have a perfect right, if his purchase of it was in due course, a right in no way to be affected by the rights of him from whom he bought it.

Something much like negotiability, touching *property*, the common law learned long ago from equity. Purchase of land or goods for value, and without notice, cuts off equities; that is a cardinal rule of law, and always has been in courts of equity.[1] But it has never been applicable to undertakings to pay, in the case of common law contracts; applied to undertakings to pay, as purchase for value, without notice, often is, the principle has reference to bills, notes, and cheques only.

The notion of grace was even more repugnant to the common law of England, for there was nothing like it. Contracts were to be performed on the day named; no indulgence was allowed without the consent of the promisee. Indeed grace, as the term itself indicates, was at first indulgence by consent of the promisee, even in the matter of bills and notes; but the practice after a time hardened into requirement, the judges ceasing by degrees to inquire of the custom, and applying it to the contract as law.

The merchants had a long struggle before they succeeded in getting their custom recognized by law. Great judges pointed out the antagonism of the custom to most fundamental and cherished conceptions of the law of England. The urgency of commerce however prevailed, though only step by step. First foreign bills of exchange, as they were and are called, were by a clever fiction in pleading admitted to a place in the common law; a fiction by which

[1] 'Market overt' may also be noticed.

it was made to *seem* that the custom after all was nothing less than a sister of the common law, bearing under a strange garb the family likeness.[1] Then the door having been opened, inland bills were after a season and much debate similarly admitted. The door was now closed, though once and again some judge appears to have opened it stealthily to let in a wandering promissory note. But the fear of promissory notes was so great, the danger that the common law would be 'eaten away' was so threatening, that the courts on the whole, led by their greatest judge, Lord Holt, successfully resisted the pressure from without. Parliament was finally called in aid, and responded. Promissory notes were admitted into the law on an equality with bills of exchange by the Statute of 3 & 4 Anne, c. 9.

If the custom of merchants brought something new to the law of England, it received at the same time something new from that law. The common law doctrine of consideration is indigenous to English soil; the custom of merchants knew nothing of it before the custom was admitted into the jurisprudence of England. A common law principle was now added to a foreign product; and while neither the common law nor what must now be called the law merchant has undergone any essential change in the contact of each with the other, certain minor modifications of each, in the mingling of the two, have taken place. This is more manifest in those cases, to be considered later, in which some contract of the common law, such as a contract of suretyship, has been annexed to one of our contracts of the law merchant. But the same is true in regard to the common law doctrine of consideration.

That doctrine was imposed upon an unwilling custom; but it was not imposed in the usual way, for the force of

[1] See Rastell's Entries, 338 (A. D. 1595); Dunlop v. Silver, 1 Cranch, 367.

the custom was granted expression in part. In a suit upon any simple written contract of the common law it is incumbent upon the plaintiff to give some express evidence of consideration; production of the writing is no evidence upon the point, unless the language of it shows consideration. In the case of a suit upon a bill, note, or cheque however, while it is still necessary that the plaintiff should prove consideration, he proves it, prima facie, by producing the paper in evidence. The promise to pay is presumed to have been based upon consideration. So far the old law appears to have made concession to the custom, which treated the paper as the sufficient evidence, presumptively, of the liability of the promisor.

§ 2. Characteristics of Bills, Notes, and Cheques.

These then are the characteristics of paper of the law merchant, or bills, notes, and cheques: namely, negotiability (with its incidents), grace, and presumptive consideration. These are the *ordinary* characteristics of such paper; negotiability is not necessary; that is, it is not necessary to a bill or note, in order to give the paper grace and to bring it within the favoring rule concerning consideration, that the instrument should be negotiable. Nor is grace necessary; that is, it is not necessary to a bill or note, in order to give it negotiability, that it should be entitled to grace. Cheques too are commonly negotiable, though not entitled to grace. But there is some conflict of authority whether an unnegotiable note — and the doubt would in principle apply as well to a similar bill or cheque — carries the presumption of consideration; though the words 'value received,' or the like, commonly used, would be enough, prima facie, to meet the requirement of the law.

§ 3. Definitions: Order of Subjects.

To conclude this Introduction: A promissory note is a written promise, and a bill of exchange a written order, to pay to a certain person, or to the order of a certain person, or to bearer, a certain sum of money, absolutely. A cheque is a written order upon a bank or banker to pay on demand (otherwise as in the case of a note or bill). 'Draft' is a term of convenience, signifying either a bill of exchange or a cheque. Bills of exchange and cheques are foreign or inland; those drawn in one state or country and payable in another are foreign;[1] all others are inland. Paper is negotiable only when made payable, in terms or plain intent, to 'order,' or to 'bearer.'

The following are examples of the three kinds of instrument: —

1. Boston, Jan. 1, 1892. Six months after date I promise to pay to A (or to A or order, or to the order of A, or to bearer) One Thousand Dollars. Value received. B.

2. (Date.) Thirty days after sight (or after date, or at sight) pay (as above). To C (individual, partnership, bank or other corporation).

3. (Date.) Pay (as above, 'Value received' being usually omitted). To the Eagle Bank, Boston.

The law however prescribes no particular form of words for any of these instruments; it is satisfied if the essentials of the instrument are stated, however inartificially or with whatever prolixity.

The person who executes, that is, signs, a promissory

---

[1] Bank of United States v. Daniel, 12 Peters, 32. Compare Bills of Exchange Act, 4, (1). But see Grimshaw v. Bender, 6 Mass. 156. That cheques may be cheques though drawn in one country and payable in another, see Heywood v. Pickering, L. R. 9 Q. B. 428; Roberts v. Corbin, 26 Iowa, 315.

note is called the maker, not drawer; the person who executes a bill of exchange is called the drawer, not maker; the person who executes a cheque is generally called the drawer, sometimes the maker. The names, through carelessness or indifference, are now and then confused; but the contract of the maker of a note differs radically from that of the drawer of a bill, and it is best therefore to give to each its recognized name. The contract of one who executes a cheque is anomalous; it is not that of drawer of a bill or of maker of a note; but on the whole the better usage gives to the person the name of drawer.

The person to whom, by name, a note, a bill, or a cheque is made payable is called the payee; the person upon whom a bill or a cheque is drawn, that is, the person called upon to make payment, is called the drawee, and in case of acceptance by him (the instrument being a bill of exchange), acceptor. When the payee, or other person at the same time or afterwards, puts his name upon the paper, the act is called indorsement, and the party an indorser. The person to whom the paper is then or afterwards passed is called indorsee or holder. The term holder is sometimes applied to the payee; the term indorsee is applied to a holder after an indorsement, even though the indorsement be not immediately to him.

After the chapter on Physical Requisites, the nature of the several contracts of the parties incurring liability will be considered, and in the order following: maker, acceptor, drawer, indorser. Directly afterwards the effect of adding certain contracts of the common law to those of the law merchant will be examined. Then turning from the parties liable under their particular contracts to those to whom they are liable, the rights of holders will be considered; more especially of bona fide holders for value, for the rights of payees will already, indirectly, have been disposed of. Thus matters in common to all the several contracts before particularly described and distinguished will come under examination.

§ 4. Contract.

The law merchant adopts the doctrines of the common law in regard to the essentials of contract; whatever the form of the contract in question, — whether that of maker, acceptor, drawer, or indorser, or other party, — it must be supported by valuable consideration, there must be union of minds, and the parties liable must be competent to contract. And that is true not only between immediate parties, but between mediate parties as well. Thus, there must be a valuable consideration not merely to support an action by the payee of a promissory note against the maker, — there must somewhere be a valuable consideration to support an action against the maker by the payee's indorsee. So if there be a want of union of minds between the maker and the payee, there will be a want of union of minds, upon the same facts, between the maker and the payee's indorsee; and so if the maker is incompetent to contract with the payee, he is incompetent to contract with the payee's indorsee.[1]

§ 5. 'Law Merchant:' 'Common Law.'

The custom of merchants then has, with judicial and it may be statutory accretions, become the law merchant; and the student should bear in mind that 'law merchant' and 'common law,' in such phrases as 'contract of the law merchant' and 'contract of the common law,' are used in this book by way of contrast, the former term referring to the law of bills, notes, and cheques; the latter to the com-

---

[1] See Chapter 13.

mon law proper. Properly speaking, the law of bills, notes, and cheques is, as we have seen, no part of the common law; or if received speech makes too strongly against that statement, it is at all events a separable addition to the common law, and everywhere to be distinguished from that native English product.

CHAPTER II.

PHYSICAL REQUISITES: ANALYSIS OF DEFINITION.

[*The student should refer to the definition given in the Introduction, p. 6.*]

§ 1. Written Promise: Written Order.

Promissory notes, bills of exchange, and cheques must be in writing; no oral promise or order would be treated on the same footing, though the oral undertaking might be a perfectly good contract, a contract of the common law. The requirement of a writing is not a requirement of statute, but of the law merchant as derived from the custom of merchants. Generally speaking, the whole of the note, bill, or cheque must be in writing; but a mistake obvious on the face of the instrument could be corrected by a suit brought for the purpose, or perhaps in an action upon the instrument on breach of the contract.[1]

The law merchant however has never prescribed any particular writing material, or any particular material for receiving the writing. The instrument may be written with pencil as well as with ink,[2] and, it seems, upon any material firm enough of itself to hold the writing.

A promissory note in common form, as shown in the example, contains a promise, expressed by that word. That however is unnecessary; but what will satisfy the

---

[1] See Conner v. Routh, 7 How. (Miss.) 176. See post, Chapter 13, § 3.
[2] See Geary v. Physic, 5 Barn. & C. 234; Brown v. Butcher's Bank, 6 Hill, 443; L. C. 121; Reed v. Roark, 14 Texas, 329.

definition, — and the definition is nothing less than a rule of law, — which requires a promise, is not clearly determined. It is generally laid down that the promise must be express; hence that the mere fact that a debt is acknowledged is not enough, for that would but raise an *implied* promise. For example: 'Due C & B $ 17.14' is not, it seems, a promissory note, for want of an express promise to pay.[1]

But to say that a promise must be express is not to say that the word 'promise' must be used; a promise is express when either the word 'promise,' or any equivalent word or expression, is used.

What is the equivalent of 'promise'? That is the difficult question — difficult so far at least as principle is concerned, for the equivalency is often arbitrary. Thus: Setting any certain time for payment in express terms appears to be accepted as an equivalent; and this even though the words of time are 'on demand.' For example: 'Due J A $94.91 on demand' is a promissory note; it being deemed an express promise to pay.[2] The use of words of negotiability is also an equivalent. For example: 'Due R, or bearer, $200.26.' This on like ground is a promissory note.[3] The use of the words 'for value received' is held insufficient. For example: 'Due C & B $17.14, value received,' is not a promissory note; the words 'value received' being deemed not an equivalent of 'promise.'[4] And so it has been held of the words 'to be accountable' in an instrument such as this: 'I have received the sum of £20 which I borrowed of you, and I have to be accountable for the said sum with interest.'[5]

[1] See Currier v. Lockwood, 40 Conn. 349.
[2] Smith v. Allen, 5 Day, 337; Kimball v. Huntington, 10 Wend. 675.
[3] Russell v. Whipple, 2 Cowen, 536.
[4] Currier v. Lockwood, 40 Conn. 349; two judges dissenting
[5] Horne v. Redfearn, 4 Bing. N. C. 433. See White v. North, 3 Ex. 689, 690. 'To be accountable' was deemed to mean that credit would

When an equivalent of 'promise' is used, it matters not how the acknowledgment of debt is made. The foregoing would be examples of what are commonly called 'due bills' (with an actual promise). Another way in which the acknowledgment is sometimes made, oftener in England than in this country, but sometimes here, is by what is called from the letters used an 'I O U.' For example: 'I O U £20 to be paid on the 22d inst.' is a promissory note.[1] Again: 'S has deposited in the State Bank $1000, payable to himself on return of this certificate' is a good promissory note, though a certificate of deposit.[2]

It is no more necessary in the case of a bill of exchange that the word 'order' be used than that the word 'promise' be used in a promissory note. Any equivalent word or expression will satisfy the definition; but it seems here that the law does not give such loose rein to interpretation as we have just seen in regard to the word 'promise.' That is, the equivalent word or expression is to be a real equivalent, in the common acceptation. Still it is not necessary that the words, literally taken, should be imperative; the language may be that of courtesy and politeness in form, as often it is, and yet be imperative in the eye of the law. For example: 'Please let the bearer have $50. I will arrange it with you this noon' is a good bill of exchange, as containing an 'order' to pay.[3] Again: 'Mr. B will oblige Mr. A by paying C or order $100' would be a good bill on the same footing. A little less however might be fatal. For example: 'Please let bearer have £7, and place it to my account, and you will much

be given in account and the balance paid. But see Miller v. Austin, 13 How. 218.

[1] Brooks v. Elkins, 2 Mees. & W. 74.
[2] Klauber v. Biggerstaff, 47 Wis. 551.
[3] Bissenthall v. Williams, 1 Duv. 329.

oblige me' is *deemed* not a bill of exchange for want of an 'order' or the equivalent.[1] Again: 'We hereby authorize you to pay on our account to the order of G £6000' at certain times, in stated instalments, is not a bill of exchange, for the same reason.[2]

§ 2. THE PAYEE.

'To pay to a certain person, or to the order of a certain person, or to bearer.' The payee must be a person certain, that is, existing, and must be ascertainable at the execution of the instrument unless it is payable to bearer. But though the paper be not payable to bearer, the person need not be ascertained or identified on the instrument; enough that he is so referred to as to be ascertainable by evidence ab extra. For example: 'Pay to the executor of A, deceased,' contains a good designation of the payee of the bill, though the description requires evidence from without to identify the person intended.[3] Indeed, a mistake in the name, where a name of the payee is given, may be made good by evidence.[4]

The definition is satisfied by the use of any mercantile phrase in place of the name of a payee, so long as no fictitious person is designated. For example: 'Pay to bills payable or order' is a good designation of the payee; the meaning being that the instrument is payable to the person to whom the 'bills' are 'payable,' that is, ordinarily to the drawer.

The rule requiring the payee to be a real existing person is in England statutory, as is the whole law of bills and notes; but the statute probably expresses the rule of the law merchant on the subject. In some states, by statute,

---

[1] Little v. Slackford, Moody & M. 171. Sed quære.
[2] Hamilton v. Spottiswoode, 4 Ex. 200.
[3] Adams v. King, 16 Ill. 169.
[4] Jacobs v. Benson, 39 Maine, 132.

a bill payable to an obviously fictitious person may be treated as payable to bearer, that is, to a real person. Such is the law of England also.[1]

Perhaps because the law of bills and notes is derived from custom, the rule in regard to the payee is held to mean that the instrument cannot be made payable to either of two different persons. As a matter of fact, it would be contrary to the custom of merchants to execute paper in that way. But whatever the reason, the law does not permit such a designation of the payee, though the instrument might still be good as evidence of debt. For example: 'Good to A or B for $181.80, value received,' is not a promissory note for want of proper designation of the payee, though it may be declared upon and used as evidence of debt (in a suit against A and B jointly).[2] No such rule, it may be noticed, applies to the contract of maker.[3]

§ 3. Money.

That these instruments must be payable in money has always been held essential, and the custom of merchants to that effect has received the sanction of statute, — the statutes merely expressing the force of the custom. Thus in England, the statute of Anne already referred to, by which promissory notes were adopted into the law, refers in terms to promises to pay 'money;' and the same word is used in the similar American statutes.

---

[1] See Vagliano v. Bank of England, 1891, A. C. 107.

[2] Osgood v. Pearsons, 4 Gray, 455, citing Blanckenhagen v. Blundell, 2 B. & Ald. 417. See also Carpenter v. Farnsworth, 106 Mass. 561. But see Westgate v. Healy, 4 R. I. 523.

[3] 'We, or either of us,' is not an uncommon form of promise in a note; it is perfectly good. But compare Ferris v. Bond, 4 Barn. & Ald. 679, which, however, is consistent with the text. Whether a bill or cheque could be drawn by 'A or B' may be doubted.

By 'money' is meant, in strictness, that which by law is tenderable for debt, that is, assuming that no provision is made for payment in anything else. If the instrument is not payable in money, or in what the courts judicially know to be equivalent to money, it is not an instrument of the law merchant. For example: 'We promise to pay A or order $1000 in cotton' is not a promissory note.[1] Again: 'Pay to A or order £1000 in good East India bonds' is not a bill of exchange (or a cheque).[2] Again: 'I promise to pay A or order $140 in carpenter's work' is not a promissory note.[3] Again: 'Pay A or order $1000 in current funds' or 'in currency' is by some courts deemed not a bill (or a cheque).[4] Again: 'We promise to pay to the order of A, twelve months after date, in Buffalo, N. Y., $2500, in *Canada money*,' being a New York contract, is not, it is held, a promissory note, because it is not payable in the money of this country or in what the court can judicially know to be the equivalent.[5]

The rule itself is accepted by all courts; but the courts have not been agreed in applying it, as cases referred to in

[1] Auerbach v. Pritchett, 58 Ala. 451.
[2] Buller, N. P. 272; Chalmers, Bills, 13 (Benjamin).
[3] Quinby v. Merritt, 11 Humph. 439.
[4] Wright v. Hart, 44 Penn. St. 454. But see White v. Richmond, 16 Ohio, 5; Klauber v. Biggerstaff, 47 Wis. 551. See Frank v. Wessels, 64 N. Y. 155. It has very often been held that instruments payable in current bank notes are not payable in money. See the cases just cited and, among others, Little v. Phenix Bank, 7 Hill, 359, affirming 2 Hill, 425; McDowell v. Keller, 4 Cold. 258; Irvine v. Lowry, 14 Peters, 293. In Graham v. Adams, 5 Ark. 261, it was held that a note or bond payable 'in good current money of the State' was payable in gold and silver. To the same effect, Cockrill v. Kirkpatrick, 9 Mo. 688. Secus of a promise to pay 'in Arkansas money of the Fayetteville Branch.' Hawkins v. Watkins, 5 Ark. 481. Further, see the cases cited in Thompson v. Sloan, 23 Wend. 71; L. C. 1.
[5] Thompson v. Sloan, 23 Wend. 71; L. C. 1.

the authority last cited show. Indeed, that authority itself has been criticised, though in a case clearly distinguishable.[1] The difficulty lies in what is to be accepted as judicially known to be equivalent to money. It is hardly safe to call anything the equivalent of money on the ground that it passes as such at certain places; such a rule would admit into the company of promissory notes promises to pay in wool or in tobacco, it may be, in some places, where in the absence of money such things may happen to pass current as payment. Nor is it safe to treat currency, unless it is the currency of the nation, as equivalent to money; for currency is apt to fluctuate, that is, to fall from its face value. The most, it seems, that the law should allow would be a promise to pay in National Bank notes, if for any reason paper should be made so payable.

In some States promises to pay in things not money have been treated as standing in part on the footing of paper of the law merchant. The presumption of consideration has been applied to them; while negotiability has been denied them.[2] But the favor is generally considered as misplaced; the fact that the paper is payable in commodities being deemed enough to put it upon the footing of an ordinary contract of the common law.

§ 4. Certainty of Sum.

Further, the sum payable must be certain. But the meaning to be given to the rule is in certain respects a

---

[1] Black v. Ward, 27 Mich. 191, 194. There has been an inclination to favor the paper where the sum is payable in the local State currency. Mitchell v. Hewitt, 5 Smedes & M. 361; Drake v. Markle, 21 Ind. 433; Butler v. Paine, 8 Minn. 324; Cockrill v. Kirkpatrick, 9 Mo. 688; White v. Richmond, 16 Ohio, 5; Swetland v. Creigh, 15 Ohio, 118.

[2] Jones v. Fales, 4 Mass. 245, 254. See also Denison v. Tyson, 17 Vt. 549; Dewey v. Washburn, 12 Vt. 580.

matter of doubt. It is clear that the sum cannot be fluctuating so as to be unascertainable at the time of making the instrument, as where it is to rise or fall *indefinitely* according to the happening of an uncertain event. For example (hypothetical): 'Pay to A or order, thirty days after sight, $1000 or less according to the market value of 10 shares of Moon Mining stock at that time' would not be a bill of exchange for want of designation of a sum certain. But perhaps the case would be different where the only uncertainty was between two fixed sums, as in the case of a promise or an order to pay $1000, or $500 if a particular event happened before the time of payment of the larger sum. Here the sum would be ascertainable at the outset; it would be either $1000 or $500; there could be no indefinite fluctuation in such a case.[1] But some cases appear to be opposed to this view. For example: 'Two years from date, for value received, we, or either of us, promise to pay to W or bearer $60, with use; said W agrees that if $50 be paid on the first day of January, 1843, it shall cancel this note;' that is deemed not a promissory note.[2] Greater or more common difficulty arises with regard to cases where the principal sum payable is certain, but to it something further is to be added in a subsidiary way, dependent upon some event, or uncertain in amount. In some parts of the country it is not uncommon to add to the principal sum promised another stated sum by way of attorney fee, in case suit should be brought upon the instrument. In many cases it has been held that this additional stipulation does not affect the nature of the instrument.[3] But

---

[1] Compare the case of time of payment 'on or before,' infra, § 5.

[2] Fralick v. Norton, 2 Mich. 130.

[3] Sperry v. Horr, 32 Iowa, 184; Seaton v. Scovill, 18 Kans. 433; Garr v. Louisville Banking Co., 11 Bush, 180; Stoneman v. Pyle, 35 Ind. 103; Nickerson v. Sheldon, 33 Ill. 372; Dietrich v. Bayhi, 23 La. An. 767.

in other cases the contrary is held;[1] and in some cases it is held that the addition may violate the usury laws, or other statutes, or public policy, and for that reason render the instrument void or subject to any special provision of the laws.[2] Another instance of the difficulty occurs where payment is promised at a stated time 'or before,' with deduction of interest for the time if payment is made before the day set. Some of the courts have held that the sum payable is rendered uncertain by the provision for anticipation;[3] other courts would, it seems, hold the contrary, on the ground that it is enough that the principal sum payable, in such cases, is certain.[4] The latter appears to be the better rule. Still another instance occurs where the promise to pay is, 'with current exchange.' A similar conflict of authority exists in regard to such cases; but the better rule, and also the weight of authority, treat the provision as not affecting the subject of certainty of amount.[5]

Provisions accelerating the time of payment on non-payment of interest when due have no effect upon the character of the paper; that is, they do not make the sum payable uncertain. For example: the defendant is guarantor and the plaintiff is holder of an instrument promising to pay a certain sum of money, with interest in instalments, and

[1] Woods v. North, 84 Penn. St. 407; First National Bank v. Gay, 63 Mo. 33.

[2] Witherspoon v. Musselman, 14 Bush, 214; Shelton v. Gill, 11 Ohio, 417; Myer v. Hart, 40 Mich. 517.

[3] Stults v. Silva, 119 Mass. 137; Way v. Smith, 111 Mass. 523; Hubbard v. Mosely, 11 Gray, 170.

[4] Compare Helmer v. Krolich, 36 Mich. 371; Mattison v. Marks, 31 Mich. 421, doubting Hubbard v. Mosely, supra. The question in these, as in some of the Massachusetts cases, related to certainty of time, but there would be the same question of certainty in amount ordinarily.

[5] Smith v. Kendall, 9 Mich. 241; Johnson v. Frisbie, 15 Mich. 286; Sperry v. Horr, 32 Iowa, 184. But see Lowe v. Bliss, 24 Ill. 168.

being thus far a promissory note, but with an added provision that in case of default in the payment of any instalment of interest when due, the principal sum shall, at the holder's election, at once become due. The instrument is a promissory note, the added provision not affecting it in that respect.[1]

§ 5. 'Absolutely': Certainty of Time.

It is an invariable rule, or a rule with at most but a single exception, that the promise or order must be absolute; any condition or contingency expressed in it would have the effect to reduce the instrument from the high level of the law merchant to the lower level of the common law. The condition or contingency need not appear in terms, — 'upon condition,' 'if,' 'in the event that,' or the like, — in order to defeat the instrument as a contract of the law merchant; the same effect is produced if in substance and reality the promise or order is conditional or contingent. Thus, to make the paper payable out of some particular designated fund would have that effect, in ordinary cases, because the fund might not exist or be available at the time of payment. For example: 'One month from date I promise to pay to A or order $1000 out of the net proceeds of ore to be obtained from the mine in the lot of land this day conveyed to me by B' is not a promissory note, being payable upon the contingency of obtaining the required amount of ore out of the mine.[2]

It makes no difference that the event upon which the promise or order is made happens, or that the particular fund exists and is available when payment is due, so that the promise or order may be binding; it is fatal to the contract as a contract of the law merchant that when the

---

[1] Sea v. Glover, 1 Bradw. (Ill.) 335.
[2] Worden v. Dodge, 4 Denio, 159; L. C. 8.

promise or order was made, payment was dependent upon condition or contingency. For example: 'Due K $1000 when he is twenty-one years of age' is not a promissory note though K lived to become, shortly afterwards, twenty-one.[1]

It may be remarked that an order to pay over the whole or any part of a specified fund will ordinarily amount to an assignment of the same,[2] and that that of itself would be fatal to the conception of a bill of exchange or a cheque. A bill or a cheque can rise no higher than an undertaking; it signifies a debt, not a transfer of money or other property.

It will not affect the instrument as paper of the law merchant that language unnecessary to such paper is used in it, provided the additional language does not make the promise or order conditional or contingent. To add a provision for reimbursement, in the case of an order to pay, would not affect the paper as a bill of exchange, for that would not be directing *payment* to be made out of the particular fund or source; and whether the fund or source for reimbursement existed or was available would make no difference. For example: 'Pay to the order of A $1000, one month from date, and reimburse yourself out of funds in your hands due me' is a bill of exchange, regardless of the reimbursement clause[3] or of the existence of any debt due the drawer. Again: 'On the 1st of August next please pay to G or order £600, on account of moneys advanced by me to S,' is a bill of exchange regardless of the clause following the sum.[4] So too the

---

[1] Kelley *v.* Hemmingway, 13 Ill. 604; L. C. 10.

[2] See Attorney-Gen. *v.* Continental Ins. Co., 71 N. Y. 325.

[3] Kelly *v.* Brooklyn, 4 Hill, 263; Coursin *v.* Ledlie, 31 Penn. St. 506; Corbett *v.* Clark, 45 Wis. 403.

[4] Griffin *v.* Weatherby, L. R. 3 Q. B. 753, overruling Banbury *v.* Lisset, 2 Strange, 1211.

consideration for the undertaking may be stated, if no condition is created in the promise or order. For example: 'Pay to A or order $1000 one month from date, *for stock*' is a bill of exchange.[1] It is immaterial that the additional language may express a condition or contingency, provided that the condition or contingency is no part of the promise or order to pay. That is to say, to a note, a bill, or a cheque may be added a contract of the common law, as has already been stated.

But it may sometimes require careful consideration to determine whether the additional language forms part of the promise or order. Thus, while it is clear that the fact that it is recited in an instrument promising to pay money, that other paper or property is deposited with it as collateral, and that the same may be sold if such instrument is not paid at its maturity, will not prevent that instrument from being a promissory note; still if it is recited in the instrument that the instrument itself is held as collateral, it will be perceived upon reflection that the contrary is true and that the promise is now made conditional. For example: 'Six months after date I promise to pay to the order of myself $2400, value received, to be held as collateral security for the payment of B's note, December 5th, 6 months, for $968.41,' and other notes, is not a promissory note; for in legal effect it is a promise to pay *if* the notes to which it is collateral are not paid.[2] So too while an insurance note is not reduced to a contract of the common law by adding the words 'On policy 33,386,'[3] the contrary would be true if the words were 'subject to the policy,' or the like.[4]

---

[1] See Coffman v. Campbell, 87 Ill. 98.

[2] Haskell v. Lambert, 16 Gray, 592.

[3] Taylor v. Curry, 109 Mass. 36. The policy provided for a set-off of notes due the company.

[4] American Bank v. Blanchard, 7 Allen, 333.

The promise is not conditional by reason of the fact that it designates a particular place of payment; nor is acceptance conditional for designating a place of payment. It is not necessary to make demand of payment at that or at any other place in order to fix the liability of the maker or the acceptor; it is the duty of such party to come and pay. For example: 'Three years and two months after date I promise to pay M or order, at the office of the Bank of the United States, at Nashville, $4880.99, value received,' is a promissory note, and not conditional, touching the liability of the *maker*, upon demand at the place named or anywhere else.[1]

That proceeds, however, upon the ground that the very fact of non-payment by the maker or the acceptor on the day of the maturity of the paper is a breach of his contract, a rule peculiar largely to the law merchant. But if it should be desirable to bring an action upon the day of the maturity of the paper, it would be necessary to make a demand, otherwise there could be no dishonor, — that is, breach of the contract, — on that day, until indeed the close of business hours, and then it would perhaps be too late to sue on that day.

There is one exception to the rule requiring demand to be made after maturity, to fix the liability of the maker of a note or the acceptor of a bill, — namely, where the promise or order is made performable at a certain designated place *only.* Such language would certainly make the paper payable upon a condition; but it is probable that a condition of that kind would not affect it, as a contract of the law merchant.

It is obvious, and the fact has already been noticed, that the promise or order is not performable absolutely if the time of payment is not certain to come to pass. For example: 'I promise to pay to A or order $1000 when the

---

[1] Wallace v. McConnell, 13 Peters, 136; L. C. 65.

estate of B is settled up' is deemed not a promise to pay absolutely, because the estate of B may never be 'settled up.'[1] Again: 'I promise to pay to A or order $1000 as soon as crops can be sold or the money raised from any other source' is not a promise to pay absolutely.[2] Again: 'At sight after the arrival and discharge of coal per brig G pay to the order of myself $1500, value received,' is not an order to pay absolutely.[3]

Certainty of time, however, does not mean a fixed and stated day of month and year; or as it is sometimes put, certainty here does not mean definiteness. Nothing is more common than promises to pay 'on demand,' or orders to pay 'at sight,' or at a certain time 'after sight;' such instruments are respectively as good promissory notes or bills of exchange as if payment was to be made upon a day stated.

All that the law requires is that the time of payment shall be sure to arrive, as, for instance, in the case of a promise to pay on the death of a person named. Indeed, physical certainty appears not to be required; moral certainty being deemed sufficient, as in the case of a promise by the government to pay a sum when it pays certain other debts which it owes.[4]

Some confusion however exists, as certain of the examples already given and others show, in regard to the meaning of the rule in cases in which the time of payment is left indefinite without giving power to the holder to put an end to the indefiniteness. But by the better view such a state of things will not prevent the paper from being a

---

[1] Husband v. Epling, 81 Ill. 172. But there would come an end of time for making claims against the estate; and would not the estate be, practically speaking, 'settled up'? The time would seem to be only indefinite in such a case, not uncertain to come to pass.

[2] Nunez v. Dantel, 19 Wall. 560.

[3] Grant v. Wood, 12 Gray, 220.

[4] Andrews v. Franklin, 1 Strange, 24; Evans v. Underwood, 1 Wils. 262.

promissory note (or a bill of exchange if one should ever be drawn in that way). If the time of payment is sure to come to pass sooner or later, that is enough; when, sooner or later, it does come to pass, the instrument may be sued upon, in case of breach, as a promissory note.

Confusion on this point has arisen in recent cases of promises to pay at a time stated 'or before,' at the maker's election.[1] But the instrument is payable at the time stated at all events; the time of payment is certain to come to pass; the maker may choose to shorten the matter, — that is all.[2] Another difficulty with such cases, arising from the fact that the total sum payable is in one sense uncertain, has already been noticed.[3]

No time of payment at all need be stated; the paper in that case will in law be payable on demand, and that, as has already been stated, is enough. The common cheque is a familiar example. An undertaking to pay within a reasonable time meets the requirement of the law merchant; for a reasonable time is deemed sure to come; and an undertaking will often be construed as performable within a reasonable time where the matter of time is left wholly indefinite in the language used. For example: 'I promise to pay to A or order $1000 when convenient' is construed a promise to pay within reasonable time, and hence within a time certain.[4] Again: 'I promise to pay to A or bearer $75, one year from date, and if there is not enough realized by good management in one year, to have more time to pay,' is a promise to pay within a year, or at the end of a reasonable time thereafter, if enough should not be

---

[1] Stults v. Silva, 119 Mass. 137; Way v. Smith, 111 Mass. 523; Hubbard v. Mosely, 11 Gray, 170.

[2] Hehner v. Krolich, 36 Mich. 371; Mattison v. Marks, 31 Mich. 421.

[3] Supra, § 4.

[4] Works v. Hershey, 35 Iowa, 340.

realized out of the business within a year; and the promise is therefore deemed to be performable at a time certain.[1]

Again, the time of payment may be put at the election of the holder not merely by making the instrument payable in one payment on demand, but by making it payable in parts at the pleasure of the holder. For example: 'I promise to pay to A $125 in such manner and proportion, and at such times and place, as A may require' is payable absolutely, being payable in law in instalments on demand.[2]

Indeed, the time of payment may be put in the alternative, one of the alternatives being wholly uncertain, if the *holder* has his election which of the alternatives to take; that is, if the holder has the right to insist upon payment, at the time certain set in the instrument, the law merchant is satisfied.

§ 6. Signature.

Any of these instruments may be signed in pencil as well as in ink;[3] and though it is unusual to sign in any other way than by writing the name, that is not necessary, provided only the signature adopted was intended as an execution of the particular contract. Any party may sign with his mark, or he may substitute for his name a cipher, figures, or what he will; but if the name of the party is not signed, the holder has it to show that what the party did write was intended to answer the purpose of a signature.[4] There must be a signature in some form

---

[1] Capron *v.* Capron, 44 Vt. 410.

[2] Goshen Turnpike *v.* Hurtin, 9 Johns. 217. See Washington Ins. Co. *v.* Miller, 26 Vt. 77; White *v.* Smith, 77 Ill. 351.

[3] Geary *v.* Physic, 5 Barn. & C. 234; Brown *v.* Butchers' Bank, 6 Hill, 443; L. C. 121.

[4] See Brown *v.* Butchers' Bank, supra, where the figures '1, 2, 8,'

upon the paper itself. It could not be shown that the want of a signature was due to mistake or oversight; though a suit in equity could, it seems, be maintained in a proper case to correct an omission in signing due to mistake.[1]

were held a good indorsement on evidence of the intention; and the same case, referring to George v. Surrey, Moody & M. 516, as to signature by mark.

[1] See Lancaster Bank v. Taylor, 100 Mass. 18; Beard v. Dedolph, 29 Wis. 136; Brown v. McHugh, 35 Mich. 50, 52. These are cases of omitted indorsement; but the principle is probably general.

CHAPTER III.

THE MAKER'S CONTRACT.

§ 1. Signature.

The contract of the maker of a promissory note differs in one respect from that of any other party to a contract of the law merchant; the writing itself shows, apart from grace, what the contract is. One has but to read the note to see that it is an absolute undertaking to pay.

The contract itself may be executed in any way, so far as the signature of the maker is concerned. Ordinarily the maker signs the note at the right lower corner; but that is not necessary. His signature written anywhere on the paper will bind him as maker if that was the intention. It may even be written in the body of the promise, as where the note reads, 'I, A B, promise to pay,' etc. provided that it was intended that the name as written there should answer the purpose of a signature.[1]

There is this difference, however: Where the signature is placed at the end of the note, the intention is fixed; the signing in that way is an execution of the note as matter of law, in the absence of fraud practised upon the maker in regard to the instrument itself. But if the signature be out of the usual place, it is then a question of fact whether the supposed signature was intended as an execution of the instrument; the burden being upon the holder to show that it was so intended.[2] The simplest kind of

---

[1] Taylor v. Dobbin, 1 Strange, 399.

[2] Compare In re Booth, 127 N. Y. 109; Watts v. Pub. Admr., 4 Wend. 168; Catlett v. Catlett, 55 Mo. 330; Armstrong v. Armstrong, 29 Ala. 538. These are cases of wills.

contract is the one now assumed to be in question, where the promise is made by one person only. That is the typical case, the case from which to start,—the case from which all others are more or less variants.

§ 2. Joint and Several Signature.

The note may be signed by more than one person; and then, according to the intention manifested, it will be the several note of each, or the joint note of all, or it will be either the one or the other as the holder may choose to treat it. The question which of these it is, will be a question to be ascertained from the writing itself. The language of the note may in terms state the intention; as where it reads, 'We jointly promise,' or 'We jointly and severally,' or 'We or either of us,' or 'I, A B, as principal, and I, C D, as surety, jointly and severally promise;' or the language may not in terms declare the intention. In the latter case the intention is a matter for construction, on the language used, the rule whereof appears to be this: If there is nothing to indicate a different intention, the promise of the makers is to be deemed joint. For example (hypothetical): 'We promise to pay to A or order $1000, six months from date,' followed by the signatures of the makers, would be a joint promissory note, as there is nothing in the language to indicate that the makers intended to bind themselves severally.

Where the promise is joint, there is this addition to the typical case of a promise by one person only, that the promise is now the indivisible undertaking of two or more. Apart from statute there can be but one right of action for the breach of the contract in such a case, and hence when that right of action is pursued to its end, obviously nothing more can be done. There are not as many rights of action as there are parties; and if suit should be brought against one without objection, and judgment should be obtained against him, then though the judgment should prove fruitless, no action could be brought against the others.[1] Where the promise is several, there are as many rights of action — on which of course as many judgments may be obtained — as there are makers; though as there is but one debt, one satisfaction satisfies all rights of action and all judgments. Where the promise is joint and several, the holder has an election; he may treat the makers as liable in either way.[2]

One further point touching joint promises may be noticed. The promise may be made by partners or not. If made by partners, any of the partnership may act for the firm; and accordingly, a refusal to pay, on the day of maturity, made by any one of the partners, would be a breach of contract by all, so that suit could be brought, on the same day, upon the note (of course it would be against all the partners). But if the joint promisors were not partners, and no agency existed between them, there could be no breach of the contract before the close of the day of maturity, except by demand upon and refusal by all.

Another modification of the typical case occurs where one of the promisors undertakes as surety. If the fact of suretyship is shown upon the note, the holder must govern himself accordingly. The surety is still a maker, — that is, he promises to pay; but he promises sub modo, — he promises subject to certain restrictions imposed by the

---

[1] King v. Hoare, 13 Mees. & W. 494; Sessions v. Johnson, 95 U. S. 347; Bigelow, Estoppel, 104–109. 5th ed.

[2] 'If two bind themselves by contract *jointly and severally*, they may both be joined as defendants in one action; or either or each of them may be sued in a separate action. For when the contract is in this form, the obligation created by it may be treated as either joint or several, at the election of the party who is entitled to recover for the breach of it.' Gould, Pleading, § 69.

suretyship upon the holder of the note. The holder must not have dealings affecting the contract, such as agreements to extend the time of payment, behind the surety's back.[1] Otherwise, however, the surety stands in the same situation as the principal maker. If the fact of the suretyship is a private matter, understood only between the principal and the surety himself, it has no bearing upon the rights of the holder; towards him there might as well have been no special understanding. But should he have notice of the understanding at the time of taking the note, or should he afterwards receive or acquire notice, then, by the better view, he would have to govern his conduct as if the fact were shown upon the paper itself.[2]

§ 3. SIGNING AS AGENT.

How ought a man to sign a promissory note who intends to exempt himself from liability? This question arises constantly in cases of alleged (or actual) agency. A, who in point of fact is treasurer or otherwise agent of B, has occasion to execute a promissory note solely on behalf of B; how is he to do it? If he wishes to exempt himself, he should do so in terms or by plain if not necessary implication; otherwise his signature — that is, signing his own name to the note — will bind him as maker, whether the principal is bound or not.

The agent does not exempt himself from liability within the rule just stated — 'in terms or by plain if not necessary implication' — by adding words which are merely *descriptive* of the position which the agent holds.

---

[1] On this subject, further infra.
[2] The case referred to in the text is suretyship in the ordinary sense, not in the sense which would make an accommodative acceptor, for example, a surety. As to cases of that sort, see Farmers' Bank v. Rathbone, 26 Vt. 19; L. C. 622.

It does not affect a man's liability in a written (or a verbal) contract to describe himself; that at most serves but to identify him. Of this nature the law considers all such words as 'agent,' 'trustee,' 'treasurer,' or the like, following a man's name. That may be harsh, for in many cases the intention may be overturned; but it is settled construction. For example: 'Two months after date pay to the order of T $4469.76, value received, and charge the same to the account of D. F. & Co., agts. Piscataqua F. & M. Ins. Co.,' binds D. F. & Co., the added words being deemed mere description of the position held by them; it does not indicate that the instrument was executed in their office or character of agents.[1] Again: 'One year from date we promise to pay to A or order $1000, value received. A B, C D, trustees of First Parish,' binds A B and C D, for the same reason.[2]

The general rule is plain, and it must be applied, — the language must be interpreted by itself alone. The application of the law to all but simple cases like those of the examples is, however, often troublesome, and consequently sometimes inconsistent. If in the first of the examples the signing had been 'D. F. & Co., agts. *for* Piscataqua F. & M. Ins. Co.,' it seems that D. F. & Co. would not have been liable. The instrument would, it seems, have shown 'in terms' that they were acting in their office and character of agents.[3] But if it had read 'D. F. & Co., agts. *of*,' &c., the language would probably

---

[1] Tucker Manuf. Co. *v.* Fairbanks, 98 Mass. 101. It does not affect the case that the instrument was a bill of exchange, of which the 'agents' were drawers.

[2] See Id.; Shoe and Leather Bank *v.* Dix, 123 Mass. 148.

[3] Id., referring to Ballou *v.* Talbot, 16 Mass. 461, as an authoritative decision, where a note was signed 'J T, agent for D P,' and J T was held not liable. Jefts *v.* York, 4 Cush. 372; Page *v.* Wight, 14 Allen, 182. But see DeWitt *v.* Walton, 5 Seld. 571, where the signature 'D H, agent for the Churchman' was held to bind D H.

have been treated as merely descriptive of the position held, and hence not as exempting the signers.[1]

On the other hand, while a signing by 'A B for C D,' or 'for C D, A B' is the note of C D, if authorized, though the name of C D is not mentioned in the body of the note, still if the note is signed by the name of the agent only, it is laid down that it is his note though the body of the instrument make it a promise 'for' or 'on behalf of' the principal.[2]

It is sometimes said that to exempt the 'agent' from liability, in a case in which he might have acted in his character of agent, he ought to name his principal and further express in words the intention of binding the principal alone, — that is, he should show that the act is the act of the principal. But though it *may* be necessary to do that, in order to make the promise a promise of the principal, it is held unnecessary to do so in order to exempt the agent. If he has done that in express terms, that will be sufficient to exempt him. For example: 'We as trustees, but not individually, promise to pay,' &c., followed by the signatures of the makers (with the word 'trustees' added), the signers having authority to make the note as trustees, would not bind the signers personally.[3]

It does not impose liability upon the 'agent' that words which alone would be mere description are added to the signature, if elsewhere the promise is put as the act of the principal (or as we have just seen, if the agent expressly exempts himself). For example: 'I, as treasurer of the Congregational Society, or my successors in office, promise to pay,' &c., signed 'S R, Treasurer,' is not the note of S R.[4]

---

[1] Tucker Manuf. Co. v. Fairbanks, 98 Mass. 101.
[2] Barlow v. Congregational Society, 8 Allen, 460, 463.
[3] Tucker Manuf Co. v. Fairbanks, 98 Mass. 101.
[4] Barlow v. Congregational Society, 8 Allen, 460.

§ 4. Anomalous Signature of Stranger.

The last variant from the typical case — the last to be noticed — is an anomalous kind of undertaking, and one that has much exercised the courts. The case is this: After a promissory note has been executed in the usual way, a third person, who may or may not have been a stranger to the consideration between the maker and the payee, puts his name upon the back of the paper (or anywhere else, so that it is not with that of the maker), as a further assurance in favor of the payee. Now this act, though often spoken of as a kind of indorsement or as anomalous indorsement, is not properly speaking an indorsement; while the paper is in the hands of the payee it cannot be indorsed by another, according to the meaning of indorsement in the law merchant; the payee of paper payable to order must be the first indorser.

It is true that the courts of some States treat the party as an indorser, as far as they can; such courts will not admit that he can be treated in any way as on the footing of a maker of the note, and probably that conforms with what was the actual intention in most cases; but still those courts treat the party not as an indorser proper, but as an indorser sub modo.[1] Certain other courts meet the difficulties of the anomalous contract well, by treating it as a contract but imperfectly expressed, or rather as expressed but in part; refusing to regard it as a written contract within the meaning of the rule which excludes parol evidence to vary the terms of the writing. And accordingly, the contract being regarded as an open one, they receive evidence to show what, in point of fact, was

---

[1] Coulter v. Richmond, 59 N. Y. 478; Hall v. Newcomb, 7 Hill, 416; Clouston v. Barbiere, 4 Sneed, 336.

the understanding of the parties in the execution of the particular engagement.[1]

Another course, more commonly followed than either of the foregoing ones, proceeds to treat the contract in the way of an arbitrary presumption; the party being regarded as in the situation of a maker of the note.[2] If he signed the paper when it was executed, he is a co-maker and joint maker with the real maker; if he signed at some later time, he is still a maker, though not a joint maker, — a maker by way of guarantor or surety.[3] In the first of the two cases his liability is supported by the same consideration which supports that of the real maker; in the second, it must be supported by a new consideration of its own. Probably for some purposes the party would be treated as a surety even in the first case, where he is held to be joint maker; for it is to be remembered that a surety may be a joint maker with his principal. The courts which adopt this course admit evidence to show the time when the anomalous contract was signed, giving effect to the undertaking accordingly; but that is the extent to which they allow the contract to be affected by evidence.[4]

All this, however, supposes that the anomalous signing was for the further security of the payee;[5] if that was

[1] Sylvester v. Downer, 20 Vt. 355. See Eilbert v. Finkbeiner, 68 Penn. St. 243; Carr v. Rowland, 14 Texas, 275; Good v. Martin, 95 U. S. 90; Rey v. Simpson, 22 How. 341.

[2] Union Bank v. Willis, 8 Met. 504; Rodocanachi v. Buttrick, 125 Mass. 134; Phillips v. Cox, 61 Ind. 345; Herbage v. McEntee, 40 Mich. 337; Semple v. Turner, 65 Mo. 696. The rule has been modified by statute in Massachusetts. See Rodocanachi v. Buttrick, supra.

[3] Rodocanachi v. Buttrick, supra; Way v. Butterworth, 108 Mass. 509; Greenough v. Smead, 3 Ohio St. 415; Seymour v. Mickey, 15 Ohio St. 515.

[4] Wright v. Morse, 9 Gray, 337.

[5] There is much real, and still more seeming conflict of authority in regard to cases of anomalous signature; but most of the cases, of

not the case, if the signing was not intended to make the party liable to the payee, but to add security, with indorsement by the payee, to a purchaser of the paper, then the signing is not deemed anomalous at all, — it is indorsement proper, by all the authorities, if the payee also has indorsed.[1]

which there is a multitude, will fall under one of the three classes of the text.

[1] Bigelow v. Colton, 13 Gray, 309; Clapp v. Rice, Id. 403; Greenough v. Smead, 3 Ohio St. 415; Seymour v. Leyman, 10 Ohio St. 283.

CHAPTER IV.

THE ACCEPTOR'S CONTRACT.

§ 1. Acceptance Proper: Modes and Effect.

The drawee as such of a bill of exchange (or of a cheque) is under no liability whatever to the holder; to the holder he has not bound himself in contract, and he cannot be liable to the holder in tort upon refusal to honor the paper because as drawee he owes no duty to him; until acceptance he owes no duty to any one unless it be to the drawer.

Acceptance is the act by which the drawee of a bill of exchange, whether foreign or inland, signifies his undertaking, according to the law merchant, to pay the bill. Possibly a cheque might be accepted; but it is probable that a professed acceptance of a cheque would amount in law to a certification of it, which is a very different thing from acceptance.

By acceptance, the drawee contracts much as the maker of a promissory note contracts; he binds himself to the holder absolutely to pay, according to the tenor of the bill. No one else than the drawee (except perhaps as surety or guarantor *with* the drawee) can assume the position and liability of acceptor. For example: A draws a bill on B, payable to the order of C. B writes his name across the face of the bill, or elsewhere upon it. B is an acceptor, bound absolutely to pay the bill. Again: A draws a bill on B, payable to the order of C. D writes the word 'accepted' across the face of the bill, and signs his name thereto. D is not an acceptor of the bill.[1]

The law merchant permits acceptance to be signified orally or in writing. In some States the law merchant has been modified on this point by statute; thus, the statutes of certain States require that acceptance shall be in writing and signed by the drawee or by his lawful agent. Such statutes, however, are complied with by the signature alone of the party; that is at once a writing and a signature.[2]

According to the law merchant — that is, apart from statute — written acceptance may be made in any way and anywhere, if upon the bill, so long as there is an intention to accept. There are in use, however, certain brief modes of acceptance by which, because they conform to recognized custom, the law understands the intention directly, as much so as if the drawee were to write out in full and sign his undertaking to pay the bill at maturity. In these cases the intention to accept is fixed by the particular act; no different intention can be shown, unless, indeed, by fraud and mistake, or perhaps by mistake without fraud, the alleged acceptor was led to signing one instrument when he supposed he was signing another.[3] The customary modes of acceptance thus recognized by law are the following: Writing the word 'accepted,' or writing the name of the drawee, or any substitute for his name, upon the face of the bill; either of these alone,

---

[1] Davis v. Clarke, 6 Q. B. 16; May v. Kelly, 27 Ala. 497. There could be no protest and notice, such as would bind the drawer, on D's refusal to pay, for the drawer never requested him to pay.

[2] Spear v. Pratt, 2 Hill, 582; L. C. 32.

[3] Compare Foster v. Mackinnon, L. R. 4 C. P. 704; L. C. 554; indorsement procured by fraud as to the instrument. Such cases must be distinguished from fraudulent representations in regard to the consideration.

written by the drawee or by his agent, has a fixed meaning in law, to wit, acceptance.[1]

There are other modes which, because they have not the force of recognized custom, but still apparently signify acceptance, are deemed presumptively to be a manifestation of intention to accept; that is, they are deemed prima facie acceptance. The commonest of these are the following: Writing upon the bill 'presented,' or 'seen,' or the day of the month; these or any other words written by the drawee, which are consistent with the idea of acceptance, are held to amount to acceptance unless they are shown to have been written with a different intention.[2]

Whether oral acceptance of a bill of exchange is equivalent, by the law merchant, to written acceptance for all purposes is not clear; but assuming that it may be, the case should clearly show a present acceptance as distinguished from an undertaking to accept at some other time, such as a promise to accept the bill when it is produced for the purpose.

The oral acceptance of a bill of exchange is not a promise to answer for the debt or default of another, to wit, the drawer, and hence is not rendered invalid by the Statute of Frauds. The drawee's acceptance of a bill is a promise to pay a debt of his own; for the promise is supported by a consideration moving from the drawee to the holder, and that as well in cases in which there has been no barter of commodities or the like, as in cases in which there has been such a transaction. The case is this: Before accept-

---

[1] See Spear v. Pratt, 2 Hill, 582; L. C. 32. It may be that in some States the contract would be treated as not a written one, and that the courts would accordingly treat such acts as only prima facie acceptance. Compare what is said on Indorsement, in note to § 1, Chapter VI.

[2] See Spear v. Pratt, supra. It has been held that a signature of the drawee following the words, 'Paid on this order forty dollars' amounts to an acceptance of the whole. Peterson v. Hubbard, 28 Mich. 197. But see Cook v. Baldwin, 120 Mass. 317; Bassett v. Haines, 9 Cal. 261.

ance the holder had a contingent right of action, presently available, against the drawer, dependent upon refusal of the drawee to accept and the taking of certain steps. That right is taken away by the act of the drawee in accepting the bill; and so there is a case of detriment to the promisee.[1] Perhaps the result would be different if, instead of a bill of exchange, the instrument were something else, — as, for instance, an order to pay money upon some stated condition; in such a case acceptance might not affect any existing rights.[2]

§ 2. Quasi-Acceptance: Modes and Effect.

Thus far of acceptance proper, according to the tenor of the bill. Other acts are often called acceptance with some qualifying term; thus we have acceptance 'by giving credit to the bill,' 'conditional' acceptance, acceptance 'supra protest,' acceptance 'in case of need,' and 'virtual' acceptance. These are at best but cases of quasi-acceptance; none of them has the effect of acceptance proper. They will now be severally explained.

Acceptance 'by giving credit to the bill' is unusual, and in the nature of things operates only between the drawee and the particular holder who presented the bill for acceptance. This kind of acceptance arises by inference from the drawee's keeping the bill presented to him

---

[1] See Pierce v. Kittredge, 115 Mass. 374, 376. On the consideration compare also Arpin v. Owens, 140 Mass. 144, a case of acceptance *after* the holder had taken the bill; but the reasoning is indirect and artificial, where a plain and satisfactory reason was at hand.

[2] See Manley v. Geagan, 105 Mass. 445. But was not the instrument in that case, though called for distinction an 'order,' a bill of exchange? Further, as to the Statute of Frauds in such cases, see Curtis v. Brown, 5 Cush. 488, showing a conflict of authority between the courts of Massachusetts and of New York, where the consideration moves between the drawer and the (oral) acceptor.

for his acceptance for a very considerable length of time, obviously beyond what is proper for deciding what to do, or by any other act on his part, having the effect to induce the holder reasonably to suppose that the bill has been honored, or, as it is put, to 'give a credit to the bill,' and so to induce the holder to refrain from taking the steps necessary to fix the liability of the drawer and the indorsers, if the bill has been indorsed.[1] Liability in such a case is absolute; but this kind of acceptance necessarily puts a stop to the circulation of the bill, since the bill remains in the hands of the drawee till sued upon; hence the acceptance operates only between the immediate parties, as was just said. The drawee may keep the bill a reasonable time, as for the matter of a day, in deciding whether to accept or not.

'Conditional' acceptance explains itself in part; it is a case in which the drawee of a bill annexes some written condition to his acceptance, and he is liable only upon the performance or happening of the condition. The holder may, if he will, receive such an acceptance, without destroying the peculiar quality of the instrument as a contract of the law merchant. That is to say, the instrument will still be a bill of exchange having, if suitably drawn, negotiability and days of grace. The difference will be noticed between expressing a condition in the bill itself as signed by the drawer, and adding a condition in the acceptance.

The addition of the condition has, however, its own consequences, not appearing upon the face of the now modified bill. The drawer of the bill, and any indorser or other party whose name may appear upon it, undertook that the drawee should accept the bill as drawn, not some modification of it. The modification in the condition is, in other

---

[1] Hough v. Loring, 24 Pick. 254; Dunavan v. Flynn, 118 Mass. 537; Hall v. Steel, 68 Ill. 231.

words, a new term, to which the assent of the drawer and any other parties to the paper must be obtained, or their undertaking necessarily fails. The holder then receives a conditional acceptance, or any other acceptance which varies the tenor of the bill as executed by the drawer, on pain of discharging all non-assenting parties. All parties subsequent to the conditional acceptance, however, contract subject to such acceptance. If the holder wished to retain the benefit of the undertaking of the prior parties, he should have treated the refusal of the drawee to accept the bill as drawn as a dishonor of it. But having received the conditional acceptance, the holder must show that the condition has been performed or has happened.

Acceptance 'supra protest' is not common in this country, though it is sometimes met with. This kind of acceptance differs radically from acceptance proper, and from any of the quasi-acceptances yet described, for it is not only the act, in ordinary cases, of another than the drawee, but it imposes a liability much like that of an indorser. This sort of acceptance arises where, upon dishonor by the drawee, followed by a protest, — whence the term 'supra protest,' — a third person ordinarily, who may or may not be a party to the bill, accepts it for the honor of the drawer or of any other party or parties, or of all the parties. This acceptance is often called acceptance 'for honor.'

The contract of the acceptor supra protest, or for honor, is an undertaking to pay if, upon a further presentment of the bill to the drawee for payment, at maturity, it is again dishonored and duly protested, and due notice of the dishonor is given to such acceptor; otherwise not. For example (hypothetical): A draws a bill on B, payable to C or order. B refuses to accept the bill on presentment, whereupon C has it protested. D then accepts the bill 'for the honor' of A. At its maturity C presents the bill to B for payment, who again dishonors it. C takes no further steps. D is not liable.

Ordinarily, as has been intimated above, some one else than the drawee so accepts; but the drawee may himself accept supra protest, if he was not bound to accept in the ordinary way. He may in that way himself become holder of the bill, and hence entitled to maintain suit upon it. For example: A draws a bill of exchange upon B, payable to the order of C. C presents the bill for acceptance to B, who, not being under any legal obligation to accept, refuses, and then accepts the bill, after protest, for the honor of the drawer, and purchases it from C for value. B now has the rights of a holder, and at the maturity of the bill, on taking proper steps, can hold A.[1]

The next of these quasi-acceptances is acceptance 'in case of need.' That occurs where the drawer, to prevent a possible miscarriage by the refusal of the drawee, himself directs the holder, by writing on the bill, to apply 'in case of need' to some third person named thereby. This, like acceptance supra protest, is not common in America; but it is occasionally met with, mainly, it is to be supposed, on bills drawn abroad.

Acceptance 'in case of need,' like acceptance 'supra protest,' is given after protest of the bill, though it is possible that protest may not be necessary under the English law. In practice the holder, after having had the bill protested, takes it to the person named, and receives his acceptance or refusal. If he accepts, he assumes a conditional liability substantially like that of an acceptor supra protest. A slight change in the example last put, to suit the facts, will make it an example of the present subject.

The last of these quasi-acceptances to be considered is 'vir-

---

[1] Compare Swope v. Ross, 40 Penn. St. 186; L. C. 618. Further, on acceptance supra protest, see Schimmelpennich v. Bayard, 1 Peters, 264; Konig v. Bayard, Id. 250.

tual' acceptance. 'Virtual' acceptance is a term applied to promises to accept, as distinguished from present acceptance proper. The effect of the engagement is radically different from acceptance, and from any of the cases of quasi-acceptance yet described. Indeed, if the word 'virtual' were to be taken in its natural sense, to call a promise to accept a bill of exchange a 'virtual' acceptance would be very misleading. The act is neither acceptance nor of the nature of acceptance; the term 'acceptance,' with the qualifying word, is applied to it only because it is an undertaking of the drawee of the bill, which may be absolute.

But a promise to accept — that is, an undertaking to do sometime in the future what the drawer requires by an immediate act — is an affair of the common law only;[1] if it comes to a contract, it is a contract of the common law as distinguished from a contract of the law merchant. In principle it is subject to all the limitations of the common law; it does not import consideration; it has not the property of negotiability or of days of grace.

No doubt the nature of this 'virtual' acceptance has been somewhat obscured at times, partly by the very term 'virtual *acceptance*,' partly because the act relates to a contract of the law merchant. But it is clear upon the better authorities, as well as upon principle, that it has not the properties of a contract of that law. For example: A in Boston draws a bill of exchange on B in New York, payable to the order of C, and informs B by letter that he has drawn the bill. B replies by letter to A, saying, 'Your draft will be duly accepted.' D discounts and becomes holder of the bill, on C's indorsement. D cannot maintain an action against B, because the contract of B, if any

---

[1] The difference should be observed between a promise to accept thereafter, and a promise to pay; the latter would be an acceptance proper.

was created, was not negotiable or transferable.[1] For the same reason C could not maintain an action against B.

But the contract of the virtual acceptor, if a contract has been made, is absolute, if the terms of the promise are absolute; it is of course what its terms make it. It may be conditional, and often is, as well as absolute, and that without affecting the bill. It is in fact and in law a separate, independent engagement; the bill of exchange may circulate freely, and be presented for payment at maturity, without reference to its existence.

In the absence of statute, a promise to accept a bill of exchange may by the current of authority be made before or after the drawing of the bill;[2] and in favor of an existing bill, if not in favor of a non-existing bill, the promise may be either in writing or oral.[3] But the promise should clearly identify the bill, or clearly cover it by general description or general language;[4] and it is available only in favor of one who has taken the bill in reliance upon the promise to accept.[5]

It will be right to infer from the last statement that the promise to accept is not necessarily binding because it is supported by a valuable consideration, for the holder

---

[1] Worcester Bank v. Wells, 8 Met. 107; Exchange Bank v. Rice, 107 Mass. 37; s. c. 98 Mass. 288. See Henrietta Bank v. State Bank, 80 Texas, 648, 651; Grant v. Hunt, 1 C. B. 44.

[2] Coolidge v. Payson, 2 Wheat. 66; L. C. 33; Schimmelpennich v. Bayard, 1 Peters, 264; Exchange Bank v. Rice, 98 Mass. 288; Bigelow's L. C. Bills & Notes, 50–53.

[3] See Bigelow's L. C. Bills & Notes, 53. Statute has changed the rule in some States, requiring the promise to be in writing.

[4] Coolidge v. Payson, supra.

[5] Cases supra. The doctrine of a few cases (Jones v. Bank of Iowa, 34 Ill. 313; Read v. Marsh, 5 Mon. 8), that a promise to accept an *existing* bill may be sued upon as a virtual acceptance, whether the holder took the bill on the credit of the promise or not, is unsound. Exchange Bank v. Rice, 98 Mass. 288.

may not have connected himself with the promise. For example: For valuable consideration the drawee of a bill promises the payee to accept it, if presented on a certain day. The payee now indorses the bill to the plaintiff, who takes it without knowledge of the promise. Afterwards, being informed of the promise, the plaintiff presents the bill to the drawee, on the day named in the promise, for acceptance, which is refused. Payment is also refused at maturity of the bill. The drawee is not liable to the plaintiff.[1]

§ 3. Certification of Cheque.

Finally, the certification of a cheque should be noticed in this connection, if for no other purpose than to compare it with and distinguish it from acceptance. The act of certifying a cheque consists in the drawee's writing the word 'good' upon it. This binds the drawee absolutely, as acceptance binds the drawee of a bill; still it is not the same thing in effect, for, when procured by the holder, it discharges the drawer.[2] Nor are the consequences of refusal the same; indeed, certification is not required by the cheque, and refusal has no legal consequences.

It is held that the teller of a bank has no inherent power to certify cheques drawn upon his bank, that being a power to pledge the credit of the bank.[3] Probably the contrary would be true of the cashier, president, or vice-president of the bank.[4] However that may be, it is usual

---

[1] Coolidge v. Payson, 2 Wheat. 66; L. C. 33; McEvers v. Mason, 10 Johns. 207; Exchange Bank v. Rice, 98 Mass. 288; s. c. 107 Mass. 37; Worcester Bank v. Wells, 8 Met. 107.

[2] See Chapter V., § 3.

[3] Mussey v. Eagle Bank, 9 Met. 306. But see Farmers' Bank v. Butchers' Bank, 16 N. Y. 125.

[4] Merchants' Bank v. State Bank, 10 Wall. 604.

in cities to confer upon some officer of the bank, generally the cashier, power to certify the cheques of customers of the bank in so far as they have funds on deposit. And of such cases it is held that certification binds the bank, in favor of an innocent holder for value, though in point of fact the drawer had at the time no funds in the bank. It matters not whether the certification in such a case was due to mistake of the bank officer or not.[1] The certification means, not that the drawer has funds at the time of the certification, and will continue to have them when payment is demanded, but that the bank will pay the sum to the holder on demand.[2]

[1] Farmers' Bank v. Butchers' Bank, and Merchants' Bank v. State Bank, supra.
[2] Mussey v. Eagle Bank, 9 Met. 306.

CHAPTER V.

THE DRAWER'S CONTRACT.

§ 1. Drawer, Maker, Indorser.

The contract of the drawer of a bill of exchange must be set in bold contrast with that of the maker of a promissory note; in no way are the two in themselves alike. Physically unlike the contract of the maker, the contract of the drawer, whether of a bill or of a cheque, does not appear upon the face of the writing; radically unlike the contract of the maker, the contract of the drawer of a bill is conditional and secondary.

Aside from its merely physical properties, the contract of the drawer of a bill of exchange is in the main like that of an indorser. The drawer stands in the position of first indorser, in order of contract; thus the order of parties to an accepted bill is this: (1) acceptor; (2) drawer, virtually as first indorser; (3) payee, virtually as second indorser, though literally first, or such indorser, if any, as follows negotiation; and then, (4) any subsequent indorsers in order. If the bill is not accepted, the order of parties begins with the drawer, still virtually as first indorser, and then proceeds as in the case of an accepted bill. This part of the drawer's contract is treated in the chapter on the Indorser's Contract, post, Chapter VI.

§ 2. Right to Draw: Reasonable Ground.

Looking a little deeper, there are, between the contract of drawer and that of indorser, several substantial legal differences arising from the very nature of things. A man who draws a bill of exchange is naturally and legally supposed to have something to draw upon in the hands of the drawee, or at all events he is supposed to have a reasonable expectation that the draft will be accepted and paid by the drawee; that is, the drawer is supposed to stand in close relation to the drawee, and to have good ground accordingly for drawing. An indorser, however, is not supposed to know, and, in fact, generally does not know, anything about the state of things between the drawer and the drawee; and though his indorsement is, by a useful fiction, treated as equivalent in many respects to drawing a bill, and when special, as where the indorsement itself is to 'order,' is also in form like a bill in brief, still it is not a drawing by one having or supposed to have funds with the drawee, or knowledge of the action to be taken by him; that is, the indorser as such is not supposed to stand in any special relation to the drawee.

It results from this difference of situation, that the drawing of a bill of exchange (or a cheque) may operate as a fraud; and a drawing which may operate as a fraud should and does put the drawer in a different position from that of an honest drawer, and different therefore from that of an indorser, — different not merely as regards his liability by some other branch of law, but different as regards his liability under the law merchant. The drawer in such a case becomes, upon dishonor of the paper, if not by the very act of drawing, substantially the maker of a promissory note. For example: A draws a bill of exchange on B, payable to the order of C, having no reasonable ground to believe that the bill will be honored by B; and it is not honored by him. A is liable to C without notice of the dishonor.[1]

---

[1] Hopkirk v. Page, 2 Brock. 20; L. C. 96; Robinson v. Ames, 20 Johns. 146; Orear v. McDonald, 9 Gill, 350; Wood v. Price, 46 Ill. 435; Harness v. Davies Sav. Assoc., 46 Mo. 356; Dickens v. Beal, 10

But one is not lightly to be deemed guilty of fraud; and it does not necessarily make one guilty of fraud to draw without having provided and left with the drawee funds with which to pay one's draft, for one may still have reasonable ground to expect that the draft will be honored. Reasonable ground for drawing is the test.[1] The exact state of accounts between the drawer and the drawee may not be known by the drawer at the time of drawing; the accounts may be fluctuating from time to time, and balanced only at considerable intervals; and the drawer may reasonably suppose that the balance is in his favor to the amount of the draft; or though he may know that the balance is against him, he may have had assurance from the drawee that the paper will be honored; or he may have felt reasonably justified in drawing from practice between himself and the drawee in such cases. Drawing is not a fraud under circumstances of the kind.[2]

The holder, however, makes a case, it seems, against the drawer, by showing that he had no funds in the hands of the drawee when the bill or cheque was presented; it is then for the drawer to show, if he can, that, notwithstanding the want of funds, he had reasonable ground to believe that the paper would be honored, and hence that the usual steps for fixing the liability of a drawer should have been taken.[3]

Peters, 577; Brown v. Maffey, 15 East, 216; Rucker v. Hiller, 16 East, 43. It seems that the drawer would be liable without any demand upon the drawee; for why demand payment of a bill unreasonably drawn?

[1] See the cases just cited, to which many others might be added. A few early cases, following the discredited decision in Bikerdike v. Bollman, 1 T. R. 405, are contra. See Foard v. Womack, 2 Ala. 368; Tarver v. Nance, 5 Ala. 712; and certain New York cases, in which, however, the point was not raised. The true rule in New York conforms with the text. Robinson v. Ames, 20 Johns. 146.

[2] See Dickens v. Beal, 10 Peters, 572; Hopkirk v. Page, 2 Brock. 20; L. C. 96.

[3] Harness v. Davies Sav. Assoc., 46 Mo. 357; Story, Bills, § 312.

The 'reasonable ground' of the rule may relate either to the time of the drawing of the instrument, or to the time of presentment. Hence, the drawer may fall without the protection of the rule even where he had funds applicable to the draft at first, or on the way, to meet it, for he may withdraw or intercept them, and then have no reasonable ground to expect that the paper will be honored.

In regard to what amounts to reasonable ground, it is laid down that there must be something more than that which would excite an idle hope or a bare expectation, — something more than a remote probability. There must be a prospect such as would create a full, sober expectation or strong probability that the paper will be honored; such a state of things as would induce a merchant of common prudence and fair regard for his commercial credit to draw the draft.[1] The fact that the drawee is indebted to the drawer would create, presumptively, a case of the kind, though in point of fact the drawer have no funds in the drawee's hands.[2] The case would probably be different if the existence of the debt were in dispute. For example: A draws a bill of exchange on B, for an amount which A expects to recover against B in a contested suit by A against B. A has drawn without funds or reasonable ground to draw.[3]

The drawer may have reasonable ground to draw in certain cases, before any debt exists, by having an indisputable expectation of one, as where, having made a consignment to another, he draws before the consignment has reached the consignee.[4] Nor does it affect the case

---

[1] See cases in note 1, p. 48.

[2] Walker v. Rogers, 40 Ill. 278.

[3] Benoist v. Creditors, 18 La. 522; Williams v. Brashear, 19 La. 370. The second of these cases shows that the test of absence of funds is not conclusive; only the absence of reasonable ground is conclusive.

[4] Dickins v. Beal, 10 Peters, 572; Orear v. McDonald, 9 Gill, 350; Grosvenor v. Stone, 8 Pick. 79.

that the consignment, by depreciation of value, may have become insufficient to meet the bill, for that was not to be foreseen;[1] if it *was* foreseen by the drawer, or was understood by him to be inevitable, the case would probably be different. Again, it makes no difference, and for the same reason, that the consignment may never have reached the consignee.[2] So again the drawer has reasonable ground, where a debtor of his requests him to draw on a certain person, who is represented by the debtor to be indebted to him, especially where the drawee accepts (afterwards refusing to pay).[3] But the drawer of a bill who has no funds with the drawee, except that he has supplied him with goods on credit, which credit does not expire till long after the bill becomes due, has no reasonable ground to draw.[4]

The fact that the bill may have been accepted by the drawee has, by the weight of authority, no *decisive* bearing upon the question of the right of the drawer to draw.[5] Acceptance may perhaps require the holder to await the maturity of the bill, and then present it again for payment, though that is by no means clear; but whether that be the case or not, acceptance does not certainly show that the drawer had reasonable ground; at most it but indicates a presumptive right to draw, and hence only presumptively entitles the drawer to insist upon the usual steps for fixing his liability.[6]

[1] Robinson *v.* Ames, 20 Johns. 146. See Rucker *v.* Hiller, 16 East, 43.

[2] Byles, Bills. 301, 13th Eng. ed.

[3] Byles, ut supra, citing Latitte *v.* Slatter, 6 Bing. 623.

[4] Id., citing Claridge *v.* Dalton, 4 Maule & S. 226.

[5] See Rhett *v.* Poe, 2 How. 457; Valk *v.* Simmons, 4 Mason, 113; Allen *v.* King, 4 McLean, 128; Kinsley *v.* Robinson, 21 Pick. 327; Gillespie *v.* Cammack, 3 La. An. 248; Foard *v.* Womack, 2 Ala. 368, 371; Hoffman *v.* Smith, 1 Caines, 157, 160. But see Pons *v.* Kelly, 2 Hayw. 45, 47; Richie *v.* McCoy, 13 Smedes & M. 541. See also Orear *v.* McDonald, 9 Gill, 350, 358.

[6] See 2 Daniel, Neg. Inst. § 1082.

Another special feature of a drawer's contract is that where the drawer draws upon himself he is not entitled to notice if the paper is dishonored; for, drawing upon himself, he was in honor bound to accept. He may accordingly be treated as the maker of a promissory note.[1] In that view it seems to be unnecessary to make any demand of acceptance or payment of him. The same is true where a corporation or a partnership draws upon itself, or where one draws upon a partnership of which one is a member; and so also, it seems, of the case of drawing paper by one partnership upon another, where the defendant drawer is a member of both.

§ 3. Drawer of Cheque : Certification of Cheque.

What has been said in the last section applies mainly to bills of exchange, though it is proper to notice that the drawer of a cheque may, for some special reason not relating to funds, have had no reasonable ground to draw, and so be liable much like the maker of a note.[2] But the contract of drawer of a cheque is in itself peculiar, as was observed in the Introduction.

The peculiarity of the contract in question is due, of course, to the special nature of a cheque. Cheques have sometimes been called bills, in cases in which it was not necessary to observe any distinction between the two kinds of paper; but it is never safe to assume that things which are alike are the same, and it is certain that cheques are not, even in substance, bills of exchange.

A bill of exchange is supposed to have been drawn, as has already been seen, either upon funds in the hands of the drawee, *or* upon reasonable ground to believe that the

---

[1] Fairchild *v.* Ogdensburgh R. R. Co., 15 N. Y. 337; Miller *v.* Thomson, 3 Man. & G. 576.
[2] See Carew *v.* Duckworth, L. R. 4 Ex. 313.

drawee will honor it ; a cheque is always supposed to have been drawn upon funds. The drawer of a cheque draws upon his own banker, who, where the transaction is rightful on the part of the drawer, holds money of the drawer subject to his order as manifested by cheques. A bill of exchange is oftener drawn upon some merchant or trader. The cheque is drawn with a view to prompt payment rather than to use as money, — though merely to put a cheque into circulation is not in itself improper, so as to discharge the parties ; a bill of exchange only performs its ordinary function when it is put into circulation; the one is drawn to obtain money, the other, often to give credit and to take the place of money as far as desired.

The consequence which the law merchant annexes to this difference is that the drawer of a dishonored cheque, not drawn upon sufficient[1] funds applicable to it, is in the position substantially of the maker of a promissory note; at all events, he is liable to the holder without notice of dishonor.[2] Indeed, the drawer of a cheque remains liable, it seems, without notice of dishonor, though he had reasonable ground to draw, provided he has not suffered prejudice by the failure to give him notice, or to make an earlier demand than was made.[3] The drawer of a bill, as we have seen, would be discharged in such a case.

The case of the drawer of a cheque thus far may be put in this way: Prima facie, the drawer is entitled to notice of dishonor ; hence, the plaintiff must offer some legal excuse for the omission when he has failed to give such notice. Still, if he can show that the drawer has not, in point of fact, suffered prejudice by the omission, the

---

[1] Carew v. Duckworth, L. R. 4 Ex. 313.

[2] Andrew v. Blackly, 11 Ohio St. 89 ; Carew v. Duckworth, supra.

[3] Pack v. Thomas, 13 Smedes & M. 11 ; Mohawk Bank v. Broderick, 10 Wend. 304, affirmed, 13 Wend. 133 ; True v. Thomas, 16 Maine, 36. See Keene v. Beard, 8 C. B. N. S. 372 ; L. C. 156.

plaintiff can maintain his action against him. The drawer is, in a word, treated as the principal debtor sub modo; he is not discharged either by failure to make presentment within the time required in the case of a bill of exchange payable (like a cheque) on demand, or by want of notice of dishonor upon presentment and refusal to pay, unless the drawer has suffered some loss or prejudice thereby, and then only to the extent of his loss.[1] Reasonable ground to draw will not help the drawer of a cheque in such a case. For example (hypothetical): A draws a cheque on his banker B, payable to C or order. C holds the cheque for a week; within which time, on any day, he might reasonably have presented it to B for payment. When the cheque was drawn, B was solvent and paying his customers' cheques, and continued to do so for several days afterwards. Before the cheque is presented B stops payment, and the cheque is dishonored, and A is not notified. Subsequently B makes an arrangement with his creditors, and ultimately pays them, including A, in full. A is liable on the cheque regardless of the delay in presenting it, and the want of notice of dishonor. Again: In the same case, C omits for ten days to present the cheque, though he might have presented it on any day before. Meantime B fails; but before his failure A withdraws all his funds from B. A is not discharged by C's delay.[2] Again: In the same case B compromises with his creditors, including A, at fifty cents on the dollar. A is liable on the cheque for half the sum named in it. Again: In the same case A leaves all his funds with B, and loses the whole. A now is discharged by reason of C's delay.[3]

[1] Heywood v. Pickering, L. R. 9 Q. B. 428; Robinson v. Hawksford, 9 Q. B. 52; Little v. Phenix Bank, 2 Hill, 425, 428; Bell v. Alexander, 21 Gratt. 1; Morrison v. McCartney, 30 Mo. 183; Griffin v. Kemp, 46 Ind. 172. See Keene v. Beard, 8 C. B. N. S. 372; L. C. 156.

[2] Kinyon v. Stanton, 44 Wis. 479.

[3] Id.; Jones v. Heiliger, 36 Wis. 149. In all of these cases the

On the other hand, the holder of a cheque is protected (with an exception to be mentioned in the next paragraph) where he has exercised the diligence which would satisfy the law in the like case of a bill of exchange; in such a case no showing of loss or prejudice due to failure to exercise greater diligence would be heard. For example: The holder of a cheque which he receives on Saturday morning presents it on Monday afternoon in banking hours, and the cheque is dishonored, — the bank having stopped payment Monday at noon. The holder might have presented the paper on Saturday, or on Monday before noon, when it would have been paid. The diligence required in the case of a bill of exchange has been exercised, and the drawer is not discharged.[1]

But if prejudice result by reason of the holder's failing to exercise the diligence which would be required if the cheque had been a bill of exchange, the drawer will be discharged to the extent of such prejudice. Whether the delay is in demand of payment or in the giving of notice of dishonor, or in both, makes no difference.

This, however, supposes that the delay in making demand of payment is not due to keeping the cheque out in circulation. The difference between a cheque and a bill in that respect has already been noticed; a bill (not payable on demand?) may be kept out in circulation for a long period of time without affecting the liability of any of the parties, though the drawee fail, meantime, to the prejudice of the drawer; whereas, a cheque should with reasonable prompt-

drawer of a bill would be discharged. It should be remembered that neither a cheque nor a bill of exchange operates as an assignment of the fund or (until acceptance, in the case of a bill) makes the drawee a debtor to the holder. In Illinois, however, drawing a cheque operates as an assignment of the amount called for. Munn v. Burch, 25 Ill. 35.

[1] See Story, Notes, § 493; Bills, §§ 470, 471; Burkhalter v. Second Nat. Bank, 42 N. Y. 538; Simpson v. Pacific Ins. Co., 44 Cal 139.

ness be presented for payment, which means, if the holder and drawee reside in the same place, on the day, or day after, it is taken,[1] or, if they reside in different places, that it should be sent forward to be presented for payment on the day, or day after, it is taken, excluding in either case non-secular days, — unless a sufficient reason for not doing so is shown; that, on pain of discharging the drawer in the event of prejudice to him by the default.[2] That is what is meant, it seems, by the statement sometimes made, that the holder of a cheque is bound to greater diligence than the holder of a bill.[3]

Another substantial difference between the contract of drawer and indorser is created by certification, as it is called, of a cheque. That act consists in the drawee's writing the word 'good,' or perhaps some equivalent word, on the cheque. The act differs essentially in legal effect from the acceptance of a bill of exchange. Accepting a bill in no way affects the liability of the drawer, except in so far as it prevents immediate recourse (on refusal) against the drawer, — that is, the drawer of a bill remains a party to it after acceptance, as before, and liable upon it in case of dishonor by the acceptor. Certifying a cheque, on the other hand, if done at the instance and for the benefit of the holder, has the effect to discharge the drawer entirely.[4]

[1] Smith v. Miller, 43 N. Y. 171; s. c. 52 N. Y. 545; Burkhalter v. Second Nat. Bank, 42 N. Y. 538; Simpson v. Pacific Ins. Co., 44 Cal. 139; Alexander v. Burchfield, 7 Man. & G. 1061.

[2] Prideaux v. Criddle, L. R. 4 Q. B. 455. See Woodruff v. Plant, 41 Conn. 344.

[3] Mohawk Bank v. Broderick, 10 Wend. 304, 307, affirmed, 13 Wend. 133; Gough v. Staats, 13 Wend. 549, 551, 552.

[4] Minot v. Russ, 156 Mass. 458; First Nat. Bank v. Whitman, 94 U. S. 343, 345; First Nat. Bank v. Leach, 52 N. Y. 350; Born v. First Nat. Bank, 123 Ind. 78; National Com'l Bank v. Miller, 77 Ala. 168.

That rule has been supposed to proceed upon the ground that the act of certification amounts to a payment of the cheque between the drawer and the drawee, his banker. The drawee charges the sum to the account of the drawer as he would upon a cash payment, and becomes himself absolute debtor, like the maker of a promissory note, to the holder. The money deposited to the credit of the drawer is diminished by so much as the certified cheque calls for; the sum represented by the cheque is no longer the drawer's in any way.[1]

Assuming that to be the true ground upon which the rule is based, it would seem to make no difference whether the cheque were certified at the instance of the payee (or later holder) or of the drawer; and the practice in regard to charging the sum against the drawer, as money of his now appropriated by the drawee to paying the cheque, is the same in either case. But the latest authorities put the discharge of the drawer on the ground that the holder has brought about the drawer's discharge by making the bank his debtor. 'By his own act he makes the bank his debtor, and releases the drawer of the cheque.'[2] Hence, when the *drawer* procures the certification, so as to pass the cheque the more readily, he remains liable; and so most of the courts which have considered the question hold.[3] The drawer thus becomes practically a guarantor of the bank's solvency.

§ 4. Presentment for Acceptance.

For most purposes there is no occasion for separating the contract of drawer from that of indorser in regard to

---

[1] First Nat. Bank *v.* Leach, 52 N. Y. 350; Metropolitan Nat. Bank *v* Jones, 12 L. R. N. 402.

[2] Born *v.* First Nat. Bank, 123 Ind. 78; Minot *v.* Russ, 156 Mass. 458.

[3] See Minot *v.* Russ, supra; Bickford *v.* First Nat. Bank, 42 Ill. 238; Rounds *v.* Smith, Id. 245; Andrews *v.* German Nat. Bank, 9 Heisk. 211; Mutual Nat. Bank *v.* Rotgé, 28 La. An. 933.

presentment for acceptance; what is true of the one case is true of the other, and hence the subject will be reserved, in the main, for consideration with the other subjects belonging in common to drawing and indorsement, and treated under the latter head as the larger one.

There is one phase, however, of the law relating to presentment for acceptance which is peculiar to the drawer's contract; unless, indeed, there happen to be an indorsement upon the paper when it is so presented, in which case the law would apply to the indorsement as well. A bill of exchange payable at a stated time after date need not be presented for acceptance.[1] However, according to the more general understanding of the law merchant, the drawer's contract, in the case of a bill of exchange, looks, in all cases in which the bill is not payable on demand, to an acceptance as well as to payment by the drawee. That is, the drawer is understood to engage in favor of the payee, or subsequent holder, that the drawee will give him, at any time, the special security of acceptance; which of course, in the case of paper payable after date, or a stated time after sight, may be long before the maturity of the bill, and thus be a matter of great importance.

That undertaking of the drawer may be broken by the refusal of the drawee to accept the bill; there being then, upon due notice (which the law requires), a breach of contract on the part of the drawer, he is in principle, and by the current of authority, liable on the bill at once, regardless of the fact that payment of the bill, by the *drawee*, may not be required by the order for a long time thereafter. For example: A draws a bill of exchange on B. in favor of C, dated Jan. 1, 1893, payable three months after date. On Jan. 2, 1893, C presents the bill to B for acceptance, and acceptance is refused; the paper is duly

---

[1] Walker v. Stetson, 19 Ohio St. 400; L. C. 314.

protested, and A is duly notified. A is liable on the bill at once; C need not wait until the time stated in the bill before suing.[1]

The real meaning then of the drawer's contract in such cases, in the eye of the law merchant, is that the holder shall have the drawee's acceptance, which being given, he shall then have payment by the drawee at the stated time; but that, if the drawee refuse acceptance, the sum shall be due at once from the drawer; though it must be remembered that it is part of the drawer's contract, in ordinary cases, that there shall be due protest and notice of dishonor, whether on non-acceptance or non-payment after acceptance. Indeed, though presentment for acceptance may be unnecessary, protest and notice are required on pain of *discharging* the drawer, and not merely for the purpose of fixing his liability.

All this, it must be understood, is applicable to paper payable at, or at a stated time after, sight, and not merely to paper payable at, or at a stated time after, date, for presentment for acceptance in the former case is necessary. And, as has already been intimated, if there happen to be an indorsement upon the paper, the indorser also may be made liable, and sued at once; for his contract, as well as that of the drawer, is broken.

In Pennsylvania, however, a special view of the law merchant upon the foregoing subject obtains. It is there held that where presentment for acceptance is made in a case in which the step is unnecessary, as it is where the paper is payable at a stated time after date, presentment for acceptance, if refused, is to be regarded as nugatory, — that is, no rights can arise against the drawer. The holder must wait until the stated time for payment arrives, and then

---

[1] 3 Kent, 95; Bank of Washington *v.* Triplett, 1 Peters, 25; Union Bank *v.* Hyde, 6 Wheat. 572; Weldon *v.* Buck, 4 Johns. 144; Mason *v.* Franklin, 3 Johns. 202; Thompson *v.* Cumming, 2 Leigh, 321.

present the paper for payment as if nothing before had been done.[1] If presentment was *necessary*, refusal to accept would probably give an immediate right of action, in Pennsylvania as well as elsewhere, assuming that all steps were taken; for now the holder has done an act which the drawer required him to do.

[1] House v. Adams, 48 Penn. St. 261.

CHAPTER VI.

THE INDORSER'S CONTRACT.

§ 1. Definition, Modes, and Formality of Indorsement.

In accordance with what was said in the chapter relating to the Drawer's Contract, all that part of the drawer's contract which is of the same tenor as the contract of an indorser will be considered under the present head, and that too without further mention, except so far as may be needful, of the drawer. That is to say, all that hereafter appears in regard to the indorser's contract will apply equally to the contract of drawer; what is peculiar to the drawer's contract having been considered in Chapter IV. 'Indorser's Contract' should be taken, therefore, to mean Contracts of Indorser and Drawer, so far as alike.

Indorsement is an act whereby a person, not being acceptor or quasi-acceptor, surety or guarantor proper, writes his name upon a duly executed, negotiable bill of exchange, promissory note, or cheque,[1] with or without terms of contract or liability, according to the law merchant, or writes an equivalent contract on a separate paper, annexed or not to the bill, note, or cheque; to which act the drawing of a bill of exchange is in substance, for the purposes now in hand, an equivalent.

The act may be done by the holder of the paper, or by one having no interest in it. When done by the holder,

---

[1] A negotiable cheque may be indorsed. Keene v. Beard, 8 C. B. N. S. 372.

indorsement is an order upon the maker, drawee, or acceptor to pay the sum named to the next holder named, or to his order, or to the bearer, and has accordingly much the effect of drawing a bill of exchange; when done by one having no interest in the paper, indorsement merely adds security to the instrument.

If the instrument is on its face, or by indorsement, payable to order, indorsement by the holder is necessary to pass the title by the law merchant; that is, to give to the next holder legal ownership and a corresponding right of action upon the instrument. If the instrument is on its face, or by indorsement, payable to bearer, indorsement is not necessary to pass the title. If the instrument is on its face payable to a person named, without words of negotiability, there can be no indorsement of it; but if on its face there are words of negotiability, it may be indorsed after an indorsement making it payable to a person named, without addition.

Where indorsement is required to pass the (legal) title, transfer without indorsement, though with full intent to pass title, passes only an equitable title to the paper. Standing on such a title, the new holder can have no better rights than the person from whom he took the paper. For example: A is payee of a note payable to his order, but illegal in his hands. He transfers the paper to B for value and without notice, but without indorsement. The note is invalid in B's hands.[1]

[1] Lancaster Bank v. Taylor, 100 Mass. 18; Beard v. Dedolph, 29 Wis. 136. But if the omission of indorsement was due to mistake, the transferee could compel indorsement by suit in equity. Brown v. McHugh, 35 Mich. 50, 52. And if that proceeding were before maturity and before knowledge of the invalidity of the paper, the result would be to give the transferee a perfect title, as if there had been an indorsement in the first place. Lancaster Bank v. Taylor, supra. After maturity it would be too late, according to that case, and also according to Whistler v. Forster, 14 C. B. N. S. 248. But see Beard v. Dedolph, supra.

By the law merchant, indorsement need not be in the name of the indorser; enough that it is his act, intended as indorsement. For example: The payee of a bill of exchange payable to his order writes upon the bill '1, 2, 8,' as a substitute for his signature as indorser, and transfers the instrument to the plaintiff. The act is indorsement.[1] Again: The wife of the payee in such a case, acting as the authorized agent of the payee, writes her own name upon the note. That is indorsement by the payee.[2]

When indorsement is required, in order to pass title, the act must be done by him who has the legal title, — that is, generally by him to whose order it is payable, — though the entire beneficial interest be in another. Thus, one to whose order as trustee a promissory note is payable must indorse it, to pass the title to another; indorsement by the cestui que trust would pass the equitable title only, and payment could not be enforced in favor of the indorsee. So where paper is made payable to A, to the order of B, the meaning is that it is payable to A only upon the order of B; hence, B must indorse it in order to give to A the full right of legal ownership. Again, upon the death of the holder of paper the legal title passes to his executor if he left a will, or to his administrator if he died intestate; and this though the deceased gave the paper by will specifically to another. Hence, the executor must indorse it to pass title, if it is payable to order, to give the legatee the right to sue upon or to transfer it.[3]

The rule of indorsement finds frequent expression in cases of paper payable or indorsed to a partnership. The legal title being in the partnership, nothing short of an

---

[1] Brown v. Butchers' Bank, 6 Hill, 443; L. C. 121.

[2] Stevens v. Beals, 10 Cush. 291.

[3] Crist v. Crist, 1 Cart. (Ind.) 570. See also Hersey v. Elliot, 67 Maine, 526. The executor or administrator will indorse 'without recourse.'

act by the firm can be indorsement. It makes no difference to whom the paper is to be passed; one of the partners, acting merely in his own right, could not indorse the paper even to his sole co-partner.[1] Of course the partner might indorse the paper over as the act of the partnership; and it would make no difference that he did it in his own name, if the act were the act of the firm.[2] Nor would the act be ineffective because the paper was indorsed over to one of the partners. Such indorsee could not, indeed, maintain an action upon the paper against the partnership; but his right of action would be perfect against other parties.[3]

Upon the death of a member of the partnership, the survivors may indorse, in the name of the partnership, paper payable or indorsed to the firm. The survivors acquire by survivorship full and complete title to such paper for the purpose of settling the affairs of the now dissolved partnership, and hence, for indorsing over the paper; the proceeds going to the benefit of the estate of the deceased partner to the extent of his interest.[4]

A different rule prevails, it seems, in those cases in which indorsement of the firm paper is not necessary to pass title; that is, where the paper is payable to bearer, or is already indorsed in blank. In such a case it does not follow that because the legal title and ownership may be in a partnership the partnership indorsement is necessary to pass the paper, even while the partnership continues to exist unchanged. No indorsement by a member of the partner-

---

[1] Estabrook v. Smith, 6 Gray, 570; Robb v. Bailey, 13 La. An. 457.

[2] Estabrook v. Smith, supra.

[3] So a note made by a partnership payable to the order of one of the partners may be indorsed over by the payee so as to give a good title to his indorsee. Thayer v. Buffum, 11 Met. 398.

[4] Story, Promissory Notes, § 125; Crawshay v. Collins, 15 Ves. 218 226; Jones v. Thorn, 2 Mart. N. S. 463.

ship in his own right would pass title in favor of a person having notice of the wrongful act; but the paper itself would not carry notice, and one who purchased for value and without notice would acquire a perfect title. And upon death of one of the partners, it would not be necessary, it seems, for the survivors to indorse such paper over as surviving partners.[1]

There is much doubt whether the same rule would apply concerning such cases of indorsement where the firm has been dissolved, not by death, but by the act of the parties, or by the law. There are authorities which deny the power of one of the partners to indorse the paper over in such a case,[2] even though that partner have authority to settle up the partnership business.[3] The contrary would be true, however, if the indorsee had no notice of the dissolution,[4] or if the paper was payable or indorsed to the particular partner (for the partnership) who after dissolution indorsed it.[5]

A bill, note, or cheque payable to the order of one who receives it as agent for another is payable in law to his principal's order; and no indorsement by the agent is needed to give the principal or any subsequent holder a perfect title. For example: A promissory note is payable to the order of 'A, Cashier' of a bank. The note is payable to the order of the bank, and the cashier's indorsement is not necessary to pass the title.[6]

Again there can be no transfer by indorsement which passes less than the entire title to the paper. A part

[1] Attwood v. Rattenbury, 6 J. B. Moore, 579; Bigelow's L. C. Bills & Notes, 136.
[2] Sanford v. Mickles, 4 Johns. 224.
[3] Abel v. Sutton, 3 Esp. 108; Humphries v. Chastain, 5 Ga. 166; Foltz v. Pourie, 2 Desaus. Eq. 40.
[4] Cony v. Wheelock, 33 Maine, 366.
[5] Temple v. Seaver, 11 Cush. 314.
[6] First Nat. Bank v. Hall, 44 N. Y. 395.

interest in the paper could no doubt be transferred, because alienation is an incident of property; but the transfer would be in virtue of the common law, and the rights of the parties in respect of the transaction would be rights of the common law, not of the law merchant. The law merchant knows nothing of such transactions; the transferee could not sue either prior parties or the supposed 'indorser' himself, in any action upon the paper.[1]

Indorsement is a technical act by the law merchant, and can be effected only in certain ways. In the first place the act, as the definition states, must be in writing; in the second place it must be with intent to indorse according to the law merchant. The first of these rules, as well as the second, is a requirement of the law merchant, not of any statute. In regard to the second, the intent is fixed, according to the current of authority: (1) when the name of the indorser is written in blank upon the bill, note, or cheque; (2) when the contract is written out on the paper in the common form 'Pay to A or order,' 'Pay to the order of A,' or in equivalent words, with signature; (3) when the words written restrict present negotiability, as 'Pay to A only;' (4) when the words exempt the party from liability, as 'Without recourse;' (5) when to any of the first three modes such words as the following are added, 'Waiving notice,' or 'Waiving demand and notice,' or 'Waiving protest,' or 'Waiving protest and notice;' (6) when to any of the first three modes the words 'For collection,' or the like, are added.

[1] Douglass v. Wilkeson, 6 Wend. 637. There may, however, be acceptance for part of a bill of exchange. And there is some semblance of authority for the opinion that, *before* acceptance, there may be an indorsement as to part of the sum named. See Pownal v. Ferrand, 6 Barn. & C. 439; Beawes, pl. 286. But the better view is contra. Chitty, Bills, 235, note. See also the remark of Parke, B. on the argument in Oridge v. Sherborne, 11 Mees. & W. 374; L. C. 78, 81.

The first of these modes is called Indorsement in Blank; and though it is in blank, the law merchant supplies its terms, most of the authorities holding the terms fixed as if they had been written out at length, some authorities however treating the terms supplied by the law as expressing prima facie only the terms of agreement.[1]

The second of the modes is called Indorsement in Full; though in point of fact the terms of the contract are no more fully expressed than are those of the drawer of a bill of exchange by the language of the bill. An equivalent to the common form of indorsement ('Pay to A or order,' 'Pay to the order of A') is 'pay to A,' though at first suggestion that would appear to be substantially different. But the paper itself being negotiable, it is held that a particular indorsement like that mentioned shows no intention to put an end to the negotiability of the instrument, and hence it is deemed only a short way of saying 'Pay to A or order.'[2]

The third mode is called Indorsement in Full Restrictive. The intent to cut off the further circulation of the paper is plain in such an indorsement; and because

---

[1] Some courts hold that indorsement in blank is not to be treated as a written contract within the rule which excludes parol evidence to vary a contract in writing; and they accordingly hold that such indorsement does not fix the intention to indorse according to the law merchant, except by prima facie presumption. Ross v. Espy, 66 Penn. St. 481; Hill v. Ely, 5 Serg. & R. 363; Harrison v. McKim, 18 Iowa, 485; Iser v. Cohen, 1 Baxt. 421. But the better authorities treat the act as fixing absolutely the intent to indorse, with its consequences in the law merchant. Bank of United States v. Dunn, 6 Peters, 51; Bigelow v. Colton, 13 Gray, 309; Dale v. Gear, 38 Conn. 15; Charles v. Denio, 42 Wis. 56; Eaton v. McMahon, Id. 484; Rodney v. Wilson, 67 Mo. 123; Doolittle v. Ferry, 20 Kans. 230. See also Davis v. Brown, 94 U. S. 423, where it is held that a contemporaneous *written* agreement might be shown to vary the indorser's liability.

[2] Leavitt v. Putnam, 3 Comst. 494; L. C. 129.

the indorser, being owner of the paper, has naturally the right to transfer it, subject to such restrictions as he will, the courts will, it seems, support the particular restriction. Any holder after A, therefore, can have no better title than that of assignee.[1]

The fourth mode is called Indorsement without Recourse, or sans Recours. Here the intent is merely to pass title to the paper, without liability by way of indorsement;[2] which intent the courts will of course support. This mode is resorted to, properly, only in those cases in which indorsement is necessary to transfer the title. For example: A promissory note is payable to the order of A, who is trustee of the payee. It is needful to transfer the title of a third person, and A, who is unwilling to incur the liability of indorser, indorses it, 'Pay to the order of B,' signing his name and adding (or writing before his signature) 'Without recourse.'

Of the fifth mode, in its varieties, — which are varieties of substance, — nothing need be said at present; the subject comes up later, necessarily, when we come to consider the steps required to fix the indorser's liability.

The sixth mode is called Indorsement for Collection. The meaning of it is that the indorser desires to have collection made by some agent, usually a bank or the Clearing House. It is notice that the indorser does not transfer the ownership of the paper, and hence that he does not intend to incur the liability of an indorser, an intent which the law will uphold.[3]

In other cases than the foregoing, the question whether the writing amounts to indorsement will depend upon the

---

[1] See Leavitt v. Putnam, supra.

[2] The indorser may, however, be liable as a vendor, if it should turn out that the paper, or any prior signature, was not genuine. Dumont v. Williamson, 18 Ohio St. 515.

[3] Sweeny v. Easter, 1 Wall. 166, 173.

reasonable construction to be placed upon the language used, helped out as it may be in some cases by external evidence. For example: Above the defendant's signature, upon the back of a negotiable promissory note, was written, 'Rec'd one year's interest on the within, May 10, 1871.' This imports merely an acknowledgment of interest paid, and to hold the signer as indorser it must be proved by external evidence that the signature had no connection, or not the connection apparent, with the words quoted.[1]

Any writing by the holder importing a transfer of his title, right, or interest in the instrument, if containing nothing inconsistent with the idea of indorsement, will, it seems, be construed to mean indorsement. For example: The holder of a negotiable note writes on the back of it, 'I this day sold and delivered to A the within note,' adding his signature. This is deemed an indorsement.[2] Again: In like case the writing is, 'I hereby sell and assign to A all my right and title to this note.' followed by signature. This is deemed an indorsement.[3] Again: The defendant writes on the back of a negotiable note an agreement by himself to pay the note 'as if by me indorsed.' This is deemed an indorsement.[4]

It is competent by the law merchant for an indorser to make a transfer of negotiable paper upon some special condition stated in the writing. Such an indorsement would not take away the negotiable or other properties of the paper,[5] nor would it necessarily prevent the act from being indorsement. If the condition were not performed, the property of the instrument would revest in the

---

[1] Clark v. Whiting, 45 Conn. 149.
[2] Adams v. Blethen, 66 Maine, 19.
[3] Sears v. Lantz, 47 Iowa, 658.
[4] Pinnes v. Ely, 4 McLean, 173.
[5] Tappen v. Ely, 15 Wend. 362.

indorser, assuming that the condition were a condition of the transfer.[1]

There may be a joint indorsement, as where the indorsement is by partners, or where it is by several persons united in interest in the transaction. It will not make an indorsement by two or more a joint indorsement that they indorse at the same time, though they may have been led to do so by the same inducement; their interest in the transaction must be joint, — they must have undertaken to share the contract together.[2] When such is the case they are all joint indorsers towards the holder. Between themselves, however, they are not indorsers at all; that is, one of them could not maintain an action against one of his associates as an indorser,[3] nor indeed could one without his associates, after taking up the paper, maintain an action against any party to it.

It is not necessary that the writing should be upon the bill, note, or cheque; though if elsewhere, some clear and distinctive manifestation of intent to indorse must be shown. This may be by annexing to the instrument a written indorsement,[4] which may be in any of the forms just designated. But to write upon the paper, or to annex to it a writing of any other import than that of indorsement, as the term is defined above, though the writing be by the holder himself, and the bill, note, or cheque be at the same time transferred to the person in whose favor such writing runs, will not, according to the better authorities, be indorsement or the equivalent of indorsement.[5]

---

[1] Robertson v. Kensington, 4 Taunt. 30.
[2] Shaw v. Knox, 98 Mass. 214.
[3] Id.
[4] Folger v. Chase, 18 Pick. 63.
[5] Tuttle v. Bartholomew, 12 Met. 452; Belcher v. Smith, 7 Cush. 482; Spies v. Gilmore, 1 Comst. 321; Hall v. Newcomb, 7 Hill, 416; Cottrell v. Conklin, 4 Duer, 453; Waterbury v. Sinclair, 26 Barb. 455.

Special contracts of the kind belong by nature to the common law; they will be considered in a later chapter.

§ 2. Apparent Indorsement.

What appears on its face to be an ordinary indorsement may often be shown to be something else, and that consistently with regarding the terms to be supplied by law, in order to make out the contract, as fixed; for that assumes that there is nothing in the circumstances, as distinguished from the actual terms, of the contract to affect it. Thus while evidence may not be admissible to show that what appears to be an indorsement in blank was understood to have been intended as indorsement without recourse, evidence of the time and circumstances under which it was made is admissible, and this may vary its effect materially, even to making it on the one hand practically an indorsement without recourse, or on the other of raising the grade of liability, or indeed of modifying it in any one of several ways.

Thus, an indorser may show that his own indorsement was made at the same time with that of one or more other indorsements, as part of one common transaction by which the parties named became jointly bound. That could not be done against a holder for value without notice; but it could be shown against one who had taken the paper *with* notice, so as to require him to sue them all together, if at all. And it could be shown between such indorsers themselves, if one of them, having taken up the paper, should call upon another to pay as a prior indorser; for we have already seen that joint indorsers are not indorsers at all between themselves.[1]

The time when a particular indorsement was made may

But see contra, Partridge *v.* Davis, 20 Vt. 499; Myrick *v.* Hasey, 27 Maine, 9.

[1] See Shaw *v.* Knox, 98 Mass. 214; L. C. 122.

be shown also for the purpose of affecting the order of liability. Suit can never be brought by one indorser, on taking up the paper, against a subsequent indorser; and the order in which the names appear on the paper affords only prima facie evidence of the real order in point of time. The apparent liability of one indorser to another may accordingly be shown to be apparent only and not real. For example (hypothetical): A negotiable promissory note bears the indorsements of A and B in that order. The liability of both is fixed on dishonor by the maker, and B takes up the note and brings suit against A. A may show that his indorsement, though written above that of B, was in point of fact made on a day subsequent to B's indorsement.[1]

No such evidence, however, would be received against any one who indorsed or held the paper after the indorsement by the defendant. Towards the holder in such a case it would make no difference in what order the parties in fact indorsed: he could sue prior indorsers (or other prior parties) in any order he pleased; he could bring his action against the first indorser alone as well as against the last. Enough in such a case that the defendant's liability has been fixed.

What appears to be the ordinary contract of indorsement unmodified, may be shown to be something else also in the following cases: The relation of principal and agent may be shown to exist between the plaintiff and the defendant; in such a case the agent acquires no title, — he merely holds in right of his principal. Again, it may be shown that the paper was indorsed to the holder for some special purpose, and is held in trust, as where it was indorsed for collection merely. And again the relation of principal and surety may be shown to exist between the parties, as

---

[1] As to evidence of the kind touching *anomalous* indorsement, see ante, pp. 33-35.

where the indorsement was made by the defendant at the request and for the accommodation of the plaintiff; that too would defeat liability altogether.[1] Or it might be shown, with the same result, that both plaintiff and defendant were co-sureties on the paper for another person. Or again, it might be shown that there was a defence arising from an antecedent transaction, including an agreement that the paper should be taken in sole reliance upon the responsibility of the maker or acceptor, and that it was indorsed in order to transfer the title in pursuance of such agreement, so that the attempt to enforce payment of the defendant was in the nature of a fraud.[2]

These are the chief if not the only cases in which what appears to be an ordinary indorsement may be shown to be something else, or rendered inoperative towards giving the immediate indorsee a right of action thereon. Of course want of consideration may be shown, as in other cases of contract; but that is a different thing, implying as it does that the defendant's act was a true indorsement. But where the defendant or the plaintiff makes an attempt to prove that what stands as a clear and unambiguous contract of indorsement was not intended to be such, merely by the declarations of the parties made at the time, — as by showing that the defendant indorsing in full said that he was not to be liable, and that the plaintiff received the indorsement accordingly, — that attempt, according to the current of authority, will not be allowed to succeed.[3]

---

[1] Case v. Spaulding, 24 Conn. 578.

[2] Upon this whole subject, see Dale v. Gear, 38 Conn. 15; Downer v. Cheseborough, 36 Conn. 39; Chaddock v. Vanness, 35 N. J. 517; First Nat. Bank v. National Marine Bank, 20 Minn. 63.

[3] Dale v. Gear, 38 Conn. 15, explaining Case v. Spaulding, 24 Conn. 578; Patterson v. Todd, 18 Penn. St. 426; Hill v. Ely, 5 Serg. & R. 363. The Pennsylvania courts, and those of some other States, would, contrary to the general current, admit evidence of the kind if the indorsement were in blank. Supra, p. 67, note.

§ 3. Nature of the Contract.

The contract unmodified of the indorser of an inland bill of exchange, or of a promissory note, or of a cheque, is that he will pay the sum named in the paper upon the following conditions precedent, where presentment is for payment: (1) Due presentment and demand; (2) Due notice of dishonor. Of a foreign bill of exchange: (1) Due presentment and demand; (2) Due protest; (3) Due notice of dishonor.

Where presentment of a bill of exchange is for acceptance, and acceptance is necessary, the contract of an indorser of an inland bill is for payment upon the following conditions precedent: (1) Due presentment and demand; (2) Due notice of dishonor. Of a foreign bill: (1) Due presentment and demand; (2) Due protest; (3) Due notice of dishonor. Where acceptance is not necessary, then, *in case of* due presentment for acceptance, — of an inland bill, due notice of dishonor; of a foreign bill, due protest and due notice of dishonor.

All this leads to a consideration of the steps necessary to fix the indorser's liability, transforming it from a conditional to an absolute obligation. But there is another subject which may properly be disposed of first.

§ 4. Legal Effects of Indorsement.

What is now referred to is certain legal effects of indorsement which may be called the secondary aspects of the subject.

One of these effects, though probably an apparent effect only, is seen in indorsement in full, such as 'Pay to the order of A.' What that purports on its face to be is true as well of indorsement in blank: each is an order to pay the sum named, as designated. Indeed, as we have seen, indorsement in general is said to be equivalent for certain purposes to drawing a bill. That statement, however, is only a free expression of a very general truth.

In the first place, the statement, to be exact, should be that indorsement is equivalent to drawing a bill or to drawing a cheque, according to circumstances. The indorsement of a cheque cannot properly be said to be equivalent to drawing a bill; for the question would arise at once, if the statement were made with full purpose, What kind of bill, a foreign or an inland bill? The difference is, as has just been noticed, material. The *indorsement* of a cheque cannot require protest; that would be to change the nature of the cheque. And the same may be said of indorsement of a promissory note.

It may be said, however, that indorsement is equivalent to drawing an inland bill; but why that rather than equivalent to drawing a foreign bill, — that is, why that, so far as the nature of indorsement is concerned, especially in a case in which the cheque or the note is drawn or made and payable in different States? And then in regard to indorsement of a bill of exchange, could it be said that indorsement of a foreign bill was equivalent to drawing an inland bill? That again would be to change the nature of the instrument.

This shows that so far as there is any equivalency, the equivalency must have relation to the particular instrument, — indorsement of a foreign bill to the drawing of a foreign bill, indorsement of an inland bill to the drawing of an inland bill, indorsement of a cheque to the drawing of a cheque, indorsement of a promissory note to the drawing of an inland bill.

But at best the equivalency is only for certain purposes; in no case is indorsement equivalent to the drawing of a bill for any of the special purposes considered in Chapter

V., such, for instance, as in regard to the rule of drawing without funds. Another important particular in which there is no equivalency will be noticed by referring to certain remarks on a preceding page concerning indorsement in full; where it was seen that indorsement by such words as 'Pay to A' would not cut off negotiability, whereas a bill so drawn would not be negotiable.

Indeed, the statement that indorsement is equivalent to drawing a bill is misleading in many cases, and necessary in none. It had been better in the first place had it merely been said that indorsement is an order on the drawee, acceptor, or maker to pay according to the tenor of the instrument. That would be strictly true. But the statement under consideration is too well fixed in the language of the law-books to be discarded; hence, as we must needs have it, it must be explained. We may then, though not without some hesitation, eliminate this phase of the subject from any list of real effects, of a secondary nature, of indorsement; all that is left of it, as an order to pay, being the contract of indorsement in its primary aspect.

The most important perhaps of the secondary aspects of indorsement is seen in a rule of law, not arising necessarily from the terms of the contract as primarily expressed, — that indorsement is a conclusive admission or possibly a warranty of the legal validity of the paper as it stands at the time of the indorsement.[1] That rule of law is often put as a corollary (or as growing out) of the primary rule, that the indorser undertakes to pay on the taking of certain steps; but if it is proper to express it in terms of warranty, the rule is more than that.

In so far as that rule is a corollary of the primary rule of indorsement, it merely means that in an action upon an indorsement it is not necessary for the plaintiff to prove, for example, the genuineness of *prior* signatures or of the

---

[1] See Bigelow, Estoppel, 480 et seq., 5th ed.

paper itself; enough that the indorsement is genuine. That is a well-settled rule of law, resulting immediately from the indorser's undertaking to pay on presentment, demand, and notice of dishonor (or whatever steps are required). For example: The defendant is indorser, and the plaintiff indorsee, of a promissory note payable to the order of A, and purporting to be indorsed by him. The steps (presentment, demand, and notice) necessary to fix the defendant's liability were duly taken. But it is conceded by the plaintiff, if the evidence is admissible against him, that the supposed indorsement by A is a forgery, of which fact, however, both parties were ignorant at the time of defendant's indorsement. The evidence is not admissible, and the defendant is liable notwithstanding the forgery, the indorsement being in law an admission of the genuineness of the signature in question.[1]

As a corollary, the rule is not of great importance; for it would be just as well for one to stand upon the terms of the indorser's contract as primarily expressed. That covers the whole case. But if it be correct to state the rule thus, as it sometimes is stated, that indorsement is a *warranty*, instead of a mere admission, of the validity of the paper, then the rule becomes highly important; for in that case the holder would have a right of action upon that warranty if it were untrue, and in principle it would be no answer that the plaintiff took the paper with knowledge of the real state of things. But there is ground for doubting whether such is the law; the true rule probably is, that indorsement is but an admission, conclusive, therefore, only in favor of an innocent indorsee, that the paper is genuine.[2]

---

[1] State Bank *v.* Fearing, 16 Pick. 533.

[2] See, however, Erwin *v.* Downs, 15 N. Y. 575, infra, where it appears to be held that indorsement is a true warranty of the *capacity* of prior parties. But compare Barlow *v.* Bishop, 1 East, 432.

Another instance of this effect of indorsement touching prior contracts on the paper relates to the competency of prior parties. It is sometimes said, and there is express authority for the statement, that indorsement amounts to a warranty of the capacity of all parties whose signatures appear upon the paper before, that is, at the time of, the indorsement. For example: The defendant is indorser and the plaintiff indorsee of a promissory note. The note was executed by a married woman, incompetent by law to contract, of which fact the plaintiff was aware when he took the note. The defendant's liability as indorser has been duly fixed, but he now attempts to set up the incapacity of the maker in defence. That is deemed no defence.[1]

There is ground for doubting, in this case as well as in regard to genuineness, whether it is strictly true to say that there is a *warranty* of capacity; and support is given to the doubt by the English courts, in treating analogous cases as admissions of capacity.[2] But the admission of capacity probably stands upon a different footing from the admission of genuineness. The latter should be conclusive only in favor of a holder who purchased without knowledge of the forgery; while the former may well be conclusive in favor of any holder for value after the indorsement. And the reason is, that one would never indorse paper knowing that it was not genuine, while one might well indorse genuine paper though some prior

[1] Erwin v. Downs, 15 N. Y. 575.
[2] Drayton v. Dale, 2 Barn. & C. 293; Vagliano v. Bank of England, 23 Q. B. Div. 243, 247 (reversed on other ground, 1891, A. C. 107). The language of the English Bills of Exchange Act, 55 (1), (2), should be noticed. 'Warrant' or 'warranty' is not used; and the statute here is plainly nothing but a codification of the decisions of the courts on the law merchant.

Transfer by delivery, that is, without indorsement, is a different thing, that creates a true warranty, one of right, title, genuineness, and capacity. Merriam v. Wolcott, 3 Allen, 258; Bills of Ex. Act, 58, (3).

party to it was, for instance, under twenty-one years of age,— upon the probability that the party would perform his contract. Only a holder without knowledge could have a superior claim to that of the indorser, in a case of forgery; while a holder with knowledge might well have a superior claim, in a case of incapacity.

On the whole, it is reasonable to suppose that the use of language of warranty in cases of the kind under consideration is conventional merely; that is, it is not meant that a warranty, in the proper sense, arises from indorsement, but only that an admission is made, which usually is binding. It is clear that an indorser, generally speaking, cannot plead the invalidity of the paper against prior parties; his contract does not depend upon the legality of theirs.[1] And that is all that the language of warranty now means.

Another question of a kindred nature has given the courts trouble; to wit, Does this admission by the indorser of the validity of the paper as it stands disqualify the indorser to give testimony to the invalidity of the paper in a suit against (not the indorser, but) some prior party? Such party may of course set up the invalidity of his own contract against a holder having notice; but can he produce the indorser as a witness? In the time of Lord Mansfield the question was answered in the negative; no person, it was held, could be permitted to give testimony to invalidate an instrument to which he had given his signature; having given a credit to it, he could not afterwards discredit it.[2]

But the rule was not satisfactory to the English courts, and some twelve years later, after narrowing it to negotiable instruments, they overturned it, and held the indorser

---

[1] Prescott Nat. Bank v. Butler, 157 Mass. 548, 550, using language of warranty.

[2] Walton v. Shelley, 1 T. R. 296.

competent notwithstanding his indorsement.[1] In this country there is a conflict of authority, some of the courts having followed the earlier English rule,[2] others having followed the later one,[3] while still others have adopted a middle course. It will only be necessary to state the rule adopted by courts taking the middle ground. According to that rule, the indorser is a competent witness to impeach the validity of the paper, if the plaintiff took with notice, otherwise not.[4] But the better and more general rule treats him as competent in either case. The rule of exclusion applies in any case only in regard to facts of the time of the execution of the contract sued upon.[5]

[1] Jordaine v. Lashbrooke, 7 T. R. 601.
[2] Treon v. Brown, 14 Ohio, 482.
[3] Townsend v. Bush, 1 Conn. 260; L. C. 150; Haines v. Dennett, 11 N. H. 180; Stafford v. Rice, 5 Cowen, 23; Williams v. Walbridge, 3 Wend. 415; Freeman v. Brittin, 2 Harr. (N. J.) 192; Taylor v. Beck, 3 Rand. 316; Stump v. Napier, 2 Yerg. 35.
[4] Thayer v. Crossman, 1 Met. 416; Newell v. Holton, 10 Gray, 349; Clapp v. Hanson, 15 Maine, 345. See Davis v. Brown, 94 U. S. 423.
[5] Woodhull v. Holmes, 10 Johns. 231; Skilding v. Warren, 15 Johns. 270; Strong v. Wilson, Morris, 84; Drake v. Henly, Walker (Miss.), 541.

CHAPTER VII.

INDORSER'S CONTRACT CONTINUED: PROCEEDINGS BEFORE DISHONOR.

§ 1. Presentment and Demand distinguished: Modus of the Steps.

THE first thing to be done to fix the liability of an indorser is to make presentment and demand; which in the case of promissory notes or cheques will be for payment; in the case of bills of exchange may be either for acceptance or for payment, according to circumstances. In ordinary cases it is not necessary to draw any distinction between presentment and demand, and therefore the two are often treated as one, either term — presentment or demand — being used indifferently as including all that the law so far requires.

In point of fact, however, the two are separate and distinct steps, and the law requires that both or some equivalent be taken. Sometimes it may accordingly be necessary to distinguish between the two, as where the defendant contends that one or the other was omitted. Hence the nature of each should be pointed out.

But the terms themselves fairly point out their ordinary meaning. Presentment is the act of handing over the paper to the maker, drawee, or acceptor, or at least of exhibiting it to him, with a view to payment or acceptance according to the case and the purpose; demand is a request upon the party, at the same time, to accept or pay, according to the case and the purpose. That is the ordinary meaning of the terms; and the ordinary meaning is now the subject for consideration: excuses of presentment and demand will be considered in another place.

Presentment is required by law, — (1) To enable the party called upon to judge of the genuineness of the paper, for which purpose (and for the next one) he may keep it for a short time; (2) To enable him to judge of the holder's right to the paper; (3) Where presentment is for payment that on payment he may have possession of the paper as a voucher, or for any other needful use.[1] Demand is necessary to show the holder's purpose to require the maker, drawee, or acceptor to do what has been undertaken for. There need not be any words of demand or request, however, or of presentment, if the act of the holder in presenting is understood to mean what such words would only in another way convey; not the form, but the substance, is what the law requires.

An equivalent to handing over or exhibiting the paper may, as we have intimated, satisfy the law in regard to presentment. In the case of paper not payable on its face or by notice at some bank, there can hardly be an equivalent to the handing over; there may be a waiver, of which hereafter; but waiver dispenses with the requirement instead of being an equivalent to it. But in the case of paper payable at bank the law permits an equivalent to what is naturally meant by presentment; the fact that the paper is in the bank at maturity, to the knowledge of the bank, satisfies the law, so far as presentment is concerned, where the paper is on its face payable at such bank.[2] And this upon the plain ground that it would be

---

[1] Musson v. Lake, 4 How. 262; L. C. 177. See also Arnold v. Dresser, 8 Allen, 435. The interest of the maker or acceptor in presentment is important to remember, for it explains how such party can waive rights of an indorser; the maker or acceptor waives his own rights, and those of the indorser are gone, by necessary consequence.

[2] Chicopee Bank v. Philadelphia Bank, 8 Wall. 641; L. C. 202.

a mere ceremony, in most cases of the kind, to require the holder to come to the bank which already has the paper, call for it, and stand there with it, perhaps till the close of its business hours, in waiting for the payor, or — what would be downright silliness — to offer it back to the bank in the name of presentment.

However, it is not the presence of the paper in the bank that is treated as equivalent to handing it over; it is the presence of the paper there (1) at maturity, (2) to the knowledge of the bank, that satisfies the law.[1] It is not enough that the holder has sent the paper to the bank before maturity, though that fact might be material in a suit against the bank for neglect of duty in the matter; it is not enough that the paper was in the bank at maturity, though that might be still more important in such a suit against the bank. If the bank knew nothing of the presence of the paper, the paper might as well not be there, for in such a case the bank cannot do the real thing required, — make the payment.[2]

There is another case of equivalency in relation to presentment. In cases of the kind just referred to, the paper is on its *face* payable at the bank named; but it is not uncommon in cities, and perhaps in smaller places, for the holder to send the paper to the bank with which he usually deals, for collection. In such a case the practice is for the bank to notify the maker, drawee, or acceptor that it holds the paper for collection, and requests payment. Then if the paper is left in the bank until its maturity, that will satisfy the requirement of presentment.[3] Of this case too it should be observed that it is not the notice of the bank that constitutes presentment (or demand), but the presence of the paper in the bank at maturity.

---

[1] Chicopee Bank *v.* Philadelphia Bank, 8 Wall. 641 ; L. C. 202.
[2] Id.
[3] Mechanics' Bank *v.* Merchants' Bank, 6 Met. 13, 23.

In the same cases of paper payable at bank, it is equally obvious that the law cannot insist upon demand in the ordinary sense. The paper is in the bank, and the maker or other payor knows the fact, and if he intends to pay will provide the bank with the funds before or on the day of the maturity, or may have funds on deposit generally with the bank subject to the payment of his paper. The bank accordingly has but to look at its books to see whether the party has provided for payment if he does not appear; and looking over its books, is accepted by law as a demand of payment, if done at the right time; to wit, at the close of business hours on the day of maturity. Perhaps that may not be necessary if the bank knows that there is nothing there with which to make payment; to look over the books in such a case would be idle. But that would be a case of dispensing with demand rather than making it.

It appears to answer the requirement of presentment that the holder, having the paper with him, but not exhibiting it when he makes demand, so describes it as to leave no doubt that the payor must understand of what paper the demand is made.[1] Still the paper must be produced if it is called for.[2]

§ 2. Place of Presentment.

A clear line of cleavage runs through the whole law relating to the indorser's contract between paper payable (on its face or by notice) at bank, and paper not payable at bank. With regard to the first of the two, the process of presentment has already been described in full in speaking of equivalents. But it should be observed that where

---

[1] King v. Crowell, 61 Maine, 244; Arnold v. Dresser, 8 Allen, 435; Etheridge v. Ladd, 44 Barb. 69.

[2] Ocean Bank v. Fant, 50 N. Y. 474.

paper is payable at any place designated by it, whether at bank or elsewhere, presentment should be made at that place; presentment anywhere else will be of no avail in fixing an indorser's liability, apart from waiver or sufficient modification of the contract.

The drawee of a bill of exchange may designate any place within the city or town in which the bill is payable as the place of payment,[1] but cannot require presentment in another city or town.[2] It remains to consider cases of presentment of paper payable at no place designated.

If no place of payment is designated on the paper, — in which case the paper is commonly spoken of as 'payable generally,' — it is payable in law at the place of business or of residence of the maker or acceptor; that is, in the absence of any special agreement between the parties. In regard to oral agreements changing the place of payment from that designated by law, there is some slight want of harmony in the authorities, one or two cases appearing to deny the admissibility of evidence to show such agreement.[3] But the better view treats the doctrine of place of presentment, as it is laid down by law, as intended only to supply any want of evidence, and not as fixed and absolute, and accordingly admits evidence of any agreement or understanding on the subject.[4]

In the absence, then, of agreement, the legal designation prevails; and the law, it seems, designates the place of business, if there be one, as presumptively the place for

---

[1] Troy Bank v. Lauman, 19 N. Y. 477.

[2] Niagara Bank v. Fairman Manuf. Co., 31 Barb. 403; Walker v. Bank of New York, 13 Barb. 636. But compare Mason v. Franklin, 3 Johns. 202.

[3] Pierce v. Whitney, 29 Maine, 188; Anderson v. Drake, 14 Johns. 114 (dictum); Story, Notes, § 49, and note.

[4] Pearson v. Bank of Metropolis, 1 Peters, 89; State v. Hurd, 12 Mass. 171; Sussex Bank v. Baldwin, 2 Harrison (N. J.) 487.

making presentment.[1] The place of business is (probably) preferred in law to the place of residence, because at the party's place of business rather than at his residence he expects to meet his engagements, especially to attend to calls for money. The consequence is that presentment at the residence of a maker or acceptor having a known place of business would, in principle, in the absence of sufficient reason, be insufficient in case of refusal. We say 'in principle,' for the authorities have not often had much occasion to speak plainly to the point, and many of them accordingly have been content with saying generally that presentment should be made at the place of business or of residence.[2]

There is no doubt that presentment at the place of business is good; the only doubt is whether presentment there is required. But whatever the rule on that point, 'place of business' must be taken in a real, substantial sense. It is not enough that some place has been used temporarily for the transaction of some particular piece of business, such as merely settling up old books or accounts; it must be the regular, known place for the transaction of the ordinary, general business of the party, including the payment of bills. The counting-room of a merchant would be a proper place for presentment; a mercantile clubroom ordinarily would not be. The general room of a workshop, or any part of a workshop having no office, would be no place for making presentment; the place would indeed be a place of business, but not a place of business at which the owner, in ordinary cases, would be apt to pay his bills.

---

[1] King v. Holmes, 11 Penn. St. 456; West v. Brown, 6 Ohio St. 542. See Bank of Red Oak v. Orvis, 42 Iowa, 691.

[2] See Sussex Bank v. Baldwin, 2 Harrison (N. J.) 487; Brooks v. Blaney, 62 Maine, 456; King v. Crowell, 61 Maine, 244; Malden Bank v. Baldwin, 13 Gray, 154.

Indeed, an office at which one pays one's bills, among other things, is enough to make presentment there good, if not to require presentment there. For example: The maker of a promissory note has a room, occupied also by other persons for business purposes, in which he is accustomed to receive business calls, and at which he directs such calls to be made. Presentment of the note is made there, and not at the maker's residence. The presentment is good.[1]

If, however, the maker or acceptor has no such known place of business, the holder must make demand at his residence, if, again, he has a known residence, or one which can be found by reasonable diligence. If there is neither place of business nor of residence so to be found, the holder has nothing to do in the way of presentment except to be in the town in which the paper is payable, at maturity, ready with the paper to receive payment.[2]

But the maker or acceptor may have removed; and the holder has not performed his duty in the matter of presentment by merely seeking out the last known place of business or residence of the party, and failing to find there the person sought. That is not presentment, nor is any case of excuse made by such facts. For example: The defendant is indorser of an accepted foreign bill of exchange, which has been protested for dishonor. The protest sets out a 'presentment' made 'at the late place of business' of the acceptor, 'to the person there in charge,' who answered demand of payment by saying, 'the acceptor is not here now, nor have we any funds' with which to pay. That does not disclose facts sufficient

---

[1] West v. Brown, 6 Ohio St. 542.

[2] Meyer v. Hibsher, 47 N. Y. 265; Malden Bank v. Baldwin, 13 Gray, 154.

to constitute presentment and demand; reasonable diligence requires further inquiry.¹

Indeed, it is the duty of the holder to follow the maker or acceptor upon his removal, if he has not removed beyond the State; or rather the holder should exercise reasonable diligence in attempting to follow him. If by such diligence he can find the maker or acceptor, he must do so, and make presentment in the usual way. If the maker or acceptor has removed beyond the State, since the paper was made or accepted, the holder performs his duty in the matter of place of presentment, by calling for payment at the party's last place of business or of residence according to the particular case.² Whether that is *necessary* is disputed; but by the better view it is.³ In some States, indeed, it is held that diligence must be exercised to obtain payment even where the maker or acceptor has absconded.⁴ But of such matters under the head of excuses. Of course, if the maker or acceptor lived in another State when the paper was made or accepted, the paper must be sent forward for presentment there.⁵

The place of date of the paper is prima facie evidence of the place for presentment, if no other is indicated upon it; but it is only prima facie evidence.⁶ The date, whether of place or time, is no part of the contract, and the actual fact may be shown. Even where paper is payable 'at the

---

¹ Brooks v. Blaney, 62 Maine, 456; Freeman v. Boynton, 7 Mass. 483.

² Taylor v. Snyder, 3 Denio, 145; L. C. 227.

³ Wheeler v. Field, 6 Met. 290. Contra, Gist v. Lybrand, 3 Ohio, 308; Foster v. Julien, 24 N. Y. 28, Mason, J., dis.

⁴ Pierce v. Cate, 12 Cush. 190. But see contra, Lehman v. Jones, 1 Watts & S. 126; L. C. 357; Duncan v. McCullough, 4 Serg. & R. 480.

⁵ Taylor v. Snyder, supra.

⁶ Childs v. Laflin, 55 Ill. 156; Blodgett v. Durgin, 32 Vt. 361; Taylor v. Snyder, 3 Denio, 145; L. C. 227.

office' of the maker or acceptor, the place of date does not necessarily fix the place for presentment; wherever the party's 'office' is, there presentment should be made.[1]

In the case of a bank having branches, cheques are payable at the particular branch at which the drawer keeps his account; hence presentment should be made there in all cases in which the holder has notice or is informed of the proper place.[2] He would no doubt be told where to go if he presented the paper at the wrong place, and hence could not treat the refusal as a dishonor. If not in any way informed, he may have made a good presentment, though he made it at the wrong place.

§ 3. Time of Presentment.

Coming to the question of the time of presentment, we encounter a distinction between presentment for acceptance and presentment for payment, which must first be disposed of.

Presentment for *acceptance* is necessary, as has heretofore been observed, only in the case of bills payable at or at a time after sight. But bills payable at a time stated after date may be presented for acceptance, as the drawer is generally considered to contract that the holder shall have the security, if he will, of acceptance.

With regard to bills payable at a stated time after date, the holder may make presentment, if at all, at any time he will before maturity of the bill. It is doubtful whether there could be a presentment for acceptance, in any case, after maturity; presentment after maturity would naturally be for payment. But that is not material, for all indorsers would be discharged by failure to present the

[1] Childs v. Laflin, supra.
[2] Prince v. Oriental Bank, L. R. 3 App. Cas. 325, 332; Woodland v. Fear, 7 El. & B. 519.

paper for payment at maturity, except such as had waived the requirement, and such as may have indorsed — an unusual thing — after maturity.

With regard to bills payable at or at a stated time after sight, the case is different. The law merchant requires presentment of such paper within a reasonable time; but that rule is interpreted to permit the circulation of such paper indefinitely before presentment, so that the Statute of Limitations does not run out. That is to say, the contract of the drawer and indorsers of such a bill is that the holder may present the bill at any time within the period of the Statute of Limitations, provided that the paper is kept in circulation meantime; when finally presentment for acceptance is made, the taking of the other steps required in case of dishonor will accordingly fix liability. For example: A sight bill is sent from Chicago to a distant territory on the day of its date. After some detention in the mails it reached its destination, when the holder puts it into circulation at the first opportunity, and it is then kept in circulation as well as the thinly settled condition of the territory permitted. Without unnecessary delay it is presented to the drawee thirty-five days after its date. The presentment is good.[1] Again: The defendant in London indorses to the plaintiff a bill of exchange drawn in London on A at Calcutta, payable to order sixty days after sight. The bill is dated March 5. On April 30 following the bill is indorsed by the plaintiff in England to A of Calcutta; on May 22 next the bill is sent to India, and received there early in October; shortly afterwards it is presented for acceptance, and acceptance is refused; due protest and due notice of dishonor follow. It is for the jury to say whether the bill was presented to the drawee in reasonable time; the fact that the paper was

[1] Montelius v. Charles, 76 Ill. 303.

kept out in circulation for so long time not being in itself unreasonable.¹

The bill should, however, be kept in circulation, as far as circumstances reasonably permit, or it should be presented for acceptance; it should not be locked up. To lock it up, which means to hold it when it might reasonably be passed on in circulation or sent forward for presentment, would discharge the drawer and indorsers.² What is a reasonable holding, and hence not a locking-up, must depend upon circumstances, as the examples above given show. In cases lying on the border, the question of reasonableness must ordinarily be left to the jury; in clear cases the court will rule on the facts. The court would rule that to keep a bill an entire day could not be unreasonable; it has been ruled that to hold an inland bill payable after sight in London until the fourth day after receiving it, within twenty miles of London, is not unreasonable.³

The rule, indeed, is not a hard and fast one. It may be entirely changed by custom; if there be a clear and determinate usage of trade at the place of payment, which regulates the time of presentment, that usage is considered as entering into the contract of the drawer and indorsers, and presentment must be made accordingly.⁴

It has been said that to indorse paper after maturity is equivalent to drawing a bill at sight, so far as time is concerned.⁵ But that is clearly a mistake. It cannot be necessary to present such paper for acceptance, as would

---

[1] Muilman v. D'Eguino, 2 H. Black. 565; L. C. 207.

[2] Id.; Goupy v. Harden, 7 Taunt. 159; Mellish v. Rawdon, 9 Bing. 416; Middleton Bank v. Morris, 28 Barb. 616.

[3] Fry v. Hill, 7 Taunt. 397. See Harker v. Anderson, 21 Wend. 372.

[4] Story, Bills, § 231; Mellish v. Rawdon, 9 Bing. 416.

[5] Light v. Kingsbury, 50 Mo. 331; Tyler v. Young, 30 Penn. St. 144. See Bassenhorst v. Wilby, 45 Ohio St. 333, 337.

be necessary by the general law merchant of sight bills; the paper too might be a promissory note or a cheque. The true view of the case is that indorsement after maturity amounts to an order to pay *on demand*,[1] — a subject now to be considered.

Next of presentment for payment, in the same matter of time; and first, of grace. The cardinal rule in ordinary cases is that presentment for payment must be made at maturity, — that is, on the day when by law payment is due. If the paper is payable on demand, and in England (by statute), and in one or two of our States, if it is payable at sight, the paper is not entitled to grace; it is due presently, and presentment may be made on the day of delivery, or on any other day, excepting non-secular days. In other words, the paper is at its maturity all the time. Its maturity is passed by the law merchant after the expiration of a reasonable time, a matter regulated by statute in some States, at least in regard to promissory notes. The rule applies to such paper, as well as to other kinds, that presentment after maturity is too late to fix the liability of an indorser; unless the paper is indorsed after maturity, as it may be, when it becomes due again after a reasonable time, and must be presented accordingly.[2]

In the very uncommon case of paper in which grace is excluded by the terms of the paper, — the paper not being payable on demand, — payment is due, in other words, the paper matures, as if it were an instrument of the common law instead of the law merchant. Thus, if the day of payment, reckoned literally, would fall on Sunday or any other non-secular day, it is due on the following day, and presentment for payment should be made on that day, not before, not after. If two non-secular days should come

---

[1] Pryor *v.* Bowman, 38 Iowa, 92; Leavitt *v.* Putnam, 1 Sandf. 199; Patterson *v.* Todd, 18 Penn. St. 426; Swartz *v.* Redfield, 13 Kans. 550.
[2] Bassenhorst *v.* Wilby, 45 Ohio St. 333.

together, the first being the one on which payment otherwise would be due, the paper does not reach maturity until after both those days have passed.

This leaves us with the case of paper entitled to grace. In such cases the paper reaches its maturity three days after the time at which by its terms literally taken it would be due; and presentment should be made on the last day of grace, not before, not after. If what would be the third day of grace should be Sunday or any other non-secular day, the paper matures on the second day, or on the first day of grace if the day before is also a non-secular day. Here, indeed, is said to be a survival of the original idea of days of *grace;* these were at first, according to current statement, mere favor extended by the holder, and hence, as they could not then be required, the time cannot now be increased. However lame the reasoning, supposing it to rest on fact, the law is clear and positive; grace is cut off by the law merchant, not increased, by non-secular days at payment time. For example: The defendant is indorser of a promissory note made on the first day of June and payable one month after date. Payment is demanded on the 5th of July and refused, and notice at once given to the defendant. The defendant is not liable; presentment should have been made on July 3, unless that day also was a non-secular day, in which case it should have been made on July 2.

If the instrument (entitled to grace) is on its face payable in instalments, each instalment is entitled to grace; there can be no breach of the contract, and hence no proper presentment, touching an instalment, except on the last day of grace, treating the instalment in question as if it were a separate and distinct undertaking. For example: The defendant is indorser of a promissory note dated Nov. 19, 1888, and payable by equal instalments on the 19th of November in each succeeding year for seven years. The instalment due in 1892 is the subject of the present suit; presentment for payment of which was made and refused November 22 of that year, and was followed at once by notice of dishonor. The presentment is good.[1]

A like rule would apply if it were provided, as often is the case, that if any instalment were not paid when due, the whole sum should be immediately due. The holder would have his election in such a case to sue for the instalment alone or for the whole sum, each now requiring presentment, so far as indorsers are concerned, on the same day, the last day of grace.

The rule in regard to time of presentment supposes, however, that there is no legal obstacle to presentment at maturity. Should there be such obstacle, the rule yields, and the law in most cases, if not in all,[2] suspends the requirement of performance of the duty until the removal of the obstacle; then, or rather within reasonable time thereafter, presentment must be made.

What is a 'legal obstacle,' within the meaning of this rule? It must be something not attributable to the holder, even in the way of mistake. Thus the holder could not, by way of justifying presentment after the day of maturity, show that he had made a miscalculation of the time when the paper became due, or that he had confused two instruments maturing at different times, and had taken the wrong one for the one in suit, or that in sending the paper forward to the place of payment he had made a mistake in the address which caused the delay. Mistake by the holder would be fatal.

On the other hand, 'inevitable accident,' to use a common term, would be a legal obstacle. Accident, as thus

[1] Oridge *v* Sherborne, 11 Mees. & W. 374; L. C. 78.

[2] The effect of the death of the maker or acceptor is disputed. See infra, p. 96.

brought in contrast with mistake, is some unexpected event happening without the agency direct or indirect of the person to whom it happens. The mistake of another *may* therefore be an 'accident' to the holder; so it will be if the mistake was in no proper sense due to the holder, — it is then 'inevitable accident,' and presentment may be made after the mistake has been corrected. For example: The defendants are indorsers of a bill of exchange drawn in Norwich, Connecticut, on A in Philadelphia, Pennsylvania, and accepted payable at a certain bank there. Shortly before the maturity of the bill the holder sends it to a banking-house in New York City for collection. Between New York and Philadelphia there are two mails daily, — one leaving New York at 9 A. M., the other at 4.30 P. M., each due at Philadelphia five hours after starting. On the morning before the day of maturity the cashier of the collecting bank encloses the bill, with others, in a letter addressed to the bank at which it is payable, and mails the letter in season for the afternoon mail of that day. The letter is duly put into the mail-bags, which leave New York at the time just mentioned; but by mistake of employees in the New York post-office the mail-bags containing letters for Philadelphia are directed to Washington. They are carried on accordingly to Washington, where the mistake is discovered; and the bags are now sent back to Philadelphia, reaching that city on the day after the maturity of the bill. That day is Sunday. On Monday morning the letter containing the bill in question is delivered to the bank to which it is addressed, and at which it is payable, and payment is presently refused. Protest and notice follow directly. The presentment is good, inevitable accident having prevented the making of it sooner.[1]

The existence at maturity of war between the countries

[1] Windham Bank v. Norton, 22 Conn. 213; L. C. 344.

or States in which the holder and the payor respectively reside would be another legal obstacle; and withholding presentment or attempts to make presentment until the end of the war would not affect the liability of indorsers, even though the period of limitation (for natural cases) might have expired. But within a reasonable time after the end of the war presentment should be made on pain of discharging indorsers. What time would be reasonable would in a case of doubt be for the jury; on facts leaving no ground for doubt in the matter, the court would rule. And the courts would probably be found endeavoring to narrow the region of doubt wherever they could.

A similar case would be the existence of an epidemic at the place of payment, resulting in quarantine; and it would not matter whether the quarantine was general, embracing a whole district, or a whole city, or limited only to some quarter of the city in which the paper was payable, or though it was only of the house where it was payable.

The fact that the maker or acceptor was dead when the paper matured might of course create a legal obstacle to presentment. In the first place, there may as yet be no executor or administrator, of whom alone payment could be required. Clearly no presentment could be made in such a state of things, and one of two things must be true: either the indorser's contract must hold good meantime, awaiting the qualification of a personal representative, or presentment must be excused, and the indorser's liability fixed, by taking the other steps. In some States the latter alternative appears to express the law;[1] probably the former would be more generally accepted as the better expression of it.[2]

---

[1] Hale v. Burr, 12 Mass. 86; Oriental Bank v. Blake, 22 Pick. 206; Landry v. Stansberry, 10 La. 484.

[2] Gower v. Moore, 25 Maine, 16.

In the next place, though there may be a qualified executor or administrator at the maturity of the paper, still the period of his exemption from suit (that is, from duty to pay demands against the estate) may not yet have expired. In such a case, as in the one just stated, either the indorser's contract must hold good until the period expires, when presentment must be made, or presentment must be excused, and the other steps taken. The latter alternative is adopted in some States, the former in others. For example: The defendant is indorser of a promissory note, the maker of which is dead when it matures. An administrator has been appointed and has qualified. He is exempted by law from suit for one year from the time of qualification. The note matures a month after his qualification. No presentment by the law of Massachusetts and of other States is necessary;[1] presentment by the law of Maine and probably of other States *is* necessary.[2]

But it is not enough that presentment is made on the day of maturity or other proper day; it must be made at a reasonable time of that day, though it is probable that the plaintiff makes out his case presumptively in this respect by showing that presentment was made on the right day.

In regard to time of day a distinction like that heretofore noticed between paper payable at bank and paper not payable at bank prevails. If the paper is payable at bank, or at any mercantile house having fixed hours of business, presentment should be made within such hours; to make it before or afterwards would be of no avail in the steps to fix an indorser's liability, unless indeed the bank or house

---

[1] Hale v. Burr, and other cases in note 1, p. 96. Query if *notice* is not necessary under this rule? See the statement of facts in Hale v. Burr; and see Oriental Bank v. Blake, 22 Pick. 206, holding that notice to an administrator of an indorser is necessary.

[2] Gower v. Moore, 25 Maine, 16.

of business had some one at hand to answer calls of the kind.[1] It is common for banks to have some one of its force remain for a time after the close of banking hours for such purpose; presentment accordingly would be good.[2]

The case is different if the maker, drawer, or acceptor have no place of business with early hours of closing; but the extremes of the time prescribed by law for presentment in such cases are hard to fix. It is common to say of cases of the kind that presentment may be made at any time of day between morning and night. But when does 'morning' begin and when does 'night' end within the meaning of the statement? It would be unreasonable to say that presentment might be made at any time between the beginning of day and midnight, and the law does not say so.

Payment should be called for only when, so far as time of day is concerned, it can conveniently be made. Hence it should not be called for during the hours of rest; that is, the hours ordinarily given to sleep, as, for instance, near midnight. For example: The defendant is indorser of a promissory note payable at no place designated. In the night of the day of maturity, between eleven and twelve o'clock, the holder calls up the maker, who has gone to bed, and presents the note for payment, which is refused, and notice of dishonor given. The presentment is not good.[3]

The fact that the maker or acceptor may have retired to rest will not make the presentment improper, for he may have retired in the daytime, or in the edge of the evening, because of illness, fatigue, or anything else. The only question on this point is whether the presentment was made at a *reasonable* time of day; that question, in cases in which there is serious ground for doubt, will and

---

[1] See Dana v. Sawyer, 22 Maine, 244; L. C. 225.
[2] Id. [3] Id.

should ordinarily be left to the jury. Still, the courts are inclined to push back the borders of doubt as far as they can, and so bring the case within the domain of certainty. For example: The defendant is indorser of a promissory note, payable at no designated place, and due in August. The maker lives in the country, ten miles from Boston. The note is received at maturity by a notary public, after the close of banking hours, from a bank in Boston which holds it for collection, the bank not knowing where the maker lived. After considerable inquiry the maker's place of residence is ascertained, and the notary, informed of the place, goes as soon as he can to the house, arriving there about nine o'clock in the evening. The lights of the house are out, and the inmates have gone to bed for the night. The notary calls the maker up, and presents the note for payment, and payment is refused. The presentment is good; taking into consideration the distance of the maker from the holder, the inquiry made to ascertain the maker's place of residence, and the season of the year, the time of presenting the note was reasonable.[1] Again: Presentment is made between eight or nine o'clock at the house of a grocer. The house is shut, and no one is there to give answer. The presentment *may* be good.[2]

Similar narrowing of the borders of doubt has been

[1] Farnsworth v. Allen, 4 Gray, 453. 'The question whether a presentment is within reasonable time cannot be made to depend on the private and peculiar habits of the maker of a note, not known to the holder; but it must be determined by a consideration of the circumstances which, in ordinary cases, would render it reasonable or otherwise.' Id., Bigelow, J.

[2] See Triggs v. Newnham, 10 Moore, 249; s. c. 1 Car. & P. 631; Wilkins v. Jadis, 2 Barn. & Ad. 188; Morgan v. Davison, 1 Stark. 114; Barclay v. Bailey, 2 Campb. 527. The rulings on presentment appear to have been positive in these cases; but it would be unsafe to say in general that presentment in such a case would be good. There might be 'early closing' in the trade, and no good reason shown for not making presentment at the place of business during business hours.

made in regard to presentment in the early morning. Thus presentment upon a maker at his place of residence in a city at eight o'clock in the morning has been declared too early;[1] while presentment so made in the country, at a farmer's house, would ordinarily, it seems, be reasonable.

However, rulings upon such questions are not of the same value as general rules of law, because such rulings depend so much upon the particular facts. Facts of small import in themselves often become important in cases of the kind, important enough to set aside the application of the ruling in question. The ruling is particular, not general; the examples above given cannot be taken to apply to any but very similar cases. Their chief value probably lies in their showing a disposition of the courts to extend the domain of law, and hence of certainty, as far as possible.

§ 4. Presentment, by Whom.

Presentment should be made by the holder, or by his lawful agent. According to the better rule, no one else can make presentment such as, being refused, can be treated as a step towards fixing an indorser's liability. Confusion has arisen from the fact that in certain cases a stranger in possession of the paper may make presentment for the purpose of receiving *payment;* which is only saying that payment made to such person may operate as a discharge and satisfaction of liability. That will be the case whenever the payment is made in good faith, without notice that the holder is not owner of the paper, and the paper surrendered to the party making payment. The instrument is now extinguished, and with it of course the liability of all parties to it.

But to say that payment may be made to a person not

---

[1] Lunt v. Adams, 17 Maine, 230.

entitled to receive payment is not to say that presentment by such person is good for the purpose of fixing the liability of an indorser. For that purpose presentment must be made by one who, in making it, is acting under the contract of the defendant, and who further, in the case of a promissory note or an accepted bill of exchange, can compel and not merely receive payment. The indorsement (or the drawing of bill or cheque) is an order to pay to the true holder; obviously, then, none but the true holder, — that is, the owner, or his agent, — can make a presentment that shall fulfil the terms of the indorser's contract. If presentment be good when made, as sometimes it is, by an indorser, it is good because the indorser is (not indorser, but) the authorized agent of the holder.

Upon the death of the holder, presentment should be made by his successor in title, who, as we have seen, is his executor or administrator. It should not be made by any legatee, for such person, though entitled, it may be,[1] to the money when paid, could not require payment; the maker or acceptor could refuse to pay to any one but the legal representative of the late holder.

It matters not through whose hands the paper passes in making presentment, if the act be that of the owner; the intermediate persons are only his instruments. For example: A bill of exchange is sent through the post-office to the acceptor in a letter demanding payment, and is received on the day of maturity. This is a good presentment;[2] though it would be otherwise of a mere demand of payment of paper not sent forward or lodged in the bank making demand.

---

[1] Perhaps he may not be entitled to receive it or any part of it, though it was given to him by will of the owner, for the owner may have been involved in debt, and his estate must first pay the creditors.

[2] Prideaux v. Criddle, L. R. 4 Q. B. 455; Hare v. Heaty, 10 C. B. N. S. 65.

In the case of a dishonored foreign bill of exchange there will be a double presentment; and there may be and often is in the case of an inland bill or of a promissory note. The first presentment is made by the holder of the paper or by his agent, in the ordinary way; then the paper must, if a foreign bill, *may*, if an inland bill or a note, be put into the hands of a notary public (or of some other public officer or respectable, disinterested person if no notary can be found to serve), and presentment made by him. But the action of the notary so far will be just the same, as regards time and place, as if he were holder.

In this country it is generally laid down that the notary must act in person, in the absence of statute; he cannot make presentment by a clerk or deputy.[1] Indeed, it is held that the defect in making presentment by a clerk would not be cured by the notary himself making the protest.[2] Perhaps, however, custom in large cities may be deemed to sanction the act of a deputy; that is the case in England. It is not improbable that the rule requiring personal action by the notary was due to a mere slip by an English judge.[3] In the case of inland bills and promissory notes, the act of a notary is not required at all, though it is generally permitted by statute.[4]

In some States statute authorizes presentment of a foreign bill by a notary's deputy, and in some States by

---

[1] Ocean Bank v. Williams, 102 Mass. 141; Donegan v. Wood, 49 Ala. 242; Hunt v. Maybee, 3 Seld. 266; Carter v. Union Bank, 7 Humph. 548; Smith v. Gibbs, 2 Smedes & M. 479. But see Nelson v. Fotterall, 7 Leigh, 179

[2] Smith v. Gibbs, supra.

[3] Buller, J., in Leftley v. Mills, 4 T. R. 170. See 1 Parsons, Notes and Bills, 641, note.

[4] Unless the employment of a notary is permitted by statute, notarial fees cannot be collected in such cases. Burke v. McKay, 2 How. 66, L. C. 253; Union Bank v. Hyde, 9 Wheat. 572; City Bank v. Cutter, 3 Pick. 414.

a justice of the peace. And where, in any case, no notary resides or will act in the place of payment, any public officer may act, or if no such person is at hand or will serve, then any respectable, disinterested merchant or other private citizen.[1] Perhaps witnesses should be present in such a case.[2]

§ 5. Presentment, to Whom.

Presentment may of course be made either to the maker or acceptor or to his lawful agent; and it seems that if the payor is living at the maturity of the paper, presentment *must* be made to him. Perhaps if he had become insane and placed under guardianship, presentment should be made to his guardian. Imprisonment for crime, if it affected the case at all, would probably operate as an excuse.

In case of such person's death presentment should be made, if it be required (concerning which see the remarks in the preceding section), to his executor or administrator, if one has qualified and his place of business or of residence can by reasonable diligence be found.[3] If no one has qualified as executor or administrator, or if the executor or administrator cannot be found, demand perhaps should be made upon the kindred who occupy the residence of the maker or acceptor or have possession of his property; but such a state of things would more likely be held to dispense with need of presentment.

The mere fact that the maker or acceptor has become bankrupt will not affect the rule in regard to presentment, for a man does not cease to own or control his property

---

[1] See Burke *v.* McKay, 2 How. 66; L. C. 253.

[2] 1 Parsons, Notes and Bills, 633; Chitty, Bills, 333, 9th Eng. ed.; Bayley, Bills, c 7, § 2.

[3] Gower *v.* Moore, 25 Maine, 16.

simply because he is not able to pay his debts. Much less does he cease to have friends who may help him, especially where he has been guiltless in his misfortune. But if an assignee of his estate has been appointed, by the voluntary act of the maker or acceptor, or by the law, it is not clear that presentment should not be made upon the assignee, for the estate may have proved solvent; though it appears to be held that presentment must still be made upon the bankrupt.[1]

Where a promissory note is made by one who signs his name as 'agent,' without disclosing a principal, the note, as we have seen, is the 'agent's' own undertaking as if he were principal. Presentment accordingly should be made upon him, or at all events it may properly be made upon him, though the 'agency' be real; indeed, demand may in such a case be made upon him though he may have ceased to be agent at the time of the maturity of the note.[2] If the name of the principal were given, and the undertaking made his undertaking, demand could, it seems, be made upon either, — upon the agent, because of his agency in the matter, assuming that he remained such till maturity; and upon the principal, because the promise in reality was his promise. It would not be necessary to make presentment to both, even though the promise were the joint promise of the two, because of the agency.

Where paper is made or accepted by two or more persons jointly, demand must by the better rule be made upon both or all, unless they are partners, or unless some other agency existed between them in respect of payment.[3] If they are

[1] See Nicholson v. Gouthit, 2 H. Black. 609 ; 3 Rev. Rep. 527 ; Barton v. Baker, 1 Serg. & R. 334 (notice of dishonor).

[2] Hall v. Bradbury, 40 Conn. 32.

[3] Arnold v. Dresser, 8 Allen, 435 ; Union Bank v. Willis, supra; Bank of Red Oak v. Orvis, 40 Iowa, 332 ; Willis v. Green, 5 Hill, 232 ; Gates v. Beecher, 60 N. Y. 518, denying Harris v. Clark, 10 Ohio, 5. See also Greenough v. Smead, 3 Ohio St. 415.

partners, or one of them is agent for the rest, presentment will be sufficient if made upon any one of the partners or upon the agent.¹ Upon the death of one of the joint makers or acceptors, presentment to the survivors will, it seems, be sufficient; clearly that would be the case where they were partners.

If the makers or acceptors are severally bound, presentment made to any one of them will be sufficient, for the promise is the individual promise of each, as much as if the others had not promised. And this is true as well of a 'joint and several' undertaking as of a several one merely; for the meaning of the engagement is that the parties promise in two distinct, not inseparable, ways: they promise jointly and they promise separately; that is, they are bound in either way.²

---

¹ Gates v. Beecher, supra.

² It was a mere slip of the court in Union Bank v. Willis, 8 Met. 504; L. C. 24, at the end, to say that the contract in that case was joint and several; the decision reached required the court to hold the contract joint only.

CHAPTER VIII.

INDORSER'S CONTRACT CONTINUED: PROCEEDINGS UPON DISHONOR.

§ 1. Protest.

By the law merchant, the first step necessary after the dishonor of a *foreign* bill of exchange — a step common and by statute permissible, but not necessary, in the case of inland bills, promissory notes, and cheques — is protest. This is a highly characteristic act, made, and ordinarily to be made only, by a public officer called a notary public. A notary public is an officer of international character, or at all events having international (and interstate) functions, and recognized the world over. And it is because the bill of exchange is a foreign international instrument that the services of a notary are required, if obtainable.[1]

Protest is manifested by a formal certificate, in writing under seal, of a notary, or of some one taking the place of a notary, by which he attests the dishonor of the dishonored paper. The step is wholly distinct and separate from presentment or any of the other steps necessary to fix an indorser's liability, though it is dependent for its validity upon due presentment.

Neither the law merchant nor statute has prescribed any form of words to be used in the certificate of protest; but the law merchant does require that certain facts should appear in it, in order to make it valid. These facts are the several ones going to show dishonor; to wit, due

---

[1] When the services of a notary may be performed by another, see ante, pp. 102, 103.

presentment, demand, and refusal, or an equivalent, or a sufficient excuse for omission.¹ This requires that the certificate should state time and place of presentment, and the person or persons to whom presentment was made. Thus, in regard to persons, if the bill has been accepted by more than one the certificate should state that presentment was made to all, or should state why it was not, as, for example, that the acceptors, being A and B, were partners, and that presentment was made to A.² It will not suffice for the certificate to recite that 'due presentment' was made; that would be but inference, where, because the bill is a foreign international instrument, facts should appear.

The rule of the law merchant is thus exacting because by that law the certificate of protest of a foreign bill, if the certificate is in existence and obtainable, is the only evidence of the dishonor of the bill. The drawer, who presumptively lives abroad, is entitled (and by consequence the indorsers also, since their engagement runs pari passu with his) to know authoritatively that the dishonor has been real and such as to justify the steps by which his (and their liability) is fixed and made absolute. The notarial certificate is an international document, and stands or falls by itself; its deficiencies, if there be any, cannot be made good by evidence from without, however clear the facts may be, and whether the protest be for non-acceptance or non-payment.³ On the other hand, being such a document, it is more readily received in the courts than other

---

¹ See Staniback v. Bank of Virginia, 11 Gratt. 260; People's Bank v. Brooke, 31 Md. 7; Farmers' Bank v. Allen, 18 Md. 475; Walmsley v. Acton, 44 Barb. 312; Musson v. Lake, 4 How. 262; L. C. 177.

² Otsego Bank v. Warren, 18 Barb. 290; Nave v. Richardson, 36 Mo. 130.

³ Ocean Bank v. Williams, 102 Mass. 141; Buckner v. Finley, 2 Peters, 586; Orr v. Maginnis, 7 East, 359.

written instruments. The genuineness of the notary's signature need not be proved; his seal proves that. But evidence would be admitted, no doubt, that the seal was not genuine, and so that the whole certificate was fraudulent.

Nor indeed are the statements made in the certificate conclusive evidence,[1] though they ought to be taken as strong evidence, and not so easily overturned as ordinary evidence. And the certificate is, like other written evidence of a transaction, within the general rule concerning the 'best' evidence; if the certificate exists, and can be produced, it must be produced to prove the dishonor; if it does not exist or cannot be produced, other evidence of dishonor is admissible, though proof must be furnished that the bill was in fact protested, or a sufficient excuse shown if it was not. The object of the certificate being merely to furnish evidence of sufficient dishonor, its statements of other facts, if such there be, cannot be received.

The States of the American Union, it should be remembered, are foreign to each other for the purposes of the law under consideration.[2]

Thus far of foreign bills. Of the protest of inland bills and notes and cheques the law merchant knows nothing; and hence, so far as the protest of such paper is proper, it must stand on statute or the common law. The common law has never been held to authorize it;[3] statute in many States does authorize it, and hence it must stand entirely upon the statute.[4] But statute has not put the pro-

---

[1] Spence v. Crockett, 5 Baxt. 576; Ricketts v. Pendleton, 14 Md. 320.

[2] Bank of United States v. Daniel, 12 Peters, 32, 54; Commercial Bank v. Varnum, 49 N. Y. 269.

[3] City Bank v. Cutter, 3 Pick. 414; Union Bank v. Hyde, 6 Wheat. 572; Nicholls v. Webb, 8 Wheat. 326; Kirtland v. Wanzer, 2 Duer, 278.

[4] Hence, apart from statute the protest of an inland bill or a promissory note is no evidence of the facts stated, unless the notary has

test of paper of the kind on the footing of the protest of foreign bills; it only authorizes or permits the protest. The protest of an inland bill or of a promissory note is not then an act of the high character of the protest of a foreign bill. The certificate is not to be rejected because it does not contain all that would be necessary to show due protest under the law merchant; it is evidence of dishonor as far as it goes, — its deficiencies may be supplied by external evidence.[1] Probably it might be laid aside altogether, and the facts relating to dishonor proved as if there had been no protest. At best it ought not to be received to prove anything except the dishonor, unless statute give it greater force, though that fact is perhaps sometimes overlooked in practice.

The act of the notary or other in making the presentment must, as has already been stated, take place on the day of maturity of the paper. The formal certificate of protest, whether of a foreign bill or of other paper, need not, however, be made, and commonly is not made, at the time; it may be made at any subsequent time down to the time of suit.[2] But if the full certificate is not made out at the time of the dishonor, what is called a 'noting' should then, or at all events before the following day, be made; otherwise it seems that a certificate afterwards written out will be invalid.[3] Noting consists in the making of minutes in brief of the facts to be stated in the certificate. The noting is not the protest; but if the notary should

---

deceased. Nicholls v. Webb, and Kirtland v. Wanzer, supra; Carter v. Burley, 9 N. H. 558. But see Colms v. Bank of Tennessee, 4 Baxt. 422.

[1] Wetherall v. Clagett, 28 Md. 465; Seneca Bank v. Neass, 5 Denio, 329; Magoun v. Walker, 49 Maine, 419.

[2] Bailey v. Dozier, 6 How. 23; Dennistown v. Stewart, 17 How. 606, 607.

[3] Tassel v. Lewis, Ld. Raym. 743. See Leftley v. Mills, 4 T. R. 170, 174.

die before writing out the certificate the noting may take its place if it is, or, on explanation by one who understands it becomes, intelligible. So if the certificate should be lost or destroyed without the holder's consent.

§ 2. Notice of Dishonor: Form.

The next and last step to be taken after protest, and where protest is not necessary and is not made, the next and last step after dishonor, is notice of the dishonor. Like presentment, that step is required of all paper in fixing the liability of an indorser, — that step or an equivalent, unless there be an excuse.[1] Knowledge of dishonor is not enough; the law requires the giving of notice, so as to apprise the indorser whether the holder looks to him for payment.[2]

The law merchant has not prescribed any set of words to be used in the notice; here, as in other cases, it is satisfied if its requirements are met in substance. The act to be performed is indeed less formal and more simple, and the law merchant is much less exacting, than in the matter of protest; just how much is required to make notice of dishonor good is a question upon which the authorities in certain particulars are in conflict. That which is agreed may be first stated.

The law merchant requires that the indorser should be apprised of the paper dishonored; but it is not exacting in the matter; if the indorser is correctly informed what instrument is dishonored, it matters not that there may be a mistake in the description or reference. For example:

---

[1] In regard to fixing the liability of the drawer of a cheque, see ante, pp. 52 et seq.

[2] Bank of Old Dominion v. McVeigh, 29 Gratt. 546; s. c. 26 Gratt. 785, 852; Juniata Bank v. Hale, 16 Serg. & R. 157; L. C. 359; Magruder v. Union Bank, 3 Peters, 87; s. c. 7 Peters, 287.

The defendant is indorser of a promissory note, which on due presentment has been dishonored. The note is dated '20th July, 1819,' and payable at the Bank of the United States, Chilicothe, Ohio. A written notice of dishonor is sent to the defendant, in which the note is described at length and stated to be 'dated 20th day of September, 1819;' the holder's name is not stated; in other respects the description is correct, and the notice proper. There is no other note, of which the defendant is indorser, payable at the bank named. The notice is good; the mistake of date not being, under the circumstances, misleading, and the omission of the holder's name being immaterial.'[1] Again: The defendant is indorser of a dishonored promissory note for $1400. The notice of dishonor in describing the note erroneously states the sum payable to be $1457, but otherwise the description is correct, and there is no other note signed by the person named in the notice, and indorsed by the defendant. The notice is good.[2]

The law merchant does, however, require that the notice shall apprise the indorser, with reasonable certainty, of the paper in question; a mistake which might well be misleading will be fatal, at least, if in fact it did mislead the indorser. Perhaps if he knew what paper was meant, the notice would be good, for although knowledge of dishonor is not notice, notice may perhaps be supplemented and helped by knowledge; the rule that knowledge in such a case is not what the law merchant intends by 'notice' being applicable perhaps only to cases in which no notice at all is given.

But now we have reached a difficulty. Does the law merchant — there is no other law touching the question in this country — require that the notice itself shall, expressly or by certain implication, inform the indorser

---

[1] Mills v. Bank of United States, 11 Wheat. 431; L. C. 256.
[2] Bank of Alexandria v. Swann, 9 Peters, 33.

of dishonor, and of dishonor at maturity; or is it enough that the paper was in point of fact dishonored at maturity, and that notice was given or sent at the proper time? Or again, putting it specifically, so as to raise the concrete question upon which the American courts have divided, is it enough for the holder to inform the indorser that the paper indorsed *has not been paid*, assuming that due presentment and protest, where protest is necessary, have been made?

This question has usually, if not always, arisen upon written notice, but it might arise upon oral notice. In a case of oral notice, however, it would be more easy to show that the indorser understood the notice perfectly, if such was the fact, though the language actually used in giving the information might have been scanty, so much so as to be insufficient in a written notice. For in a case of oral notice the parties are face to face, and the statement of the holder to the indorser will be apt to lead to conversation or to conduct making it clear that the notice was well understood and sufficient. Such cases then may be dismissed and give place to the difficulties arising from the language of written notice, where the parties are not face to face, and where in consequence the language of the holder is all the court has to consider.

The course of the English authorities on this point has had so much influence upon our own courts that it is desirable to call special attention to it; that will give us the real explanation of the conflicts of American authority.

To mention cases that have arisen in the English courts only within the present century, the following especially deserve attention: Notice to an indorser in the first of these cases in order of time ran : 'I am desired to apply to you for the payment of £150, due to myself on a draft drawn by Mr. Case, which I hope you will on receipt discharge, to prevent the necessity of law proceedings, which otherwise will immediately take place.' That was held not good notice, on the ground that it was no more than a demand of payment, whereas notice of dishonor was deemed necessary.[1] In a later and very famous case, in the Exchequer Chamber, the predecessor of the present English Court of Appeal, the notice ran: 'A bill of £683 drawn by ' A, upon B, 'and bearing your indorsement, has been put into our hands by the assignees of ' C, 'with directions to take measures for the recovery thereof, unless immediately paid to ' the signers of the notice. The notice was held insufficient;[2] it being considered necessary that the notice 'in express terms or by necessary implication' should assert the dishonor of the paper. Afterwards, in another case, notice that 'the bill is this day returned with *charges*' was held sufficient by the Queen's Bench; 'returned with charges' implying dishonor.[3] A few days later the following before the Common Pleas was held insufficient: 'The promissory note . . . became due yesterday, and is returned to me unpaid;' it did not disclose dishonor.[4] 'Your note . . . became due yesterday, and is returned unpaid . . . with

---

[1] Hartley *v.* Case, 4 Barn. & C. 339. The notice in this case would probably be held bad even under the rule of the more recent English cases referred to infra. See especially Furze *v.* Sharwood, 2 Q. B. 388, where the decision is declared 'perfectly correct.'

[2] Solarte *v.* Palmer, 7 Bing. 530 ; s. c. 1 Bing. N. C. 194. In this case, which has been much discussed, decided as it was in the Exchequer Chamber, the Lord Chief Justice laid down the following rule: 'The notice of dishonor should at least inform the party to whom it is addressed, either in express terms or by necessary implication, that the bill has been dishonored, and that the holder looks to him for payment of the amount.'

[3] Grugeon *v.* Smith, 6 Ad. & E. 499. See Hedger *v.* Steavenson, 2 Mees. & W. 799; Furze *v.* Sharwood, 2 Q. B. 388.

[4] Boulton *v.* Walsh, 3 Bing. N. C. 688.

1*s. 6d.* for noting' in another and still later case was held sufficient.¹

Having regard to the different forms of notice themselves, the decisions in these cases are consistent with each other; and down to and including the last one referred to, they agree in the proposition that the notice should in itself be a notice of dishonor. But the court in the last case took exception to the doctrine of the more celebrated one, that it ought to appear in the notice 'in express terms or by necessary implication,' that the paper was dishonored; considering it 'enough if it appear by *reasonable intendment*, and would be inferred by any man of business, that the bill has been presented to the acceptor, and not paid by him.'² And later judicial opinion in England appears to conform to that proposition.³ That makes the notice a very simple thing; its legal purpose being satisfied if it serve to warn the indorser of the dishonor, so that he may take steps to secure himself, if possible, against prior parties. That the notice was justified by due presentment, etc., is, therefore, a matter to be determined on the evidence at the trial, if suit should be brought, and not an essential feature of the notice itself. Still, the notice must notify of *dishonor* either in terms or by 'reasonable intendment.' The result is this, that instead of the rigid requirement laid down in the Exchequer Chamber of 'necessary implica-

---

¹ Hedger *v.* Steavenson, 2 Mees. & W. 799.

² Boulton *v.* Walsh, *supra*, was overruled in Robson *v.* Curlewis, Car. & M. 378; s. c. 2 Q. B. 421. But just before that decision came Furze *v.* Sharwood, 2 Q. B. 388, in which the court appear to have leaned towards the stricter rule in Solarte *v.* Palmer, saying, however, inter alia of the rule in Boulton *v.* Walsh, 'Perhaps it goes no farther than to require that the court must see that, by some words or other, notice of dishonor has been given.'

³ Armstrong *v.* Christiani, 5 C. B. 687; Everard *v.* Watson, 1 El. & B. 801; Paul *v.* Joel, 4 Hurl. & N. 355.

tion' of dishonor in the notice, where the fact is not expressly asserted, 'reasonable intendment' of the fact is held sufficient by the later authorities. In other words, the difference is the difference between absolute certainty of meaning and fair natural meaning.

Codification of the English law of bills and notes, which has been effected since these decisions were made, has put the matter thus: Notice of dishonor, the statute declares, 'may be given in any terms which sufficiently identify the bill, and intimate that the bill has been dishonored by non-acceptance or non-payment.'[1] The word 'intimate' suggests the words 'reasonable intendment' of the later decisions of the courts, so that those decisions appear to have prevailed.

Turning now to the American cases, but going back no further than to the first quarter of the present century, we find the Supreme Court of the United States apparently relaxing the requirement even more than have the later English authorities. The court expressly says that it is not necessary that notice of dishonor should state that payment was demanded at maturity; that it is so far sufficient if bare non-payment is stated; and that whether presentment was duly made is 'matter of evidence to be established at the trial.'[2] That is, there need be no assertion or intimation of dishonor in the notice except what is implied in sending notice of non-payment.

But as that doctrine has been somewhat canvassed, it is important to see what in fact the notice stated. The instrument was a promissory note payable at a bank in Chilicothe, Ohio. The notice, after describing the instrument, declares that it 'has been protested for non-payment, and

---

[1] Bills of Ex. Act, 49, (5). See also Benjamin's Chalmers, Bills, Art. 199. The word 'bill' in the statute is intended to include notes and cheques.

[2] Mills v. Bank of United States, 11 Wheat. 431; L. C. 256.

the holders thereof look to you.' And the court remarks that the practice in commercial cities is 'not to state in the notice the mode or place of demand, but the mere naked non-payment.' In certain other authorities the decision has been interpreted by these facts, and narrowed accordingly, so as to make it authority for some such proposition only as the following: Notice of non-payment of paper payable at a *bank* in a commercial city, construed with regard to the practice in such places, means notice of dishonor at maturity.

The distinction is thus drawn, which has already been noticed, between paper payable at bank and paper payable generally, and then the case is based more or less upon the alleged practice in large towns; so that, in the absence of such facts notice of non-payment would be insufficient, though prior steps had been duly taken. And accordingly it has been laid down that the dishonor of the paper should appear in the notice expressly or 'by necessary implication or reasonable intendment.' For example: The defendant is indorser of a promissory note, payable at no place stated, which is dishonored at maturity. Notice directly is sent to the defendant in the following language: 'I have a note signed by C E B and indorsed by you for $700, which is due this day and unpaid; payment is demanded of you.' The notice is deemed bad; the statement that it was unpaid not amounting 'by necessary implication or reasonable intendment' to an intimation that demand had been made or that the note had been in any way dishonored.[1]

The decision in this authority appears to come to the same result as that reached in the later English authorities, upon which indeed it is chiefly based. The matter is summed up by the statement of the chief justice that 'mere notice of non-payment, which does not express or imply notice of dishonor, is not such notice as will render the

[1] Gilbert v. Dennis, 3 Met. 495; L. C. 261.

indorser liable.' The sufficiency of the notice then is not a mere 'matter of evidence to be established at the trial.'

Notice of dishonor is 'implied' or conveyed by 'reasonable intendment,' according to the same authority, by mere statement of non-payment, 'where the paper is in terms, or by usage or special agreement, payable at a bank.' Such statement 'is equivalent to an averment that it is dishonored.' In other cases the statement of non-payment alone is not such an equivalent, nor does it imply or convey by reasonable intendment the dishonor of the paper, but the addition of a single word may make the equivalent; adding the word 'protested' would plainly imply dishonor.[1]

The explanation of the difference between the case of paper payable at bank and that of paper not payable at bank, in regard to the validity of a notice of 'non-payment' at maturity, lies in a fact heretofore stated. Where paper is payable at bank, presentment in the ordinary way — by exhibiting the paper — is not required; the maker or acceptor must have provided funds there with which to pay, and if he has not done so it only remains to say that the note has not been paid, to show or to indicate the dishonor. For it may be presumed that the books of the bank have been examined, if necessary, to see whether funds applicable are in the bank.

More recently, however, it has been held in another State, that notice of *dishonor* is not necessary, and that notice of non-payment is enough in any case, whether the paper is payable at bank or not, so long as proper steps in fact have already been taken. For example: The defendant is indorser of a promissory note which does not designate any place of payment. The note is dishonored at maturity, and notice is sent at once by the holder to the defendant,

---

[1] 1 Parsons, Notes & Bills, 471, citing Crawford *v.* Branch Bank, 7 Ala. 205; DeWolf *v.* Murray, 2 Sandf. 166, and other cases.

stating that the former holds a 'note indorsed by you and not paid at this date,' and demands payment. That is deemed good notice.[1]

That doctrine proceeds upon the ground that the purpose of notice of dishonor is simply to warn the indorser that he must be prepared to pay. If the indorser has doubts whether the warning is good, let him inquire; and doubts he may have as well where the steps are detailed in the notice as where they are not; he is neither better nor worse off by bare warning of non-payment, so far as the real facts in regard to the steps are concerned. But the weight of authority appears to be against such a view of the matter, and it must on the whole be said that the notice should in itself, or in the circumstances attending it, be a notice of dishonor.[2]

Authority has sometimes gone still further, and required the notice to show or intimate not only the dishonor of the paper, but dishonor of it at maturity. For example: The defendant is indorser of a promissory note, payable at no stated place, which is dishonored at maturity. The holder directly notifies the defendant in writing, stating that the note has been 'this day presented for payment' without avail, there being nothing to show that 'this day' was the day of maturity. The notice is deemed not good.[3] But that may be doubted.

[1] Cromer v. Platt, 37 Mich. 132, Graves, J. dis.
[2] See Clark v. Eldridge, 13 Met. 96; Townsend v. Lorain Bank, 2 Ohio St. 345, 355; Ransom v. Mack, 2 Hill, 587; Dole v. Gold, 5 Barb. 490; Arnold v. Kinloch, 50 Barb. 44; Armstrong v. Thruston, 11 Md. 148, 157; Lockwood v. Crawford, 18 Conn. 361; Page v. Gilbert, 60 Maine, 485.
[3] Wynn v. Alden, 4 Denio, 165. See also Townsend v. Lorain Bank, 2 Ohio St. 345; Etting v. Schuylkill Bank, 2 Barr, 355; Routh v. Robertson, 11 Smedes & M. 382. But see Crocker v. Getchell, 23 Maine, 392; Ontario Bank v. Petrie, 3 Wend. 456, overruled in Ransom v. Mack, 2 Hill, 587, 595.

Further, the notice must, generally speaking, apprise the indorser that the holder looks to him for payment. All the authorities agree in that statement as a general proposition;[1] but there has been some question of the meaning of the rule. Does the rule mean that there should be an averment in the notice that the holder looks to the indorser for payment? But implication may be as plain as assertion, and beyond doubt that is so in every case where the holder sends notice of dishonor; the sending or giving of the notice has no meaning in such a case unless it means that the holder looks to the party notified for payment. And so the courts do not require any such statement, though it is common to make one; nor perhaps is such statement necessary in notice by one indorser, though not the holder, to another. It is enough certainly that the notice proceeds from the holder or from his agent or from a notary employed by either.[2]

§ 3. Notice, by Whom.

Notice should be given (1) by the holder or by his lawful agent, or (2) by an indorser bound to pay. It cannot be given, so as to have legal effect, by any other person: except, of course, on the death of the holder, by his personal representative.

A stranger then, acting without due authority, cannot

---

[1] See § 3, infra.

[2] Bank of United States v. Carneal. 2 Peters, 543. Chanoine v. Fowler, 3 Wend. 173; L. C. 271; Furze v. Sharwood, 2 Q. B. 388. In the latter case, Lord Denman said: 'Where notice has been given by another party [i. e. an indorser] than the holder, there may be good sense in requiring that it shall be accompanied by a direct demand of payment or a statement that it will be required of the party addressed; but in no case has the absence of such information been held to vitiate a notice in other respects complete, and which has come directly from the holder.'

give valid notice of dishonor; and the reason makes the rule sensible and just, — an unauthorized stranger cannot apprise the indorser of what he is entitled to know, to wit. that the holder (or other party) will look to him for payment.[1] For the same reason it was at one time held that an indorser could not give valid notice, in his own behalf; he could not inform the party notified that the holder would look to him for payment, unless he was authorized by the holder to act for him; and in that case it would not be the indorser's notice. But the contrary rule now prevails. For example: The defendant is drawer of a bill of exchange, of which the plaintiff is an indorser, having indorsed it in favor of W who had discounted and so purchased the bill. On discounting the bill W left it with the plaintiff's clerk, with instructions to him to obtain payment or give notice of dishonor. The clerk does give such notice to the defendant at the proper time, but he gives it, not in the name of W but in the name of the plaintiff.[2] The notice is good.[3]

But though an indorser may give notice for his own benefit, to avail him in case he should afterwards be compelled to pay or should pay without suit — for an indorser loses none of his rights by paying voluntarily after his liability has been fixed; — can the indorser give notice which may avail the *holder* or any intermediate party? Doubt has existed on this point also, because an indorser as such is not an agent for the holder or for the next or any later indorser.

---

[1] Cases in Note 2, p. 119.

[2] The case therefore stands just as if the plaintiff indorser himself gave the notice.

[3] Chapman *v.* Keane, 3 Ad. & E. 193, overruling Tindal *v.* Brown, 1 T. R. 167; s. c. 2 T. R. 186, in which it had been held that notice should come from the holder or his agent, so as to apprise the party notified that he would be looked to for payment.

Clearly the mere fact that an indorser has given notice to a prior indorser in due time will not of itself avail the holder. But if the notifying indorser has authority from the holder or other to give the notice, his act will be the act of the holder; or if, not having authority from the holder or other, his own liability as indorser has been duly fixed, notice given by him, it is now understood, will avail the holder or intermediate indorser by what is well termed inurement.[1] It is necessary, however, that the liability of the notifying indorser should have been duly fixed (unless by reason of waiver it was already absolute); otherwise the indorser, being under no liability, is a mere stranger. For example: The defendant is indorser of a bill of exchange, subsequently indorsed by A to the plaintiff. The bill is dishonored at maturity, and A immediately gives notice to the defendant. The plaintiff has not given notice at all, and has not authorized A to give notice for him. The defendant is not liable; the notice by A not inuring to the plaintiff's benefit because A's liability has not been fixed.[2]

One or two early cases, as reported, appear to give sanction to a doctrine that the acceptor of a bill, and, by parity of reasoning, the maker of a note, may give notice available for the holder.[3] But that is probably to be explained on the ground that the acceptor or maker was the author-

---

[1] 'The plaintiff insists that the notice given by the bank shall inure to his benefit. If the notice had been in time and valid, it would by law have inured to his benefit,' etc. Reese, J., in Simpson v. Turney, 5 Humph. 419; L. C. 291. The student should observe that inurement is not agency.

[2] See Lysaght v. Bryant, 9 C. B. 46, the converse case, the notifying indorser having been duly notified by the holder and plaintiff. 'It seems from the cases that the holder of a bill may avail himself of a notice given in due time by a prior indorser, *provided* he himself is in a condition to sue the party by whom the notice was given.' Id., Cresswell, J. See also Harrison v. Ruscoe, 15 Mees. & W. 231.

[3] Rosher v. Kieran, 4 Camp. 87; Shaw v. Croft, Chitty, Bills, 494.

ized agent of the holder in the matter; otherwise the doctrine is unsound.[1] There must be an agency, if the notice is not given by an indorser, at the time of giving the notice, and in the act of giving it.[2]

§ 4. Notice, to Whom.

Notice may be sent to the indorser or to his lawful agent. If two or more have indorsed the paper jointly, notice must be sent to each of them, if by due diligence that can be done;[3] unless there should be an agency between them, in which case notice to the one who is agent will be sufficient to bind all. Otherwise notice to part of the number would not bind even them, since they are liable only with the rest. If the joint indorsers are partners, notice to one will suffice.[4]

In the event of the death of an indorser, notice should be given to his personal representative if there be such; if there be several, notice to one of them is notice to all.[5] But even though there should be no personal representative of the deceased indorser, it is still the duty of the holder to exercise reasonable diligence towards informing those interested in his estate of the dishonor of the paper.[6] It has accordingly been held that if notice is sent to the last place of residence or of business of the indorser, that is enough, prima facie, to fix the liability of his estate, since it may reasonably be assumed that the notice will reach those who are chiefly interested.[7] So, too, notice

---

[1] Bayley, Bills, 254, 5th ed.; Thompson, Bills, 359, Wilson's ed.
[2] See New York Co. v. Selma Sav. Bank, 51 Ala. 305.
[3] State Bank v. Slaughter, 7 Blackf. 133; Beals v. Peck, 12 Barb. 245; Willis v. Green, 5 Hill, 232; Miser v. Trovinger, 7 Ohio St. 281.
[4] Gowan v. Jackson, 20 Johns. 176; Bouldin v. Page, 24 Mo. 594.
[5] Beals v. Peck, 12 Barb. 245.
[6] Goodnow v. Warren, 122 Mass. 79.
[7] Id.

may be sent to one named as executor in the will of an indorser, though the person named has not qualified; for the fact that the indorser has named him as his executor is enough to indicate that he will take an interest in the estate, even though he should decline the office, and inform those directly concerned.[1] But it would not satisfy the law to send notice to a person *afterwards* appointed administrator, not being a person to whom the estate would pass.[2]

Notice to the personal representative should, it seems, be sent addressed to him by name, if his name can be ascertained by reasonable diligence, and not 'to the executor' or 'administrator' or 'personal representatives' of the indorser; though notice so addressed will in any case be good if received in due time.[3] On the death of a partner, in the case of partnership indorsement, notice should be given to the survivor,[4] and also perhaps to the personal representative of the deceased.[5]

§ 5. Notice, How.

The law merchant requires that the indorser shall be notified of the dishonor with reasonable expeditiousness; and hence it cannot be, and is not indifferent to, methods of giving notice. That is to say, the presumably more direct and expeditious method must be adopted, unless it can be shown that the notice reached the indorser, notwithstanding the method used, as soon as it would have done had

---

[1] Shoenberger v. Lancaster Sav. Inst., 28 Penn. St. 459.

[2] Goodnow v. Warren, 122 Mass. 79; Mathewson v. Strafford Bank, 45 N. H. 104.

[3] Smalley v. Wright, 40 N. J. 471; Linderman v. Guldin, 34 Penn. St. 54.

[4] Slocomb v. De Lizardi, 21 La. An. 355.

[5] Cocke v. Bank of Tennessee, 6 Hump. 51. But see Dabney v. Stidger, 4 Smedes & M. 749. See Hubbard v. Matthews, 54 N. Y. 43

the method preferred by law been used. And the law merchant has defined, with some degree of nicety, if not of over-nicety, the methods preferred.

Before postal communications had become as frequent and as perfect as they now are, the courts had declared that where the party to be notified resided or did business in the same town in which the notifying party resided or did business, the method to be preferred was by 'personal' act, which means notifying the defendant to his face or leaving written notice for him at his place of business or of residence. The mail was supposed not to be so expeditious; and hence notice sent through the post-office, in such a case, was deemed insufficient unless it was in fact received, and received no later than the latest day on which it would have been good if orally given. And so, generally speaking, the law stands at this day. For example: The defendant is indorser and the plaintiff holder of a promissory note, the note being in the hands of a bank for collection at the place of residence of the defendant. Upon the note there is a memorandum, written by the defendant, in these words: 'Third indorser,' the defendant, 'lives at V.,' the place just referred to. The collecting bank, in due time, by a notary public, puts a letter in the post-office at V., containing notice of the dishonor of the paper. There is no evidence that the letter is received, nor is there any evidence of usage at V. to mail notices of dishonor in such cases. The defendant is not liable, the memorandum on the note not being an authorization of notice by the mail.[1]

To that rule, which in more recent times has often been regretted, three exceptions at least have come to be made, one being perhaps contemporaneous with it: to wit, (1) If the parties live or do business in a place in which letters are regularly and daily delivered by carriers of the govern-

[1] Bowling v. Harrison, 6 How. 248; L. C. 285.

ment, or perhaps by private carriers, the notice may be sent through the mail. (2) An indorser who, residing in a different town from that of the holder, has himself received due notice through the mail, may notify a prior indorser by the mail, though that indorser resides in the same town in which he, the notifying indorser, resides, and though the practice of delivering letters does not prevail there. (3) Where the parties live in different villages or perhaps districts of one town, the mail may be used for sending notice. For example (hypothetical): The defendant is indorser and the plaintiff holder of a dishonored promissory note, both parties living in Chicago. Notice of the dishonor may be given by mail. Again: The defendant is indorser of a bill of exchange payable in Philadelphia to A or order, who lives in Providence; A indorses the bill to a bank in Providence; that bank indorses it over to another bank in New York, which latter bank indorses it for collection to a bank in Philadelphia. The bill is dishonored, and the collecting bank causes notices to be made out for all the parties, and sends them seasonably to the bank in New York; that bank sends notice seasonably to the bank in Providence, inclosing a notice for the defendant; and the bank in Providence now places this last-named notice in the post-office properly addressed. The defendant's liability under the circumstances is duly fixed.[1] Again: The defendant is indorser and the plaintiff holder of a promissory note which has been dishonored. The parties both reside in the town of S., but the defendant resides in another part of the town from the plaintiff, in a distinct village, C., where he usually receives his mail. The plaintiff mails notice of dishonor to the defendant seasonably, addressed to him at C. The defendant's liability is duly fixed.[2]

[1] Eagle Bank v. Hathaway, 5 Met. 212.
[2] Shaylor v. Mix, 4 Allen, 351. The defendant, however, received the notice.

When, indeed, notice through the mail is proper, the mere mailing the notice, if seasonable, is enough to fix the liability of the indorser; the law merchant does not expect the holder to see that the post-office delivers it or that the indorser has received it in any other way. For example: The defendant is indorser and the plaintiff holder of a promissory note, the former living in Boston, the latter in Philadelphia. The note is payable in Philadelphia, is dishonored, and protested by a notary. The notary thereupon mails in Philadelphia a letter containing the notice to the defendant in Boston. It does not appear that the defendant has ever received the letter. The defendant's liability is duly fixed.[1]

Indeed, authority, proceeding more or less upon custom in cities, has gone still further and treated notice by mail, when proper at all, as good against all parties to whom notices may be inclosed in a single letter addressed to a later indorser. So to do is deemed exercising due diligence, and hence whether the letter or the notices are ever received is immaterial. For example: The defendant is third indorser and the plaintiffs are holders of a promissory note. Before maturity of the note the plaintiffs send it for collection to their agent, a bank in Boston, which bank indorses it and sends it to its own agent, a bank in New York. At maturity payment is demanded and refused, and the note duly protested. Notices of dishonor are thereupon addressed by the notary to each of the indorsers and sent in a letter to the bank in Boston, duly addressed and mailed in the post-office in New York. This letter, with inclosures, is lost and never received by the bank or by the defendant. The liability of the defendant is deemed to have been duly fixed, due diligence having been exercised according to the usage and practice of merchants

[1] Munn v. Baldwin, 6 Mass. 316. See also Shelton v. Carpenter, 60 Ala. 201; Jones v. Wardell, 6 Watts & S. 399.

and bankers, and it being immaterial that the last indorser held the note for collection only.[1]

An agent, in giving notice, is treated as if he were principal; hence whether notice to be given by such person should be by 'personal' act or by mail is to be determined by *his* situation towards the indorser, not by the situation of the principal towards the indorser.[2]

A private messenger may be employed in any case to carry the notice, even in those cases in which the mail is the preferred means. But where the employment of a messenger is not presumptively the method to be adopted (as it would be in a village in which both parties resided, there being no delivery there by carriers, and as it would not be where they reside in different towns), the notice by messenger will be good only in case it is delivered to the indorser personally, or at his place of business or of residence, not later than the latest day on which it would reach its destination in due course of the mail.

Notice may be sent to the several indorsers in succession. For example: A promissory note is indorsed by five persons successively. The holder may notify the fifth indorser; the fifth indorser may then notify the fourth; the fourth may then notify the third; and so on back to the first. Each notice so given, if seasonable, will fix liability.[3]

Notice by what is aptly termed inurement has already been referred to in the section relating to the persons who may give or send notice. The subject belongs equally

---

[1] Wamesit Bank *v.* Buttrick, 11 Gray, 387. But see Van Brunt *v.* Vaughn, 47 Iowa, 145, where the notice is treated as good *provided* the party to whom the notices are directed himself sends them on.

[2] Manchester Bank *v.* Fellows, 28 N. H. 302; Bowling *v.* Harrison, 6 How. 248; L. C. 285.

[3] Shelburne Falls Bank *v.* Townsley, 107 Mass. 444; s. c. 102 Mass. 177. When each notice is seasonable, see infra, § 6.

to the present section, and it may accordingly be stated here that one of the methods of notice is by inurement; and that may be explained by the following example: The defendant is first of three indorsers of a promissory note of which the plaintiff is holder. The note being dishonored at maturity, the holder gives due notice to the third indorser, and the third indorser gives due notice to defendant (or to the second indorser, who duly notifies the defendant). The plaintiff is entitled to recover, the intermediate notice (or notices) given inuring to his benefit.[1]

§ 6. Notice, When.

Notice of dishonor may be given by the holder either on the day of the dishonor, being the day of maturity,[2] or on the first following secular day; and it must be given on one of those two days unless a sufficient reason is shown for omitting to do so, or the indorser will be discharged. There is, however, no case in which, by the law merchant, notice must be given on the day of dishonor, however easily it might have been done, and whatever the consequences of not doing so. For example: The defendant is indorser and the plaintiff holder of a promissory note payable in Alexandria, Virginia, which matures August 25. On that day it is dishonored. On the next day notice is sent to the defendant by mail in Washington, where he resides. The notice is seasonable; the law merchant requiring, not the utmost, but only ordinary, reasonable diligence.[3]

It should be remarked that, although what the law merchant requires in the matter of fixing the liability of

---

[1] See Simpson v. Turney, 5 Humph. 419; L. C. 291, where, however, the intermediate notice was too late.

[2] King v. Crowell, 61 Maine, 244; Howard v. Ives, 1 Hill, 263.

[3] Bank of Alexandria v. Swann, 9 Peters, 33; L. C. 293.

the indorser, whether in respect of presentment, protest, or notice, is only in terms 'reasonable diligence;' still what constitutes reasonable diligence is often defined, presumptively and only presumptively, within narrow limits. And the point under consideration is an example. Reasonable diligence only is required; but that is interpreted by the law to mean, that presumptively notice should be given on one of the two days mentioned in the rule.

If the day following maturity and dishonor should be a non-secular day, or if, where the mail may be used there is no departure of the mail on the next day after maturity, the holder may wait in the one case until the first secular day, in the other, until the next departure of the mail after the day of maturity, however long that may be. It matters not that there was a regular departure of the mail on the day of maturity and dishonor. It will be observed that, while the occurrence of non-secular days cuts off grace, such occurrence *adds* to the time for giving notice.

The length of time allowed to the holder for giving notice is not varied at all by the circumstance that there may be several indorsements upon the paper, and that he may wish to notify some other indorser than the last one. The holder may himself notify any indorser he will, notifying or not notifying others; but he has no more time for giving notice to the first or an intermediate indorser than to the last. It does not matter that as much or more time would be taken if notices were sent successively back from the last to the defendant indorser. For example (hypothetical): The defendant is first indorser and the plaintiff holder of a promissory note upon which there are five successive indorsements. Two days after the maturity and dishonor of the note, the plaintiff notifies the defendant, though the day after maturity was a secular day, with departure of mail during business hours. The notice is not seasonable.[1]

There is, however, some doubt concerning the meaning of the rule that the holder has until the day after maturity, or other day according to circumstances. The rule clearly does not mean that notice must be posted, where the mail may be used, on that day at all events. Not to speak of excuses, of which later, the only mail on the day in question may depart at an unseasonable hour in the morning for business; in such a case the law treats that day as if it were a non-secular day, so far as the sending of notice is concerned.[2] But supposing that there is a departure of the mail after business hours have opened, on the day after dishonor, must the holder deposit his notice in the post-office in time for that mail?

It has been said that the holder has an entire day after the dishonor for giving notice; and that has sometimes been interpreted to mean that the holder has until the end of that day, so that the notice need not leave until the departure of the mail a day later. For example: A promissory note is due January 2. Demand is made, and payment refused on that day. Notice of dishonor is deposited in the post-office for the defendant at 10 o'clock at night, January 3; there have been departures of the mail since business hours of the morning to the place of the defendant's residence, but the last mail has already departed, and the notice cannot go before January 4. The mailing of the notice is deemed seasonable.[2]

That doctrine, though having the support of a great

---

[1] See Simpson v. Turney, 5 Humph. 419; L. C. 291.

[2] See Lawson v. Farmers' Bank, 1 Ohio St. 206; L. C. 295, 302; 3 Kent, 106, note. 'Notice put into the post-office on the next day at any time of the day, so as to be ready to go by the first mail that goes *thereafter*, is due notice, though it may not be mailed in season to go by the mail of the day next after the day of the default.'

judge, has been seriously questioned, and indeed denied by judicial authority to be a correct statement of the law merchant; the rule, so far as there is a rule so expressed, that the holder has an 'entire day' for giving notice, being considered only a general, and not an exact statement of the law. The true rule is accordingly deemed to be that the holder ought to avail himself at latest of some departure of the mail after the opening of business hours, if there be such mail, on the day following the dishonor. For example: The defendant, residing in Salem, Ohio, is indorser of a bill of exchange held by the plaintiffs, residing in Pittsburgh, Pennsylvania. The bill is dishonored and protested July 27. There is one, and only one, daily departure of the mail from Pittsburgh to Salem: to wit, at 9.10 o'clock A. M., which is after reasonable business hours of the day. Notice to the defendant is deposited in the mail on July 28, but too late for the mail of that day. The notice is deemed not seasonable; due diligence has not been exercised.[1]

The rule declared in the case given in this example has this in its favor, that it was laid down upon mature consideration and upon a review of the authorities. A question which before had been but slightly considered has now been answered by deliberate judicial authority; and the rule is accordingly to be taken, it seems, as the better declaration of the law merchant.

Reasonable diligence, narrowly defined in certain cases, but not in others, is after all, as we have seen, the requirement in all cases.[2] Accordingly the point of beginning, in reckoning the time for giving notice, is not the day after maturity, but the day after that on which the holder, after exercising reasonable diligence, is in a position to

---

[1] Lawson v. Farmers' Bank, supra.

[2] Bank of Utica v. Bender, 21 Wend. 643; L. C. 329; Gladwell v. Turner, L. R. 5 Ex 59.

give notice.[1] For example: The defendant is drawer and the plaintiff holder of a bill of exchange dishonored at maturity. On the morning after the dishonor of the bill, the holder, not knowing where the defendant lives, applies to one of the indorsers at his house for information, but not finding him at home, calls again at 5.30 in the afternoon, and now obtaining from him the defendant's address, posts notice the same evening after six o'clock. The defendant's liability is fixed, though he does not receive the notice on the day on which it was posted as he would have done had the notice been posted before six o'clock.[2]

It would have made no difference in the example had it appeared that the whole of the day and evening had been consumed, and all of the next day or week, in reasonable endeavor to find the address of the defendant; time reasonably consumed in finding the defendant or his address is to be deducted from the account.[3] Nor, as has already been seen, would it have made any difference had the notice never been received, the mail being a proper vehicle for conveying it.

Thus far of the time of notice when given by the holder. The time allowed an *indorser* is, generally speaking, the same as would be allowed if he were holder. He may give notice on the day on which he received notice; he must give notice either on that day, or on the first succeeding secular day on which there is a departure of the mail to the indorser's place of residence where the mail may be used, unless the first succeeding secular day is the day after maturity, and the only mail goes out before seasonable business in the morning, in which case the indorser, like the holder, has till the next mail. And,

---

[1] Gladwell v. Turner, supra.

[2] Id.

[3] Fugitt v. Nixon, 44 Mo. 295; Manchester Bank v. Fellows, 28 N. H. 302.

like the holder, he has no more time for giving notice to a remote than to the last indorser.

There is one case in which, it seems, an indorser may have more time for giving notice than a holder. Notice of dishonor might be received by an indorser on Sunday or some other non-secular day; but in such a case the indorser would not be bound to regard it until the first secular day following, so that the receiving of the notice could be reckoned, at the indorser's election, as from such secular day. Accordingly, the indorser would have that day and the next, even to the next secular day, if the morrow after the day from which the reckoning is begun should be non-secular, and until a departure of the mail, as already explained. For example (hypothetical): The defendant is first, and the plaintiff second, indorser of a promissory note. Due notice of dishonor has been sent to the plaintiff. The notice is received on Sunday, July 3. The following day being a holiday, the plaintiff treats the 5th of July as if it were the day on which he received the notice, and mails notice to the defendant on the 6th of July (or if there is no departure of the mail to the destination of the notice on the 6th, or if the only departure is before reasonable business of that day, then so as to go by the first mail afterwards). The notice is (probably) seasonable.[1]

Notice may, however, be sent, whether by the holder or by an indorser, on Sunday or other non-secular day, since notice is merely warning. So it is said.[2]

An agent for collection is treated as holder for the purpose of giving notice of dishonor, and his principal, if he indorsed the paper, is accordingly treated as an ordinary indorser; that is, the case is regarded as if it were not a case of agency. In other words, the real holder and

---

[1] See Wright v. Shawcross, 2 Barn. & Ald. 501, note; Bray v. Hadwen, 5 Maule & S. 68; Deblieux v. Bullard, 1 Rob. (La.) 66.

[2] Deblieux v. Bullard, supra.

owner, if an indorser, stands upon the footing of an indorser in regard to the question of time in giving notice of dishonor. Thus the agent has the same time for notifying his principal which any other holder would have; and the principal has the same time he would have if the agent had been owner of the paper.[1]

Paper may have been indorsed after maturity, and serious question has arisen concerning time of notice in such a case. It has sometimes been considered that the rules pertaining to indorsement of paper before maturity should not apply, in their strictness, if at all, to such a case; and accordingly notice of dishonor as late as two months after the dishonor, on the special demand now required,[2] has been deemed within reasonable time.[3] It has even been stated that notice is altogether dispensed with in such a case.[4] But the better view appears to be that the rules of ordinary indorsement apply. Indorsers of paper payable on its face on demand are entitled to notice in all respects as in other cases; and why the rule should be otherwise of paper indorsed after maturity, which now is in law payable on demand, it would be difficult to explain.[5]

---

[1] Lawson v. Farmers' Bank, 1 Ohio St. 206; L. C. 295, 307; Bank of United States v. Davis, 2 Hill, 452; Church v. Barlow, 9 Pick. 547; Crocker v. Getchell, 23 Maine, 392; Manchester Bank v. Fellows, 28 N. H. 302; Bray v. Hadwen, 5 Maule & S. 68; Prideaux v. Criddle, L. R. 4 Q. B. 455

[2] The paper having been indorsed after maturity, a new contract in regard to presentment arises, to wit, that the undertaking of the maker or acceptor is to pay on demand. See ante, p. 92.

[3] Van Hoesen v. Van Alstyne, 3 Wend. 75. See also McKinney v. Crawford, 8 Serg. & R. 351; Gray v. Bell, 3 Rich. 71; Chadwick v. Jeffers, 1 Rich. 397.

[4] Gray v. Bell, supra, O'Neall. J.

[5] See Bassenhorst v. Wilby, 45 Ohio St. 333; Lockwood v. Crawford, 18 Conn. 361; Bishop v. Dexter, 2 Conn. 419; Berry v. Robinson, 9 Johns. 121; Course v. Shackleford, 2 Nott & M. 283; Poole v. Tolleson, 1 McCord, 199; Ecfert v. Des Coudres, 1 Mill, 69.

§ 7. Notice, Where.

The question where notice is to be given or sent has been indirectly answered already, in part; for we have seen that where the holder and the indorser reside in the same town the notice should be given to the indorser personally or left at his place of business or of residence, and that when they live in different places it should be sent to the indorser's address as far as ascertainable by reasonable diligence. That goes far towards answering the whole question now raised.

Notice may, however, be given to the indorser personally anywhere, wherever the holder or notifying indorser may happen to find him, so far as place is concerned; it may be given to him in his house or counting room, in the cars, or on the street, so long as it is good in other respects.[1] And that because the notice is mere warning, and not intended or expected to be followed then and there by payment, as is presentment for payment.

It may be that the indorser has post-office addresses in different towns, or it may be that there are several post-offices within the same town at each of which the indorser is accustomed to receive his mail. In such a case a letter containing the notice may be addressed to the indorser at any one of such post-offices, or to the town without naming any particular post-office; and the proper deposit of the letter in the mail, whether at the post-office or in boxes placed for receiving mail, will itself be notice. Such act would be exercising reasonable diligence, and what may become of the letter will be immaterial.[2]

Where, however, there are several post-offices in the town of the indorser, notice by letter addressed to the indorser at the town generally is sufficient, unless the indorser

---

[1] See Hyslop v. Jones, 3 McLean, 96.
[2] See Roberts v. Taft, 120 Mass. 169.

has been accustomed to receive his letters at one of the offices in particular, and to have his letters addressed to him there. In other words, the holder makes out a presumptive case, so far, by proving that notice was sent to the indorser in a letter by mail addressed to the town generally. But that presumptive case may be met by the indorser by showing that he usually received his letters at one office only, and that the fact might have been learned by reasonable inquiry. Without such evidence it might still be true that the indorser received his mail at any of the post-offices.[1] If, however, the letter was in fact received in due time, it would make no difference that there may have been a mistake in the address.[2]

The post-office address of the defendant is still a matter of first importance; that rather than the precise locality of his residence. And hence where the indorser's address is known to the notifying party, and the latter sends notice addressed to his place of residence, that being in another town, he must see to it, it seems, that the indorser receives the notice and receives it in due time. Clearly where an indorser receives his mail usually in the town of his residence, but sometimes in another town, notice should be sent to the post-office of his town. For example: The defendant is indorser and the plaintiff holder of a dishonored promissory note; the two living in different towns. The defendant sometimes receives his letters at the post-office of the town in which the plaintiff resides, but usually at the post-office of his own town. The plaintiff drops a letter in his own post-office addressed to the defendant, which is not received in due time. The defendant is discharged.[3]

Perhaps the rule would be different if the plaintiff did not know that the defendant lived in another town from

---

[1] Roberts v. Taft, supra; Morton v. Westcott, 8 Cush. 425; Saco Bank v. Sanborn, 63 Maine, 340; Downer v. Remer, 21 Wend. 10.

[2] Roberts v. Taft, supra.

[3] Shelburne Falls Bank v. Townsley, 107 Mass. 444.

the one at which the plaintiff knew that he received letters. At all events notice at the plaintiff's post-office would be good if the plaintiff, in mailing it there, acted upon information properly sought and obtained.

It is possible that the indorser may live in a very sparsely settled part of the country, and that there may be no post-office in the town in which he lives. In such a case the holder does all that is required by sending notice directed to the indorser at the nearest town having a post-office, so far as can be ascertained by reasonable inquiry.[1]

In a case of removal by the indorser, of which the holder has no notice otherwise, the indorser should inform him if he wants notice sent to his new place of residence. In the absence of notice of the change, notice of the dishonor may be sent to the indorser's former place of residence; at all events if the notifying party, not satisfied with his previous information, makes inquiry where he would be likely to receive correct information, and then acts accordingly.[2] Whether one who has some considerable time before had sufficient information of the residence of the indorser may afterwards safely act upon that information, and send notice accordingly, without inquiry at the time of sending, may in some cases raise a doubt; but it appears to be the general rule that when nothing has occurred to suggest to the notifying party a change of residence by the indorser, no inquiry further is necessary.[3]

Of cases in which the parties have lived near each other, as for instance, in some small town, the holder knowing where the indorser has lived, it may be presumed from

---

[1] Shed v. Brett, 1 Pick, 401, 411; Ireland v. Kip, 11 Johns. 232; Union Bank v. Stoker, 1 La. An. 269; Marsh v. Burr, Meigs, 68; S. C. 9 Yerg. 253.

[2] Saco Bank v. Sanborn, 63 Maine, 340.

[3] Id.; Bank of Utica v. Phillips, 3 Wend. 408; Gawtry v. Doane, 51 N. Y. 84; Berridge v. Fitzgerald, L. R. 4 Q. B. 639.

their nearness, together with any frequency of communication and notoriety of removal, that the holder was aware of the indorser's change of domicile.[1]

Temporary absence from home does not amount to removal, so as to require or even permit sending notice to the temporary place of abode; though notice received there in due time will be good. For example: The defendant is indorser and the plaintiff holder of a promissory note, both parties residing in New Jersey. Business, however, takes the defendant to Cleveland, Ohio, most of the season of the year, when the note matures, and keeps him there much of the time. About November 1 he goes from Cleveland to Chicago on business likely to take some considerable time, and informs the plaintiff that he is going there. He remains in Chicago until November 22, on which day notice of dishonor is mailed to him at that place. The notice is not received, the defendant having left for Cleveland before the notice arrived. On his return to Cleveland, he is informed by the plaintiff of what has happened. The defendant is discharged; a temporary place of abode presumptively not being a place to which notice of dishonor should be sent.[2]

It seems, however, that, where an indorser has a regular abode for a considerable time in the year, a notifying

---

[1] McVeigh v. Allen, 29 Gratt. 588, 596; Bank of Old Dominion v. McVeigh, 26 Gratt. 785; S. C. 29 Gratt. 546; Harris v. Memphis Bank, 4 Humph. 519; Bank of Utica v. Phillips, 3 Wend. 408.

[2] Walker v. Stetson, 14 Ohio St. 89; L. C. 314. Something is said of the defendant's having had no 'relations to the post-office' in Chicago, whatever that may mean. The real point is that Chicago was not the defendant's place of residence or his post-office address for the purpose in question. Query, whether Cleveland would not have been a proper place to which to send, or at which to give notice? The notice actually given there was too late, because of the delay in sending the letter to Chicago.

party, having knowledge of such place of abode, and no knowledge of his proper domicile or permanent home, may send notice to such abode, or give notice there. For example: The defendant, indorser of a promissory note held by the plaintiff, is a senator of the United States, having an abode in Washington during the session of Congress. He leaves an agent in a city near his legal domicile to attend to his business, but of that fact the plaintiff is not aware. Notice of dishonor is seasonably mailed to the defendant at Washington. The notice is deemed good.[1]

Such notice would, more clearly still, be good if the senator had given up his residence in the State he represented, and had left no one there to attend to his business.[2] Perhaps the case of a member of the Legislature at the Capitol, away from home, would fall within the principle governing the case of the example; but cases of the kind are considered to go to the verge of the law merchant.[3]

In regard to seeking information, inquiry should be made of some one from whom, or through some source of information where, trustworthy information will be apt to be given. It is usual and proper for the notifying party to make inquiry of some other party to the paper, e. g., a later indorser, in regard to the place of residence of indorsers; and such course will be especially proper, if not necessary, where the notifying party has reason to think that any party to the paper knows of such place of residence, assuming, of course, that the party having the knowledge is within reasonable reach.[4] And if a notary is employed, the holder should give him the benefit of any information he has.[5]

---

[1] Chouteau v. Webster, 6 Met. 1.
[2] Tunstall v. Walker, 2 Smedes & M. 638.
[3] Walker v. Stetson, 14 Ohio St. 89; L. C. 314, 319.
[4] Wolf v. Burgess, 59 Mo. 583; Gilchrist v. Donnell, 53 Mo. 591.
[5] Edwards v. Thomas, 66 Mo. 468.

It is not enough, it seems, to make inquiry for an indorser's place of residence at the post-office, where the indorser resides in a large city, unless indeed he has lately been employed in, or connected with, the post-office. The proper way is to consult some good city directory, and in case of removal, then at the indorser's last place of business or of residence [1]. Or, if in a case of the kind the indorser's name does not appear in the directory, then inquiry may be made of some other party, as the maker or acceptor; and if information is given, notice may be sent accordingly, whether the information given was right or not.[2] Of course, inquiry may be made of relatives of the indorser.[3] If on going to the indorser's house to give him notice, the house is found closed and unoccupied, inquiry may and perhaps should be made at the next door, if there be a house near.[4]

Inquiry should be pursued until some satisfactory, that is, apparently trustworthy, answer is given, or until it is reasonably clear that nothing useful can be found out. When, however, the apparently trustworthy information is received, inquiry may stop, and notice may be sent accordingly; and the notice will be good whether the information was correct or not.[5] For example: The defendant is indorser of a bill of exchange held by the plaintiff. On discounting the bill, the plaintiff inquires of the drawer where the defendant resides, and receives an answer, according to which he sends notice of dishonor seasonably to the defendant, nothing having occurred to lead him to doubt the correctness of the information. The notice is good, though the information is incorrect.[6]

[1] Miller v. Farmers' Bank, 30 Md. 392.
[2] Gawtry v. Doane, 51 N. Y. 84.
[3] Requa v. Collins, 51 N. Y. 144.
[4] Williams v. Bank of United States, 2 Peters, 96.
[5] Saco Bank v. Sanborn, supra; Bank of Utica v. Bender, 21 Wend. 643.
[6] Bank of Utica v. Bender, 21 Wend. 643; L. C. 329.

The place of date of a bill is presumptively the place of residence of the drawer, and so would be the place of date of an indorsement, if added, in regard to the indorser's residence; and there is good authority for the statement that the notifying party may rely upon such date if he has no reason to doubt whether the drawer or indorser lives at the particular place. For example: The defendant is drawer, and the plaintiff holder, of a bill of exchange dated at A. Notice of dishonor is directed to the defendant, in due time, at A, though A is not his place of residence, and though the plaintiff might have learned on inquiry where the defendant resides. The notice is not received. The defendant's liability is deemed duly fixed.[1]

There is also equally good authority that the notice would not be sufficient in such a case, in the absence of evidence that the plaintiff had made due inquiry for the defendant's place of residence.[2] But it is to be observed that the defendant, by dating the bill or indorsement as he has done, has himself misled the plaintiff; can the defendant afterwards object to his own act? Clearly, however, if the plaintiff had reason to know that the place of date was not the defendant's place of residence, he cannot safely treat the place of date as the proper address.[3] And of course, the place of date of a bill, note, or cheque has nothing to do with the place of address of an indorser not being also drawer or maker.[4]

[1] Burmester v. Barron, 17 Q. B. 828; Pierce v. Struthers, 27 Penn. St. 249.

[2] Lowery v. Scott, 24 Wend. 358; Spencer v. Bank of Salina, 3 Hill, 520; Carroll v. Upton, 3 Comst. 272; Taylor v. Snyder, 3 Denio, 145; L. C. 227, 237; Sprague v. Tyson, 44 Ala. 338; Tyson v. Oliver, 43 Ala. 458; Barnwell v. Mitchell, 3 Conn. 101.

[3] Pierce v. Struthers, 27 Penn. St. 249. See further, Mason v. Pritchard, 9 Heisk. 793.

[4] Lawrence v. Miller, 16 N. Y. 235, 240; Spencer v. Bank of Salina, 3 Hill, 520.

§ 8. Diligence.

The whole matter of the several steps required to fix the liability of an indorser may be summed up, as has already been stated or intimated more than once, by the statement that the law merchant requires reasonable diligence, and that only. What constitutes reasonable diligence is fixed, presumptively but not absolutely, in certain cases, as in the matter of time of presentment and time of notice of dishonor; in other cases it remains a question of fact upon all the circumstances of the case. However, when the facts are all found or admitted, the court will ordinarily determine, whatever the case, whether they show a compliance with the rule of reasonable diligence.[1]

Reasonable diligence having been exercised, the notifying party may, it seems, rest in security; it matters not now what further information may come to hand; even if it show that the information acted upon was false and the true state of things is now made known, it may be disregarded. So it has been held by high authority,[2] though the contrary has since been laid down, but in ignorance apparently of the former decision.[3]

All that has been said in the foregoing sections is said upon the assumption that no excuse for omitting the step or steps has arisen.

---

[1] Bank of Utica v. Bender, 21 Wend. 643; L. C. 329; Carroll v. Upton, 3 Comst. 272; Walker v. Stetson, 14 Ohio St. 89; L. C. 314; Bank of Columbia v. Lawrence, 1 Peters, 578; L. C. 323; Wheeler v. Field, 6 Met. 290; Peters v. Hobbs, 25 Ark. 67; Farmers' Bank v. Gunnell, 26 Gratt. 131; Tardy v. Boyd, Id. 631.

[2] Lambert v. Ghiselin, 9 How. 552.

[3] Beale v. Parrish, 20 N. Y. 407.

CHAPTER IX.

INDORSER'S CONTRACT CONTINUED: EXCUSE OF STEPS.

§ 1. Temporary Excuse.

Heretofore it has been assumed that no question of permanent excuse in regard to the steps for fixing the indorser's liability was involved, though mere delays and the reasons therefor, which may be considered temporary excuses, have been under consideration from time to time. The law in regard to temporary excuses may be thus summed up: Whenever it has become impracticable, without fault of the holder, to take the steps at the time required, the holder is excused from doing so until a reasonable time after it becomes practicable to take the steps.[1]

Now, however, we encounter cases in which one or more of the steps was omitted altogether, and the plaintiff's contention is that the taking of the step at any time was unnecessary, the law merchant finding in the facts a sufficient excuse for the omission. What facts then excuse, not some delay, but entire omission, the indorser being held, notwithstanding, as if all the steps presumptively required had been taken?

§ 2. Excuse of both Presentment and Notice.

The most common cases are waivers. There is nothing to prevent the waiver by an indorser of all the conditions

---

[1] See Windham Bank v. Norton, 22 Conn. 213; L. C. 344; Farmers' Bank v. Gunnell, 26 Gratt. 131; Tardy v. Boyd, Id. 631; Lane v. Bank of West Tennessee, 9 Heisk. 419; Dunbar v. Tyler, 44 Miss. 1; Durden v. Smith, Id. 548.

upon which his undertaking otherwise would depend. Thus he may write, in connection with his indorsement, the words 'waiving demand and notice,' or he may orally waive demand and notice; such act will make it unnecessary for the holder to take any of the steps ordinarily required for fixing liability, the word 'demand' being understood to include presentment.

An unconditional promise to pay, or assurance of payment, made by the indorser, would have a like effect; it would be equivalent to a waiver in terms of the taking of any steps. For example: The defendant is indorser and the plaintiff holder of a promissory note. The defendant being indebted to the plaintiff gives to him the note, indorsing it as security for the debt. The maker dies before the note matures, and afterwards before its maturity the plaintiff intrusts it to A for collection. A calls upon the defendant and asks him if he (A) should have the note protested against the maker's estate. The defendant replies that he need not do so, and says that the note shall be paid at maturity. A puts the note away in his portfolio, where it remains until after maturity, no steps being taken for fixing the defendant's liability. The taking of such steps is unnecessary.[1]

Indeed, when an indorser says to the holder that an arrangement for payment of the paper is about to be made, and either in direct terms or by reasonable implication requests the holder to wait or to give time, that amounts to an assurance that the paper will be paid either by the promisor or by the indorser; and hence it is a waiver of presentment and notice. For it tends to put the holder off his guard and to induce him to forego the ordinary steps, so that it would be unjust to urge the omission of those steps thereafter.[2] But it must be reasonably clear

---

[1] Sigerson v. Mathews, 20 How. 496; L. C. 371.

[2] Gove v. Vining, 7 Met. 212; Bryant v. Wilcox, 49 Cal. 47; Moyer's Appeal, 87 Penn. St. 129.

that the indorser's promise or assurance is to pay; words on occasions of the kind are not to be taken very strongly against the indorser. Thus for the indorser to say that he would 'stand good' for payment is not to say that he will pay, and is no waiver of steps.[1]

In the case of inland bills, promissory notes, and cheques, it seems that a 'waiver of protest' will have the like effect;[2] clearly it will where the parties have already given that interpretation to such words in their previous recent dealings. For example: The defendant is indorser and the plaintiff holder of a promissory note. The defendant sends to the plaintiff a writing in the following words: 'I do request that hereafter any notes that may fall due in the Union Bank [the plaintiff], on which I am or may be indorser, shall not be protested, as I will consider myself bound in the same manner as if the said notes had been or should be legally protested.' The plaintiff and defendant have had a course of dealings founded upon interpretation of the writing as a waiver of all steps. No steps to fix the defendant's liability are necessary.[3]

But the term 'protest,' in its legal sense, is obviously unsuited to any step required in the law of inland bills, promissory notes, and cheques. Still it is plain that the intention in a waiver of protest in such cases is something more than the idle one of waiving what is unnecessary; and hence a case for interpretation is raised. That may have

---

[1] Freeman v. O'Brien, 38 Iowa, 406. But this case appears to have leaned too far in favor of the indorser, in view of other facts which appear in it. An indorsement with the words 'eventually accountable' would waive presentment and notice. McDonald v. Bailey, 14 Maine, 101. So would writing the word 'Holden.' Bean v. Arnold, 16 Maine, 251.

[2] Townsend v. Lorain Bank, 2 Ohio St. 345.

[3] Union Bank v. Hyde, 6 Wheat. 572. See also Duvall v. Farmers' Bank, 7 Gill & J. 44; S. C. 9 Gill & J. 31; Bird v. Le Blanc, 6 La. An. 470; Scott v. Greer, 10 Barr, 103.

been attended to by the parties, as we have seen; if the action of the parties has not furnished an interpretation, the court must do the best it can. In the authority from which the last example is taken, it was intimated that mere naked waiver of protest would not excuse the requirement of demand and notice (and it would not, in the case of a foreign bill); but it has been decided in other cases that such a waiver would be prima facie evidence of intention to waive demand and notice, since otherwise it would have to be treated as having no effect at all.[1] And the same has been held of the anomalous expression, ' I waive demand of protest.' [2]

Waivers may be made not only before maturity, but afterwards as well, after the time for taking the steps has passed and the indorser has ceased to be under any liability.[3] It is a peculiarity of certain waivers, of which this one is an example, that their validity does not depend upon consideration or the doing or omitting to do anything in reliance upon them. Still when made after maturity, the supposed waiver must have been made with full knowledge that the indorser was discharged, in order to avail.[4] And if the indorser should actually make payment, supposing that his liability had been fixed when it had not, he could recover the money back.[5] If, however, the *facts* in the matter were known to the indorser when he made the promise to pay, or other waiver, that would be enough;

---

[1] Coddington v. Davis. 1 Comst. 186; Carpenter v. Reynolds, 42 Miss. 807; Townsend v. Lorain Bank, 2 Ohio St. 345.

[2] Porter v. Kemball, 53 Barb. 467.

[3] Sigerson v. Mathews, 20 How. 496; L. C. 371; Rindge v. Kimball, 124 Mass. 209; Matthews v. Allen, 16 Gray, 594; Lewis v. Brehme, 33 Md. 412; Freeman v. O'Brien, 38 Iowa, 406.

[4] Ross v. Hurd, 71 N. Y. 14; Freeman v. O'Brien, supra; Third Nat. Bank v. Ashworth, 105 Mass. 503; Sheridan v. Carpenter, 61 Maine, 83; Walker v. Rogers, 40 Ill. 278.

[5] Sheridan v. Carpenter, supra.

that he did not know the legal effect of them would not, it is held, help him.[1]

Again, where the maker or acceptor or other party primarily liable (for the maker or acceptor may have signed for accommodation) places an available fund in the hands of the indorser with which to indemnify him if called upon to pay, the fund being sufficient for the purpose, presentment and notice are unnecessary;[2] the indorser takes the place of the one primarily liable. There may be ground for doubting whether the steps could be omitted where the fund was insufficient to indemnify the indorser;[3] though it seems that the steps may be omitted where the entire estate of the maker or acceptor is put into the indorser's hands to indemnify him on his indorsement,[4] for in such a case too the indorser virtually takes the place of the principal debtor.

Clearly, however, where the fund in question is put into the indorser's hand to satisfy demands which he is or may become absolutely bound to pay, the steps are not made unnecessary. For example: The defendant is indorser and the plaintiff holder of a promissory note. The maker has before maturity made an assignment of his property to the indorser in trust for the benefit of his creditors, among them the indorser, to secure them against all debts due them from the maker. The steps for fixing liability are omitted. The defendant is discharged; the proper interpretation of the assignment being deemed to be that it

---

[1] Rindskopf v. Doman, 28 Ohio St. 516; Cheshire v. Taylor, 29 Iowa, 492; Third National Bank v. Ashworth, 105 Mass. 503; Matthews v. Allen, 16 Gray, 594.

[2] Beard v. Westerman, 32 Ohio St. 29; Develing v. Ferris, 18 Ohio, 170; Coddington v. Davis, 3 Denio, 16; S. C. 1 Comst. 186; Kramer v. Sandford, 4 Watts & S. 328; Perry v. Green, 4 Harrison, 61; Andrews v. Boyd, 3 Met. 434; Marshall v. Mitchell, 34 Maine, 227.

[3] See Watkins v. Crouch, 5 Leigh, 522.

[4] Bond v. Farnham, 5 Mass. 170.

was intended as an indemnity against absolute liabilities only. Hence the assignment did not make the steps unnecessary.[1]

It may be too that to excuse the steps, the fund placed in the indorser's hands should be property, or securities available immediately, such as bonds payable on demand. It has been held that the putting into an indorser's hands ordinary choses in action as collateral security, by which is probably meant choses not at once available, will not excuse the steps.[2] So if the funds in the indorser's hands have arisen from business in which the indorser is a partner with the maker or acceptor, there is no sufficient reason for omitting the steps, especially where such funds can be used only for the payment of paper at maturity.[3] So also where the funds are held by the indorser as executor or administrator of the estate of the maker or acceptor, they cannot be considered as immediately available to indemnify him; they are not put there for that purpose, and the executor or administrator cannot prefer himself.[4]

In case the indorser should prove to be the primary debtor at the outset, the maker or the acceptor having acted merely for his accommodation, he would not be entitled to presentment and notice any more than if he had appeared upon the paper in his true character. He cannot suffer prejudice by the omission, because there is no one, party to the paper, bound to indemnify him, or if there be one liable with him as principal debtor, there is no one whose liability he could affect by notice of dishonor. Indeed, much of the subject may be summed up by the state-

---

[1] Creamer *v.* Perry, 17 Pick. 332.

[2] Kramer *v.* Sandford, 4 Watts & S. 328; Seacord *v.* Miller, 3 Kern. 55; Otsego Bank *v.* Warren, 18 Barb. 290.

[3] Ray *v.* Smith, 17 Wall. 411.

[4] Juniata Bank *v.* Hale, 16 Serg. & R. 157; L. C. 359; Magruder *v.* Union Bank, 3 Peters, 87; S. C. 7 Peters, 287.

ment that if the indorser cannot possibly be prejudiced by the omission, the omission is to be excused.¹ It is enough, however, to require the steps that the indorser *may* suffer prejudice from the omission of them; the indorser is not required to show that he *has* suffered prejudice by the omission; it is for the plaintiff to show that the indorser could not possibly have suffered.²

The fact that the note, bill, or cheque has been lost does not dispense with these steps, for a copy may be used in making presentment, with an offer of indemnity against liability upon the lost instrument.³

§ 3. Excuse of Presentment.

Some excuses go no further than to justify the omission of presentment and demand, or, perhaps, but one of these two steps, for it is to be remembered that presentment and demand are separate steps, severally required in the absence of legal excuse; and, further, excuses are looked upon with scrutiny, and not allowed unless plainly made out.

First, in regard to excuses for failing to make presentment as distinguished from demand. Such a case arises where the maker or acceptor, understanding or professing to understand the errand of the holder, declines to see the paper, or expressly or virtually tells the holder that he

---

[1] Smith v. Miller, 52 N. Y. 545; Welch v. Taylor Manuf. Co., 82 Ill. 579, drawer.

[2] Foster v. Parker, 2 C. P. D. 18; also cases in note 1. Many of the cases relate to the omission of notice only, but the principle is sufficient to cover all the steps.

[3] Lane v. Bank of West Tennessee, 9 Heisk. 419. Compare Fales v. Russell, 16 Pick. 315; Tuttle v. Standish, 4 Allen, 481; Hopkins v. Adams, 20 Vt. 407; Thayer v. King, 15 Ohio, 242. These are cases of actions sustained against the maker of lost notes, of course upon copies; it follows that presentment may be made upon a copy.

need not produce it. A case of the kind would arise where the maker or acceptor, before the paper is produced, should absolutely repudiate all liability upon it, and refuse to pay it; that would be a waiver of presentment, certainly where the holder called for payment at the proper place, as, for example, at the counting-house of the maker of a note; *perhaps*, it would be a waiver wherever demand was made.[1] Mere refusal of payment, however, is no waiver of omitting presentment. For example: The defendant is indorser and the plaintiff holder of a promissory note. At maturity the plaintiff, not having the note with him, calls upon the maker, and demands payment, which is refused. The defendant is discharged, the refusal being no waiver of the requirement of presentment.[2]

Excuse of demand will doubtless excuse presentment; but, perhaps, excuse of presentment, in the special sense of that term which distinguishes it from demand, would not make demand unnecessary. Waiver of presentment, made by an indorser after maturity, must have been made with knowledge of the omission, in order to be valid.[3]

It will not be needful to separate the two steps further, and accordingly presentment may be taken as including demand.

Removal of the maker or acceptor from the State, after the making or acceptance, excuses the holder from any duty to follow him, such as would rest upon the holder in case of removal to some other place within the State in which the paper is payable. The removal would not, according to good authority,[4] though there is also contrary

---

[1] See King *v.* Crowell, 61 Maine, 244.
[2] Arnold *v.* Dresser, 8 Allen, 435.
[3] Compare ante, p. 146.
[4] Wheeler *v.* Field, 6 Met. 290.

authority,[1] excuse the holder from making presentment at the last place of business or residence of the maker or acceptor; but presentment there would clearly be sufficient. For example: The defendant is indorser and the plaintiff holder of a promissory note payable generally and made at Troy, New York, where the maker resided at the time of making the note. Afterwards, before the maturity of the note, the maker removes to Florida, where he resides when the note matures. The plaintiff makes presentment at the maker's last abode in Troy, and not receiving payment, gives notice of dishonor presently. No presentment in Florida is made. The liability of the defendant is duly fixed.[2]

Concerning the effect of absconding there is some conflict of authority. The more general doctrine is that such act excuses the holder from all duty to make presentment. For example: The defendant is indorser and the plaintiff holder of a promissory note, the maker of which, before its maturity, absconds to parts unknown; whereupon at maturity, the plaintiff, without taking other steps, gives notice of dishonor to the defendant. The defendant's liability is duly fixed.[3]

The same authorities, however, which, in case of removal beyond the State, require presentment at the last abode or place of business, recalling the doctrine that the holder is bound to exercise due diligence in endeavoring to obtain

---

[1] Foster v. Julien, 24 N. Y. 28; Gist v. Lybrand, 3 Ohio, 308. See Reid v. Morrison, 2 Watts & S. 401.

[2] See Taylor v. Snyder, 3 Denio, 145; L. C. 227. But if, as was the actual case in Taylor v. Snyder, the maker lived at the time of making the note in another State or country from that in which it was made, presentment there would be necessary. See ante, p. 88.

[3] Lehman v. Jones, 1 Watts & S. 126; L. C. 357; Reid v. Morrison, 2 Watts & S. 401; Taylor v. Snyder, supra; Spies v. Gilmore, 1 Comst. 321; Wolfe v. Jewett, 10 La. 383. The same rule prevails in the case of bills of exchange. Lehman v. Jones, supra.

payment from the maker or acceptor, refuse to accept that view of the case. These authorities require the plaintiff to show that, notwithstanding the absconding, he has exercised some diligence in order to obtain payment of the primary debtor; some inquiry should be made.[1]

The insolvency of the maker or acceptor, though known to the indorser at the time of his indorsement, is not an excuse for failing to make presentment. For example: The defendant, payee of an overdue promissory note, indorses it knowing that the maker is insolvent, the plaintiff discounting it for him at its face value. Presentment is not made within reasonable time. The defendant is discharged from liability.[2]

Waiving notice of dishonor does not excuse the holder from making presentment. For example: The defendant, an indorser of a promissory note, writes before or after his signature the words, 'Waiving notice.' The plaintiff, holder of the note at maturity, omits to make presentment of the note for payment as well as to give notice of dishonor. The defendant is discharged.[3]

In some States, contrary to the rule in others, the fact that the maker or acceptor has deceased at the time of the maturity of the note or bill, and that the paper matures before the end of the period in which his personal representative is exempt from liability to suit, excuses presentment altogether. For example: The defendant is indorser and the plaintiff holder of a promissory note due October 4. The maker dies in September preceding, and administra-

---

[1] Pierce v. Cate, 12 Cush. 195, overruling some earlier decisions and dicta.

[2] Bassenhorst v. Wilby, 45 Ohio St. 333.

[3] Berkshire Bank v. Jones, 6 Mass. 524; L. C. 369. See also Voorhies v. Attee, 29 Iowa, 49; Buchanan v. Marshall, 22 Vt. 561; Lane v. Steward, 20 Maine, 98; Backus v. Shipherd, 11 Wend. 629. But see Matthey v. Gally, 4 Cal. 62.

tion is duly granted, and notice thereof given the same month. No presentment is made at the maturity of the note or at any other time to the administrator, but notice of non-payment is given to the defendant in due season. The defendant's liability is duly fixed, presentment not being necessary.[1]

If, however, the paper should become due after the period of exemption has passed, presentment should be made.[2]

§ 4. Excuse of Protest.

As we have seen, the term 'protest,' as used by the law merchant, applies only to foreign bills of exchange, though by practice, to which the sanction of statute has widely been given, it has come to be, or rather it has long been, applied also to inland bills, promissory notes, and cheques. But the law merchant has not lost its supremacy in the matter; the protest of a foreign bill having, as we have seen, a significance not attaching to the protest of other paper. Protest in the case of a foreign bill is one definite and altogether unique act; in the case of other paper, while it naturally points to the same unique act, it has come to be used in a loose and vague sense, making it include other or even all the steps for fixing liability.

The consequence is that excuse of protest has ordinarily a definite meaning in the one case and an uncertain meaning in the other. Excuse of protest of a foreign bill, at least when in the form of a written waiver, such as 'waiving protest,' on the bill, is then in principle to be taken as referring to the distinctive act of protest, and nothing

---

[1] Hale v. Burr, 12 Mass. 86. See Oriental Bank v. Blake, 22 Pick. 206; Landry v. Stansberry, 10 La. An. 484. But see Gower v. Moore, 25 Maine, 16.

[2] Oriental Bank v. Blake, supra.

else;[1] unless perhaps the term has received a different interpretation in the practice of the parties.[2] On the other hand, waiving the protest of paper not requiring protest is an act, as has just been stated, of doubtful import; how it has been interpreted by the courts has already been seen.[3] By the better view it excuses presentment and notice.[4]

§ 5. Excuse of Notice.

What is referred to now, as in the case of excuse of presentment above considered, is excuse of notice, excluding cases of excuse of notice and other steps;[5] in other words, the cases now referred to are those in which the only question raised is upon the failure of the holder or indorser to give notice of dishonor.

Such failure is not justified by any mere waiver of presentment or demand, for such a waiver may be made in confident expectation that the maker or acceptor will be ready and anxious to pay, and will therefore offer payment without waiting to be requested.[6] Nor, it seems, will an excuse for making presentment, created by law, excuse the requirement of notice. Thus the absconding of the maker or acceptor to parts unknown, though in some States making presentment unnecessary, does not dispense with the requirement of notice.[7] So too in States in which presentment is excused by law because of the death

---

[1] That is fairly to be implied from language in Union Bank v. Hyde, 6 Wheat. 572. See also Coddington v. Davis, 1 Comst. 186.

[2] Compare Coddington v. Davis, supra.

[3] Ante, p. 146; and see the two cases just cited.

[4] Id.

[5] For those cases see § 2, supra.

[6] Compare Berkshire Bank v. Jones, 6 Mass. 524; L. C. 369, 370.

[7] Foster v. Julien, 24 N. Y. 28, 37; Michaud v. Lagarde, 4 Minn. 43. Compare Lehman v. Jones, 1 Watts & S. 126; L. C. 357, 358.

of the maker, it seems that indorsers are nevertheless entitled to notice of non-payment.[1] And a personal representative of an indorser deceased is entitled to notice as much as would the indorser himself have been had he lived.[2]

Indeed, omitting to give notice of dishonor is no more lightly to be excused than is omitting to take any of the other steps required by the law. The law merchant will not, it seems, excuse an omission to give notice except upon a waiver plainly having in view the very matter of notice; unless it is clear that notice would be of no use whatever, when, indeed, it would be unnecessary. If by possibility the indorser might suffer detriment by failing to give him notice, such failing will discharge him.[3] Accordingly, notice of dishonor is not dispensed with by reason of the fact that the maker or acceptor was insolvent all the time, and that the indorser was aware of the fact. For it does not follow, because a man is insolvent that he may not pay a particular debt, in whole or in part. A debtor is, within certain statutory restrictions, allowed to prefer his creditors; and even where his funds have passed from him, as into the hands of an assignee, friends may be ready to help him or his indorsers in the particular case.[4]

Even in the case of an express waiver of notice in terms,

---

[1] See Hale v. Burr, 12 Mass. 86, 88, where the court, speaking of demand upon the personal representative within the year of his exemption from suit, says: 'Such a demand would therefore be merely a troublesome formality, without any use; and notice to the indorser that (the promisor being dead) he will be looked to for payment, will in every respect be as advantageous to him as a previous demand upon the promisor.'

[2] Oriental Bank v. Blake, 22 Pick. 206.

[3] Foster v. Parker, 2 C. P. D. 18; Smith v. Miller, 52 N. Y. 545; Welch v. Taylor Manuf. Co., 82 Ill. 579.

[4] Barton v. Baker, 1 Serg. & R. 334, L. C. 365.

the waiving heretofore suggested should be borne in mind where the waiver was after maturity; in such a case, the act, to be valid, must have been done with knowledge that notice had not been given.[1]

There are one or two cases of excuse of notice peculiar in that they concern only the drawers of bills of exchange or of cheques. The drawer's contract has been explained in a preceding chapter, and it was there shown that one who draws a bill or a cheque, without reasonable ground to believe that it will be honored by the drawee, is treated much as if, instead of having drawn a bill, he had made a promissory note for the sum. Hence he is not entitled to notice in case of dishonor. The case may then be put, and commonly is put, in this way; that the act of drawing in such a case is deemed a fraud in the eye of the law, and notice of dishonor is accordingly unnecessary. This subject has, however, been fully dealt with in Chapter V., and need not be further considered here. It should be observed, however, that the law dispenses with notice to the drawer only; indorsers must still be notified, for they are no parties to the fraud, though it would be otherwise of an indorser who is the drawer of the bill.

To draw upon oneself, as was seen in Chapter V., also dispenses with the requirement of notice, and perhaps of presentment; and so of cases in which the drawer draws upon a partnership of which he is a member, and the like cases referred to in Chapter V. In these cases, too, the excuse extends only to the drawer; an indorser (not being drawer) is still entitled to notice.

[1] Ante, p. 146.

CHAPTER X.

ACCOMMODATION CONTRACTS.

§ 1. Nature: Consideration: Suretyship.

The legal effect of each of the contracts dealt with in the foregoing chapters will be modified somewhat, if it appears that the defendant signed the instrument without consideration for the accommodation of another party. The result is an accommodation contract, which may be described as a gift by A to B of A's credit, to be offered to another on payment of value. A contract of the kind may take any of the forms of the law merchant; a promissory note may be made or indorsed for accommodation; a bill of exchange may be drawn, accepted, or indorsed for accommodation; a cheque may be drawn or indorsed for accommodation. In a word, any party to the instrument may be an accommodation party.

Accommodation contracts of the kind too are contracts of the law merchant as much as are those which are supported by a valuable consideration at the outset. At the outset, we say, for though accommodation contracts are not so supported when first executed, a valuable consideration must spring up afterwards to make the contract binding; some one must afterwards have taken the paper for value in order to have a claim upon the accommodation party. For example (hypothetical): The defendant accepts a bill of exchange for the accommodation of the drawer, and the drawer makes a gift of the bill to the payee and plaintiff. The defendant is not liable upon his acceptance.

There is then nothing peculiar in the case so far. Nor is there anything peculiar in any other phase of the contract of an accommodation party under the law merchant in its ordinary application. Whatever would be necessary to make a case against one who had signed originally for value is equally necessary to make a case against an accommodation party; and whatever would be effective against a party who signed for value will also be effective against an accommodation party after a consideration has sprung up. What is peculiar to the situation of such a party lies in the fact that he is in a certain sense only a surety for the party for whom he has given his credit. Whatever the outward form of the contract, even though the accommodation party made as such his promissory note, and the person for whose accommodation it was made is an indorser of it, or indeed is not a party to it at all, the accommodated party or person is, between the two, the principal debtor, and the accommodation party the surety.

The accommodation party is a surety, however, not always in the full sense, but often only sub modo. It appears to have been considered at one time that he was in all cases a surety in the full ordinary sense; but the authorities now consider that the suretyship may be essentially modified by the natural character of the particular contract made by the accommodation party. Thus, if a person has accepted a bill of exchange for the accommodation of the payee, a subsequent indorsee, though with notice, may still treat him as an acceptor, not merely in point of liability in the ordinary way of acceptance, but also in regard to the more special questions of suretyship, because he has taken a principal's position. That is to say, the acceptor is not a surety towards the holder, though the holder knows that he accepted for accommodation; he is a surety only between himself and the party for whose accommodation he accepted. Accordingly, he will not be discharged by acts of the holder, which would discharge him if he were an ordinary surety, or if he were an accommodation *indorser;* for an indorser is a surety for parties before him.[1]

§ 2. Taking with Notice.

There is another doctrine touching accommodation acceptance of the greatest significance, and that is, that though the undertaking is (originally) without consideration, it stands upon a footing radically different from other cases of contracts wanting consideration. If a man makes a promissory note, accepts a bill of exchange, or indorses paper, upon the supposition that there is a valuable consideration for his undertaking when there is not, or if there is a failure of the consideration, a person taking the paper with notice, though for value, cannot hold him (with an exception which need not be mentioned here); whereas if the party's undertaking was for accommodation, he would be liable, though the holder *did* take the paper with notice or even with full knowledge, if he took it for value.

The reason is not far to seek. Where the undertaking is for accommodation, the party makes an offer by way of gift, with full understanding, of his credit, intending to respond to any one who acts upon the offer; where the undertaking is supposed by the party making it to be for value when it is not, or when the value fails, he has acted in mistake, never intending to bind himself with consideration wanting.

In the doctrines relating to suretyship and consideration are found the characteristic features of accommodation contracts. The object of the present chapter is only to call attention to and explain the general features of such contracts, as one of the forms of contract of the law mer-

[1] See post, pp. 239, 240.

chant, to show that there are such contracts, and what in general they are. The details concerning them will be dealt with more conveniently, as details of the same nature arise in connection with the other contracts of our subject. Thus, dealings with the principal debtor in their effect upon subsequent parties, the extent of the liability of accommodation parties, and other matters of detail will be considered in later chapters.

CHAPTER XI.

CONTRACTS OF GUARANTOR AND OF SURETY.

§ 1. Annexing Contracts of the Common Law: Distinction of Terms.

Thus far we have had under consideration contracts of the law merchant, with but occasional reference to contracts of the common law annexed to or connected with them. Those contracts having been severally explained, with reference to their peculiarities, nothing further would remain but a consideration of features common to them all, were it not that it often happens, as has frequently been intimated in these pages, that some contract of the common law, in the way of further assuring performance of the contract of the law merchant, has been added. The effect of adding such a contract, not upon the contract assured, for that remains unaffected, but upon the common law contract itself is now, or will from time to time become, a matter of serious importance. But in order to understand how far the assuring contract has been affected by its connection with a contract of the law merchant, we must first ascertain the very nature of the assuring contract itself, that is, its natural ordinary character, uninfluenced by such connection.

Two terms are used to signify further assurance, namely, guaranty and suretyship. These terms are often loosely employed, the one for the other, and each made to express a certain broader meaning than, strictly taken, it bears. That is especially true of the use of the term surety or suretyship. But there are situations of fact which are followed by very different rules of law, and these coincide with the meaning of the two terms in their narrower and more specific sense; at all events, it will serve a purpose of convenience, and at the same time prevent confusion, if we use the two terms in the more specific sense conforming to the situations of fact referred to.

Accordingly, we may in the first place unite the terms guaranty and suretyship under the general designation of contracts of assurance, by which will then be meant any subsidiary contract intended to secure the performance of the contract or contracts assured. Then we may separate the contract of assurance into two parts; first, supposing the assurance to be made as a separate and distinct collateral engagement, to which the name guaranty may be and commonly is given, — guaranty, that is, in the specific sense; secondly, supposing the assurance to be part and parcel of the contract assured, being an engagement then to which the name suretyship may be and commonly is given, — suretyship, that is, again in the specific sense. We shall find important legal consequences flowing from that division. But both guaranty and suretyship are undertakings to answer 'for the debt or default of another' within the meaning of the Statute of Frauds, and must accordingly be in writing and signed by the party to be bound or by his lawful agent.

§ 2. Guaranty (in specific sense).

Proceeding to the subject of guaranty in the specific sense of a separate contract, it is obvious that the assuring contract may be made either at the same time with the contract or contracts assured, or afterwards, — or, indeed, before the principal contract was made; but cases of that kind are infrequent, and would raise no peculiar legal questions. The time of the guaranty raises certain questions in regard to consideration. It should be observed that both the guaranty and the contract assured must be supported by a valuable consideration. If the contract assured is wanting in that respect, the guaranty must fall to the ground, though itself founded upon a valuable consideration; and on the other hand, though the contract assured is well supported in that respect, if the guaranty is not well supported also, it must fail. The connection of the guaranty with a contract of the law merchant in no way affects the case.

Where, however, the guaranty is made at the same time, that is, in the same general negotiations and substantially at the same time with the principal contract of the law merchant, it is not necessary that it should be supported by any separate consideration from that of the principal engagement. Both contracts being made at the same time, it matters not that the consideration more immediately and fully belongs to the principal one; the guaranty, though separate in form, in terms, and in effect, makes part of a general consideration; in other words, in common language of the books, the consideration which supports the principal contract supports the guaranty.

At this point it is necessary to guard against a possible mistake. Does the guaranty now draw from the contract of the law merchant, which it assures, any of its properties? In a suit upon the contract assured, the law merchant, as we have seen, raises a presumption of consideration to support the instrument when produced at the trial; does this presumption flow over to the guaranty? The answer must be in the negative. Not yet, certainly, has the guaranty gained anything from its connection with the more favored contract. A consideration to support the guaranty must be proved as in other cases of contracts of the common law, supposing that it is not under seal. The proof may or may not appear on the face of the guaranty or the principal contract; of which presently.

Let it next be supposed that the guaranty is made at some other time, after (or before) the making of the principal contract. Now it follows from the very requirement of a consideration to support the guaranty, that there must be a separate consideration to support the assuring engagement; that the consideration which supports the principal contract will not support the guaranty. There are one or two apparent exceptions; first, where the guaranty was agreed upon at the time of making the principal contract, and it was merely committed to writing afterwards by a sort of nunc pro tunc; and secondly, where the consideration is a continuous thing, running along at the time both of the principal contract and of the guaranty.

Another question now arises touching consideration, regardless of the time when the guaranty was made; to wit, whether the interpretation to be put upon the Statute of Frauds in regard to the necessity of a statement of consideration in the guaranty is affected by the fact that the contract assured is a contract of the law merchant, by which there is a presumption of consideration. The answer is again in the negative. If, according to the interpretation put upon the Statute of Frauds in a particular State, or according to special legislation, it is necessary in other cases that the guaranty itself should recite or refer to a consideration, it is equally necessary in the case of a guaranty of a bill, note, or cheque.

It should then be observed that in some States language indicating a consideration should appear within the guaranty, and that it will not be enough that such language is found in the contract assured. For example (hypothetical): The defendant sued upon a guaranty writes the following words upon the back of a promissory note, the contract being performable in the State of New York: 'I guaranty the payment of this note.' The face of the note reads 'For value received I promise to pay to A, or order,' etc. The defendant, by the law of New York, is not liable, there being no reference to consideration in the guaranty.

In other States the law is satisfied if there is a reference to consideration in the principal contract, as by the words 'For value' used in the last example. In still other States it is not necessary that there should be any statement of, or reference to, consideration in either the principal contract or the guaranty; it is enough that a consideration to support the guaranty existed in fact, and the fact may be shown at the trial.

The conclusion then is that in regard to the first peculiarity of the law merchant, consideration, a guaranty is little affected, if at all, by its connection with a contract of the law merchant. We may now inquire whether a guaranty is by such connection affected in the second peculiar feature of the law merchant, to wit, negotiability. In regard to that, it should be noticed that the question whether a guaranty becomes, or can become, negotiable by being annexed to a negotiable note, bill, or cheque, has two phases. The question may be (1) whether the guaranty, when written upon the note, bill, or cheque, operates as an indorsement so as to give a remote subsequent holder the rights of an indorsee against the guarantor as an indorser; or it may be (2) whether it operates as an indorsement so as to give the transferee the rights of an indorsee against prior parties.

Both questions turn upon the same considerations, it seems, so that the answer to one must be taken as the answer to the other. Unfortunately the authorities are not agreed. The earlier American authorities appear to have treated an unrestricted guaranty made by the holder of the paper (usually a promissory note), and written upon it in transferring it, as practically an indorsement; and in some States that view still prevails. That, of course, means that a general contract of guaranty, when written upon a negotiable contract of the law merchant, is to be taken as a negotiable contract as of the law merchant. For example: The defendant, payee of a negotiable promissory note, writes on the back of it, 'I guaranty the payment of the within note,' signing the same, and transfers the note to another who indorses it to the plaintiff. At maturity the plaintiff presents the note for payment, and payment being refused, gives notice at once to the defendant, as if he were an indorser. The writing quoted is deemed an indorsement, and the defendant's liability is duly fixed.[1]

But the question at once arises why should a contract of the common law, as such incapable of negotiability, become negotiable by being written upon a negotiable instrument? It is true that when written there by the holder, and followed by transfer, the holder parts with his title; but it does not follow that he parts with it as the law merchant requires in order to give the act the special features of the law merchant. Indeed, in so far as it departs in substance from the requirements of the law merchant, it falls short, or should fall short, of acquiring the features pertaining to an act done in conformity to such requirements. The law merchant knows nothing of guaranty, except in so far as indorsement is guaranty; it requires indorsement to transfer full legal title to paper payable or indorsed to order, and what indorsement is, the law merchant has carefully and consistently laid down, as we have seen. Pursuing this or some such line of reasoning, certain later authorities have refused to follow the earlier ones, considering that a guaranty is still a guaranty though written upon a negotiable instrument, and not an indorsement. For example: The defendant is maker, and the plaintiff transferee, of a prom-

---

[1] Partridge v. Davis, 20 Vt. 499. So Myrick v. Hasey, 27 Maine, 9; Leggett v. Raymond, 6 Hill, 639; Manrow v. Durham, 3 Hill, 584. But these New York cases were never satisfactory at home, and they have been overruled. Spies v. Gilmore, 1 Comst. 321; Hall v. Newcomb, 7 Hill, 416; Waterbury v. Sinclair, 26 Barb. 455.

issory note payable to A. The only writing upon the note by A is in the words, 'I hereby guaranty the within note;' but with this writing upon it A transfers the note to F and L who indorse it to the plaintiff, who now as an indorsee sues the maker. The plaintiff is not entitled to recover, the writing quoted being a guaranty, and not an indorsement or the equivalent of an indorsement.[1]

Of course, the result of such a ruling is more than technical. It is not merely a ruling that the transferee cannot sue in his own name, a ruling which would be abrogated by statute in many States, it is a ruling that no perfect legal title, such as the law merchant recognizes, has been transferred. The tranferee has acquired no more than an equitable title; and hence his demand may be defeated by the existence of equities or defences which would be available by the defendant in a suit by the payee, regardless of the rule in whose name he should sue.

The considerations above presented against allowing the guaranty to draw negotiability from the principal contract apply in principle, however general the language of the guaranty towards the holder. The contract, being a contract of the common law, is incapable of negotiability by any intention of the guarantor, however expressed, so long as his contract is expressed in the language of guaranty. Authorities, however, are not wanting which decline to take this strictly logical view; and, while not readily allowing negotiability to a simple guaranty of negotiable paper, allow negotiability to the guaranty if the intention to make it negotiable is plainly expressed upon the instrument assured.[2] It is probable, however, that the courts

---

[1] Belcher v. Smith, 7 Cush. 482; Tuttle v. Bartholomew, 12 Met. 452, overruling Blakely v. Grant, 6 Mass. 386, and Upham v. Prince, 14 Mass. 14.

[2] The guaranty of bonds and similar instruments of corporations

which treat such a guaranty as negotiable would not strain the law further by allowing negotiability to a guaranty not written upon the note, bill, or cheque. And it is certain that there could be no such thing as a negotiable guaranty of an unnegotiable instrument.

In regard to the third peculiarity of contracts of the law merchant, grace, no serious question can be raised. The guaranty itself does not draw grace from the law merchant, and is not entitled to grace under any other law, while the contract assured may or may not be. But of course there can be no breach of the guaranty until there is a breach of the principal contract, which cannot occur until the last day of grace, if the principal contract is entitled to grace.

One question more remains: Does a guaranty draw from the negotiable instrument assured the properties of indorsement touching presentment and notice? Those courts which treat the guaranty as practically an indorsement for the purpose of negotiability would probably be driven to the conclusion that the guarantor would have the right to insist upon all the steps which an indorser could require. Otherwise the contract would be very anomalous; it would be indorsement and not indorsement at the same time.

Those courts, however, which decline to treat a guaranty as the equivalent of an indorsement will find no difficulty now; the guaranty not being indorsement, the steps to fix the liability of an indorser cannot be required to fix the liability of a guarantor. The guaranty stands upon its own footing as a common law contract; what is required touching it in that aspect is now required, and nothing more.

stands upon a footing of its own. Custom or statute makes the guaranty negotiable in such cases. The text refers only to private written guaranties.

What has been said thus far must be understood as applicable to cases already referred to of anomalous indorsement — 'indorsement' by a stranger to secure the payee — whether such cases are called cases of guaranty or of suretyship.

We are now brought to suretyship in the specific sense mentioned in section 1, namely, where the assurance is part and parcel of the contract assured. And that subject may be more shortly disposed of.

The two engagements now are one, as where the instrument runs, in common form, 'I, A B, as principal, and I, C D, as surety, promise' etc., or 'We promise to pay' etc. followed by the signatures 'A B,' 'C D, surety.' And accordingly the consideration which supports the engagement of the principal supports that of the surety; there can be no occasion for any separate consideration to support the latter's contract. But the contract being within the Statute of Frauds, the same doctrine in regard to reference to consideration prevails as in the case of guaranty. Now, however, the contract of principal and surety being one, the only requirement that can be made, in the nature of things, in those States in which there must be a reference to consideration, is in the one contract signed by both principal and surety. It should be noticed in regard to that point that the contract, in such States, may be good against the principal and, for want of reference to consideration, bad against the surety; indeed it would be bad against both if the contract is joint.

No question of course can arise in regard to negotiability. The surety's contract being part of the principal's contract, it is, of necessity as much a contract of the law merchant as the principal's contract itself. And the same is to be said in regard to grace, and in regard to presentment and to most other questions.

CHAPTER XII.

HOLDER'S POSITION.

§ 1. Change of Point of View.

Thus far we have been investigating the several particular contracts of our subject, in other words, the several positions of the parties liable; now we come to the consideration of questions arising on the opposite side of the law, — questions which in general affect alike all the particular contracts heretofore under consideration. These questions will relate mainly to mediate parties; that is, to cases in which the holder is separated by at least one link from the defendant, the plaintiff accordingly being either an indorsee, or the payee of a bill of exchange. The subject of rights of immediate parties has been indirectly disposed of already.

§ 2. Right to Sue Mediate Party.

The first thing that calls for remark is that the right of the holder to sue mediate parties is a right given by the law merchant in its adoption of the custom of merchants as explained in Chapter I. That right is as perfect, when the plaintiff holds the paper conformably with the custom, as the right to sue an immediate party can be under the common law. And further, as a mere right to sue, that is, leaving out of sight any other question, the right rests upon the same footing substantially as the right of any other plaintiff suing upon a written contract of the common law; possession of the instrument thus held raises, in favor of the plaintiff, a presumptive right to it, and after maturity a presumptive right of action upon it, a right of action against mediate as well as against immediate parties.

How significant that right may be, may be seen in the statement that it will support the plaintiff in the face (1) of an admission that he holds the paper only as agent or as trustee for another, for still the law presumes that he holds it rightfully until the contrary is shown; (2) of evidence offered even to show that it is *not improbable* that he holds it as agent for another against whom the defendant has a set-off or a defence. Something more is necessary than evidence showing that it is very likely that the plaintiff has no right to the paper, or right of action upon it, after he has produced it in evidence in court with the presumption of title in his favor, and, with that, the presumption of consideration. For example: The plaintiff in a suit upon a promissory note payable to a certain corporation or bearer offers the note in evidence of his title and right to recover. The defendant denies that the plaintiff is the 'bearer' and owner of the note, alleging that it is the property of said corporation, against which the defendant has, and desires to plead, a valid set-off. The plaintiff is in fact the general agent of said corporation, having custody of all notes belonging to it; the corporation is insolvent and has no property, and the stockholders, of whom the plaintiff is one, are liable for its debts. The plaintiff is entitled to recover, and the defendant cannot have the benefit of the set-off; the evidence offered is not sufficient to rebut the presumption in favor of the plaintiff.[1]

---

[1] Pettee v. Prout, 3 Gray, 502; L. C. 385.

§ 3. Legal Defences and Equities explained.

Assuming now that no question of title to or ownership of the paper is raised, the plaintiff's right to recover will depend upon the defence set up, which may be either absolutely or presumptively sufficient. There are then two classes of defences: to the first of which, where the defence is absolute, is sometimes and may for convenience be given the name Legal or Absolute Defences; to the second, where the defence is presumptively sufficient, is given the name Equities — shortly for Equities-fixed-upon-the-holder.

These terms, however, must not be taken in their ordinary sense; in that sense they would be misleading. Equities are legal defences in the ordinary sense of defences available in suits at law, quite as much as those called legal defences. The term 'equities' is borrowed from the Court of Chancery, to express a merely outward, and after all, rather faint analogy. By an ancient rule of the Court of Chancery, adopted in modern times at law, a man who buys a legal title to property with notice of the existence in another of an equitable title takes subject to that title; he has notice of an equity. So (so far as the analogy can be traced) one who purchases or otherwise becomes owner of a bill, note, or cheque, with notice of the existence of a defence which is not absolute ('legal'), takes subject to that defence; he has notice of an 'equity.' An equity may be a perfect and complete defence between immediate parties to it, as where it consists in fraudulent misrepresentation; but at most it is only a presumptive defence against a mediate or remote holder; if the holder took the paper for value and without notice, or stands upon the rights of another who so took, the 'equity' will not avail.

The meaning given to the two terms, respectively, may be thus explained: Legal or absolute defences import either want of contract, that is, want of union of minds, want of capacity, downright illegality of contract (that is, a contract which the law wholly repudiates), alteration of the original contract, or forgery of indorsement. No liability can exist in such cases, even in favor of a bona fide holder for value. Equities, on the other hand, imply the existence of a contract between prior parties, but a contract which is invalid and hence defeasible in whole or in part. Between the parties immediately concerned, and against subsequent holders without value or having notice, these equities are perfect defences; but against a bona fide holder for value they are of no avail.

The two subjects must now be considered in detail. First, then, of Legal or Absolute Defences. That subject is considered here because it almost always appears in contests in regard to the rights of bona fide holders for value. The question then will be, what are these legal defences against which not even a bona fide holder for value can recover?

To prevent possible misapprehension, it should be stated that in strictness of language these are not defences at all; for it is incumbent upon the plaintiff to prove the existence of the contract upon which he seeks to recover. That important fact should not be obscured. The term 'defences,' in the cases about to be considered, is to be taken conventionally; and such use of the term is common enough. Thus, the books speak of the 'defence' of want of consideration in actions upon simple contract, though it is for the plaintiff to prove the consideration. But there is better justification for the use of the term in relation to the present subject, because after all the defendant has the laboring oar for the greater part. The plaintiff, who now is usually a bona fide holder for value, makes a *presumptive* case rather easily, and then the defendant must do what he can to save himself.

CHAPTER XIII.

LEGAL OR ABSOLUTE DEFENCES.

§ 1. Want of Contract: Delivery.

The first of the legal or absolute defences, in the face of which not the most favored plaintiff in the law, to wit, a bona fide holder for value, can recover, is where there is an absence of that which is essential to the creation of any contract, to wit, union of minds. Cases of the kind in the law of bills and notes commonly arise, (1) Where there has been either nothing which the law regards as a delivery of the instrument; or (2) Where, though there has been a delivery, the defendant has been made the victim of a fraud in regard to the nature of the alleged contract to which he has given his signature, or fraud (as it may be termed) in esse contractus; or (3) Where there has been an alteration in or forgery of some part of the instrument. These subjects will be considered in the order suggested; incapacity and illegality by statute will follow.

The subject of delivery cannot be disposed of by the statement that if there has been no delivery of the instrument in question, there can be no recovery upon it, for it will still be a question what is meant by delivery. And besides, the statement might be misleading; for though there may have been no delivery by the maker or acceptor, upon which any liability against him can arise, there may still have been a delivery for the purpose of creating liability against some other party. Thus, a servant may have stolen a promissory note signed by his master, from his master's drawer, and then have indorsed it and put it into circulation; in such a case, while there would be no delivery by the maker of the note so as to make *him* liable, there has been a delivery by the servant, and he and subsequent parties have incurred liability as much as if the maker had delivered the note.

Delivery in the law merchant is peculiar, not so much in the principle upon which it rests as in the not infrequent application of the principle. It is of the greatest importance that there should be a feeling of safety in purchasing a negotiable instrument, and therefore the principle of delivery is sometimes to be pressed to the utmost limit. Delivery may be effected either by intention or by negligence; that probably is a general principle, applying equally to other instruments as with instruments of the law merchant; but it is often carried further in the law merchant than elsewhere. It is not quite the same thing to say, as the books often say, that delivery may be actual or constructive, for both actual and constructive delivery may be delivery by intention; and why any delivery which has the full effect of delivery should be called constructive it is difficult to see. Such nomenclature adds, unnecessarily, a term to the situation which requires an explanation leading to nothing.

Delivery is effected by intention where either the defendant himself delivered the instrument knowingly, or where the act is done knowingly by an agent, servant, or (it seems) custodian of the defendant, though contrary to the orders of the defendant. That is, there is either a personal act by the defendant or an agency act. Such cases are clear enough in principle, but agency in the matter has sometimes perhaps been misunderstood. Thus, it has in one or two cases been supposed that where the instrument has been put into the hands of a mere custodian, — one, that is to say, having nothing to do but to keep it — the rule of agency does not apply, and hence a violation of the trust by delivery of the instrument could not create any right against the party whose confidence had thus been betrayed.[1] But that, not unlikely, may be wrong; it is not supported by the authorities upon which it is professedly based.[2]

It is true that a mere custodian is not even a special agent, in the law of agency in general; but it does not follow that he may not be treated as an agent by the law merchant. It is in this very particular, for one, that the law merchant is peculiar touching delivery; mercantile interests require the protection of the purchaser of the instrument in all cases in which it has come into his hands by an act of the defendant, by which he has intentionally parted with physical possession of it.

Delivery is effected by negligence when the defendant has done or omitted to do something contrary to the dictates of common prudence or care, — that is, contrary to what a man as prudent or careful as men usually are would do or omit, — whereby as the natural result, a result which might have been foreseen, the instrument has got into circulation. It would not be enough that the instrument got into circulation by reason of an act or an omission of the defendant; he should have been negligent, and negligent in reference to the very act of putting the paper into circulation,[3] just as in the case of intentional delivery he

---

[1] Chipman v. Tucker, 38 Wis. 43; Roberts v. McGrath, Id. 52; Roberts v. Wood, Id. 60.

[2] Burson v. Huntington, 21 Mich. 415; Baxendale v. Bennett, 3 Q. B. Div. 525. These were cases in which the paper was stolen, a very different thing. Very different too are the Wisconsin cases of Walker v. Ebert, 29 Wis. 194, and Kellogg v. Steiner, Id. 626; these were cases of fraud in esse contractus, like Foster v. Mackinnon, infra, in which there has been no conscious execution of the contract.

[3] Compare Merchants of the Staple v. Bank of England, 21 Q. B. Div. 160; Swan v. North British Co., 2 Hurl. & N. 175, 182; Arnold v.

should have parted with physical possession intentionally. If this be sound doctrine, it will follow that where the instrument got into circulation by being dropped, picked up, and passed, there has been no delivery, unless the dropping was negligent; possibly to drop a negotiable instrument, transferable by delivery, would be presumptive negligence.[1]

But a distinction is necessary at this point. If the paper has once been delivered by the maker or acceptor, whether by intention or by negligence, no question of delivery can be raised by *him* upon a loss and finding afterwards, where the paper has come to the hands of a bona fide holder for value. The maker or acceptor has delivered the paper, and that is enough so far as the question of his liability is concerned; if any one can raise the question of delivery in such a case it is only the person who lost the instrument, and at best he could do it only in an action brought against him as an indorser, — the holder would have a perfect right to the instrument.

If there be doubt about such cases, it is clear that where there has been no delivery at all, in either of the two general ways mentioned, no liability can arise against the party, maker or acceptor, from whom the paper was taken. Thus it is laid down that where a negotiable instrument is stolen or fraudulently taken from the acceptor or maker, such party cannot be required to pay it to any holder whatever; and that too though the acceptor or maker may have made the theft or fraud easy by putting the paper in an unlocked drawer in a desk to which clerks

---

Cheque Bank, 1 C. P. D. 578; Bank of Ireland *v.* Evans Charities, 5 H. L. Cas. 389; holding that the result must come about in or in immediate connection with the negligent act or omission. See Bigelow, Estoppel, 655–659, 5th ed.; also Bank of England *v.* Vagliano, 1891, A. C. 107, 115, 135, 136, 170, 171.

[1] Compare Chicopee Bank *v.* Philadelphia Bank, 8 Wall. 641; L. C. 202.

and servants and others had access.¹ For example: The plaintiff is bona fide holder for value of a promissory note signed by the defendant, and now sued upon. A third person fraudulently obtains it from the defendant upon the false representation that he is taking something else, and puts it into circulation. The defendant is not liable; there has been no delivery by him or by any act attributable to him.²

The doctrine of estoppel, sometimes applied, but for the most part doubtfully at least, against the person from whom the instrument has escaped, should never, it is well laid down, be invoked without necessity. It should be applied only in cases where the person against whom it is set up has so conducted himself, in what he has done or omitted, that, unless estopped, he would be doing something contrary to his former conduct in what he then did or omitted. That principle does not apply to a case of theft or the like, even though the party stolen from was negligent; for theft is not the natural consequence of negligence, though the negligence make it possible.³ Nor in any case of negligence, even without theft or other criminal or fraudulent act, does estoppel apply unless the negligence was in or in immediate connection with putting the paper into circulation;⁴ the negligence must have been the *cause*, the proximate, legal cause, of what happened.⁵

The statement then sometimes found even in books of the law of bills and notes, that whenever one of two innocent persons must suffer by the act of a third person,

---

¹ Baxendale v. Bennett, 3 Q. B. Div. 525.

² See Burson v. Huntington, 21 Mich. 415; Gibbs v. Linabury, 22 Mich. 479; Chapman v. Rose, 56 N. Y. 137; Kellogg v. Steiner, 29 Wis. 626; Corby v. Weddle, 57 Mo. 452; 1 Bigelow, Fraud, 618, 619.

³ Baxendale v. Bennett, supra, Bramwell, L. J.

⁴ See Arnold v. Cheque Bank, 1 C. P. D. 578, and other cases in note 3, p. 176.

⁵ See Bank of England v. Vagliano, 1891, A. C. 107, 135, and other cases in note 3, p. 176.

he who has enabled such third person to bring about the loss must bear the loss, is too broad;[1] ample confirmation will be found as we proceed. The statement indeed, like many another started when judges were feeling after the law, 'if haply they might find it,' is a dangerous one, so much so that the danger fairly overbalances its usefulness.

§ 2. WANT OF CONTRACT: FRAUD IN ESSE CONTRACTUS.

Fraud in esse contractus, as we have designated the other case of want of contract, is fraud in or by which consent, or union of minds in the supposed contract, was prevented. The case is to be distinguished sharply from fraud in its more common form of misrepresentation of facts touching the inducement or desirability of the contract, or the fraud of an agent in wrongfully filling up and delivering a blank instrument, signed by his principal. That sort of fraud does not prevent consent or union of minds in the contract; it only makes a case in which it is or may be probable that there would have been no such consent and contract as took place, had the state of things in the one case been known by the defendant, or in the other had the instrument been under his control at the moment. Fraud of that kind creates an equity only, not a legal defence.

Fraud in esse contractus may be committed in any of the various contracts with which we are concerned, and in a variety of ways; enough that consent to the particular alleged contract was never given. One of the forms which fraud of the kind assumes is misrepresentation (not of facts of inducement, but) of the very kind of contract which the party is induced to sign, or by the substitution, unperceived or misunderstood by such party, of the paper he intended to sign for another which he did not intend to sign. For example: The plaintiff is bona

---

[1] See Arnold v. Cheque Bank, supra.

fide holder for value of a bill of exchange, upon which there is an indorsement in the handwriting of the defendant, upon which indorsement the suit is brought. The defendant, a man advanced in years, is induced to write his name upon the back of the bill by the fraud of the acceptor in telling the defendant that the contract he is signing is a guaranty; only the back of the paper being shown. The defendant had previously signed a guaranty at the request of the same person, for the same purpose and amount, and he is now led to suppose that he is signing a similar guaranty to the former one (out of which no liability resulted). There has been no negligence by the defendant. The plaintiff is not entitled to recover, the defendant having been deceived, not in respect of the legal effect, but of the actual contents of the instruments.[1]

That shows again that the statement that whenever one of two innocent parties must suffer by the act of a third person, he who has enabled such third person to bring about the loss must bear the loss, can only be accepted with important qualifications.[2] The proposition is too broad even in cases of negligence, as was seen in speaking of delivery; and in the example last given there was not even negligence. The burden of the loss cannot be shifted over to the shoulders of one who never contracted, though his act or conduct may have been the occasion, if it was not the cause, of the loss.

[1] Foster v. Mackinnon, L. R. 4 C. P. 704; L. C. 554. Compare certain *statutory* cases of tricks or devices by which men have been induced by travelling agents for patent-rights and other things to sign promissory notes. Champion v. Ulmer, 70 Ill. 320. See Gibbs v. Linabury, 22 Mich. 479.

[2] If that statement were true, a man might be held as maker of a promissory note who had merely written his name upon a blank sheet of paper which another had afterwards fraudulently filled out as a promise to pay money. Of course no liability towards any one could be created in such a case. See Cline v. Guthrie, 42 Ind. 227; Caulkins v. Whisler, 29 Iowa, 495.

§ 3. Want of Contract: Alteration: Forgery: Estoppel.

Another case of want of contract arises where there has been a material, unauthorized alteration of the instrument to which the defendant gave his signature. The authorities in general declare that to alter the terms, written or printed, of a negotiable note, bill, or cheque, after the defendant's signature was written to it, is to destroy its validity against him, even in the hands of a bona fide holder for value. The reason is plain. The altered instrument is not the one he signed; and the identity of the one signed has been destroyed.[1]

A material alteration within the meaning of the rule stated may be defined thus: Any alteration (1) changing the legal effect of the instrument, (2) made with such intent, or being a final act, (3) without consent, (4) by a party to it, or by one in lawful possession of it, is a material alteration. The divisions of the definition as here given will serve as the basis of an analysis of the subject.

First, then, of alterations 'changing the legal effect of the instrument.' It was at one time considered, and it is still occasionally intimated, that a *fraudulent* alteration, material or not, would destroy the instrument, because perhaps of the wrongful intent;[2] but that doctrine has

---

[1] Wade *v.* Withington, 1 Allen, 561; Draper *v* Ward, 112 Mass. 315, Aldrich *v.* Smith, 37 Mich. 468.

[2] Pigot's Case, 11 Coke, 27 a, comment on 2d resolution. The word 'fraudulent' is not used there; but in its application to *immaterial* alterations, the language must, it seems, be understood as referring to a fraudulent intent. 'If the obligee himself,' as Coke comments in the passage referred to, 'alters the deed ... although it is in words not material, yet the deed is void.'

been generally abandoned. An immaterial alteration then cannot, by the current of authority, have the effect to prevent recovery upon the paper. For example: the plaintiff is holder for value, and the defendant, maker of a promissory note sued upon, which does not state any time of payment. The plaintiff afterwards writes in the words 'on demand,' without the defendant's consent and with fraudulent intent. The plaintiff is entitled to recover notwithstanding the alteration, the note being originally payable on demand in legal effect.[1] Again: The plaintiff is holder for value of an instrument made by the defendant, promising to pay a certain sum of money, upon a condition expressed therein, to a person named. The payee afterwards writes in the words 'or bearer' without the defendant's consent. The defendant's liability remains unchanged; the contract, being incapable of negotiability as it was executed, could not be made negotiable by adding the words in question.[2]

A like case would be made where, after a change of law not governing the instrument in question, an alteration in it is made expressing no more than what was embraced in the law by which the instrument was governed.[3] Another case of the kind would arise where an alteration was made conforming to the true intention of the parties, correcting a mistake in the writing.[4] So to add the words 'with grace' to paper entitled by law to grace, or 'without grace' to paper not entitled to grace; and so to add the legal rate of interest, as 'at six per cent,' after the words

---

[1] Aldous v. Cornwell, L. R. 3 Q. B. 573, overruling Pigot's Case, 2d resolution. See Goodenow v. Curtis, 33 Mich. 505; Curtis v. Goodenow, 24 Mich. 18. But see Bridges v. Winters, 42 Miss. 135.

[2] Goodenow v. Curtis, and Curtis v. Goodenow, supra.

[3] Bridges v. Winters, 42 Miss. 135.

[4] McRaven v. Crisler, 53 Miss. 542; Clute v. Small, 17 Wend. 238; Hervey v. Harvey, 15 Maine, 357. But see Miller v. Gilleland, 19 Penn. St. 119, by a divided court.

'with interest,' — such additions are immaterial; they have no effect upon the validity of the instrument. In such cases it makes no difference whether the defendant has consented to the alteration or not; and so of all other cases in which the alteration is immaterial.

It would be difficult to show what alterations are such as to change the legal effect of the instrument, in any other way than by specific cases. And then, too, it should be remembered that we are dealing with but part of the definition, and that all the other parts of it must also be met to make a material alteration. In other words, though in a particular case the alteration appears to change the legal effect of the instrument, it may appear that it was not 'made with such intent, or being a final act,' or one of the other facts may be wanting to make it material.

The following are some of the cases in which the alteration changes, or appears to change, the legal effect of the instrument: An alteration of the date of the instrument;[1] changing 'I promise' to 'we promise,' for such change would convert a several, or a joint and several, into a joint promise;[2] the addition of an interest clause to an instrument completed without it,[3] as for example, 'to bear legal interest,'[4] or 'interest payable annually' or 'semi-annually,' 'quarterly' or otherwise;[5] striking out the words 'after maturity' where interest is made so payable;[6] changing the name of the payee;[7] changing 'to the order of A' to

[1] Vance v. Lowther, 1 Ex. D. 176; Wood v. Steele, 6 Wall. 80; Britton v. Dierker, 46 Mo. 591; Emmons v. Meeker, 55 Ind. 321; Kennedy v. Lancaster Bank, 18 Penn. St. 347.

[2] Humphreys v. Gwillow, 13 N. H. 385.

[3] Holmes v. Trumper, 22 Mich. 427; L. C. 544; Glover v. Robbins, 49 Ala. 219. As to filling blanks in such cases, see infra.

[4] Lochnane v. Emmerson, 11 Bush, 69.

[5] Marsh v. Griffin, 42 Iowa, 403; Blakey v. Johnson, 13 Bush, 197; Lamar v. Brown, 56 Ala. 157.

[6] Brooks v. Allen, 62 Ind. 401.

[7] Stoddard v. Penniman, 108 Mass. 366; s. c. 113 Mass. 386.

'to A or bearer;'[1] adding the words 'payable at the Bank of S,'[2] though it seems that an acceptor may make a bill payable at no designated place payable at any particular place he will within the town in which by law it is payable;[3] adding another name to that of the maker of a note,[4] though the case appears to be different where another surety is added, upon delivery, to a note or bill already executed by a sure'y;[5] adding an attestation clause, for that produces a possible and probable change in the evidence of execution, proof of the signature of the attesting witness proving the execution.[6]

'Made with such intent, or being a final act.' It may be that the alteration was the result of an accident, as where the intention was to make the change in another instrument; or it may be due to mistake in regard to the terms of agreement, or in computation of amount, or in some other particular. When that is the case, it seems that the identity of the instrument is not destroyed. If the new words have been added merely, they may in principle be struck out by the one who added them on discovering the

---

[1] Union Bank v. Roberts, 45 Wis. 373.

[2] Southwark Bank v. Gross, 35 Penn. St. 80; Nazro v. Fuller, 24 Wend. 374; Whitesides v. Northern Bank, 10 Bush, 501; Burchfield v. Moore, 3 El. & B. 683.

[3] Troy Bank v. Lauman, 19 N. Y. 477. See Todd v. Bank of Kentucky, 3 Bush, 626; Whitesides v. Northern Bank, supra; of the right of an accommodation acceptor of a bill payable generally to designate a particular place of payment.

[4] Hamilton v. Hooper, 46 Iowa, 515; Lunt v. Silver, 5 Mo. App. 186; Haskell v. Champion, 30 Mo. 136; Crandall v. First Nat. Bank, 61 Ind. 349; Wallace v. Jewell, 21 Ohio St. 163; Gardner v. Walsh, 5 El. & B. 83.

[5] Crandall v. First Nat. Bank, supra; Keith v. Goodwin, 31 Vt. 268, distinguishing Gardner v. Walsh, supra, and like cases, on the ground that the addition was made after the instrument had been delivered.

[6] Adams v. Frye, 3 Met. 103.

facts; or if they are written over an erasure of the original words, and the original words cannot well be restored, they may stand, and the explanation be given at the trial.[1]

The right to make such correction appears to be limited to the person who made the change, including possibly his agents and personal representatives. After the paper has passed from his hands it is too late, for his indorsee will have taken the paper as altered, and the only right he can have is upon the altered paper. He did not take it as it stood originally, and hence cannot restore it to its original form even where that would be physically practicable. The alteration has been allowed to stand by the party who made it, and so has permanently changed the paper; it has become 'a final act.' Nor would it make any difference, it seems, that the party who made the alteration did not discover his mistake until after he had transferred the instrument; after transferring it, his rights over it are gone.

The difference between material alterations made by mistake, and alterations made with intent to change the legal effect of the instrument, is plain; in the case of mistake, the object of the act is to restore the writing to the terms agreed upon; in the case of intelligent intention to change, the object is to destroy the writing as evidence of the terms actually agreed upon. That will serve to explain some of the apparent contradictions of the authorities. Thus, it is laid down that a material alteration by a party will destroy the instrument whether it was fraudulent or not;[2] and it is also laid down that a material alteration will *not* destroy the instrument if it was not fraudulent.[3] Both statements are true. The case usually

---

[1] Compare Horst v. Wagner, 43 Iowa, 373; Krause v. Meyer, 32 Iowa, 566.

[2] Draper v. Ward, supra.

[3] Kountz v. Kennedy, 63 Penn. St. 187.

presented is one in which the alteration was suffered to remain, and the paper passed as altered to the plaintiff. The alteration is final, and authority conforms to principle, that the plaintiff, though a bona fide holder, cannot maintain an action in such a case against any of the non-consenting parties who signed the paper as it stood before the alteration. For example: The plaintiff is payee for value of what purports to be a promissory note signed by the defendants. The instrument originally read: 'For value received I promise to pay,' etc., 'with interest,' and so was signed by two persons, the defendants. The note thus executed was for the benefit of the first signer, who afterwards changes the word 'I' to 'we,' and adds after the word 'interest' the words 'at twelve per cent,' without the other defendant's knowledge, supposing himself to have the right to do so, the rate of interest not having been agreed upon when the note was executed, but being afterwards fixed between the first defendant and the plaintiff as inserted. Then the instrument so altered is delivered to the plaintiff. The plaintiff is not entitled to recover against the second defendant, either upon the instrument in its altered or in its original form, though the alteration was not fraudulent.[1]

Hence, the first of the two apparently contradictory propositions is true. But the party having made an innocent mistake, in making the alteration, may, while the instrument is still in his own hands, discover his mistake and desire to correct it, restoring the instrument to its original state. The alteration not having become final, that may be done, or the case may be treated as if it had been done, or as if no alteration had been made, if actual restoration is impracticable. Hence, the second of the two propositions also is correct. This explanation may not indeed align with some of the authorities, for the second

---

[1] Draper *v.* Ward, supra.

proposition has misled the courts in some cases, causing them to hold in general that material alterations which are not fraudulent are not fatal to the instrument; but the explanation, it is believed, shows a sound distinction.[1]

The general rule then may be expanded and stated thus: If the bill, note, or cheque be altered in a material particular, either by fraud or by an innocent mistake not corrected while the paper is in the hands of the party who made the alteration, it will be destroyed towards all non-consenting parties, and that too whether the alteration was made by the party claiming under it or by any other party to it. And no action can be maintained against non-consenting parties, either upon the altered instrument or upon the instrument as it stood before alteration, even by a bona fide holder for value.[2] The fact that the instrument may have been restored to its original form (after having been passed with the alteration) makes no difference.[3] Nor is the alteration to be deemed immaterial by reason of the fact that it is favorable to the defendant,[4] for still its legal effect is changed, and the identity of the contract signed is destroyed.[5]

---

[1] The Pennsylvania courts permit recovery by a bona fide holder for value to the amount of the instrument as originally executed, when the sum has been raised in such a way as not to excite the suspicion of a man in ordinary business. Worrall v. Gheen, 39 Penn. St. 388; Garrard v. Haddan, 67 Penn. St. 82; Phelan v. Moss, Id. 59. See also Brown v. Reed, 79 Penn. St. 370; Neff v. Horner, 63 Penn. St. 327. That is very well if the alteration was not fraudulent or otherwise final; but the Pennsylvania cases do not make the distinction.

[2] See besides the cases supra, Smith v. Mace, 44 N. H. 553; Holmes v. Trumper, 22 Mich. 427; L. C. 544; Greenfield Bank v. Stowell, 123 Mass. 196; Citizens' Bank v. Richmond, 121 Mass. 110; Woolfolk v. Bank of America, 10 Bush, 504, 517; Morehead v. Parkersburg Bank, 5 W. Va. 74; Burchfield v. Moore, 3 El. & B. 683.

[3] Citizens' Bank v. Richmond, supra.

[4] Humphreys v. Gwillow, 13 N. H. 385, 387.

[5] Id.; Draper v. Ward, 1 Allen, 561; Chism v. Toomer, 27 Ark 108.

'Without consent.' Consenting parties cannot set up an alteration; and, among others, all who have signed the contract after the alteration are consenting parties, with one exception to be stated presently. Thus, if an alteration in the date of a bill of exchange was made with the consent of the acceptor, or if he subsequently assented to it, he will be bound, and so will all other parties to it becoming such after the alteration; while the prior non-consenting parties may repudiate the instrument.[1]

The exception referred to arises in the acceptance of a bill of exchange. A bill may have been altered after it left the drawer's hands and before acceptance; in such a case, though the acceptor appears to have accepted the bill in its altered form, he has not done so in law, — he has presumably intended to accept the bill which the drawer drew. If he accepted the bill without notice of the alteration, and without negligence, he is not bound by his act. For example: The defendants being bona fide holders for value of a bill of exchange drawn upon the plaintiffs, the bill is presented to the plaintiffs for acceptance, and accepted, an alteration of the sum payable, of the date, and of the payee's name, having been made in it after it passed from the drawer's hands and before acceptance. The acceptance was without notice of the alteration and without negligence. Afterwards the plaintiffs pay the bill, and then on discovering the alteration bring the present suit to recover back the sum paid. They are entitled to recover.[2]

The reason is plain. The drawee of a bill of exchange accepts, if he does accept, on the ground that payment

---

[1] Paton v. Winter, 1 Taunt. 420; Tarleton v. Shingler, 7 C. B. 812.

[2] Compare Bank of Commerce v. Union Bank, 3 Comst. 230, bill paid at sight. See Clews v. Bank of New York, 89 N. Y. 418. Acceptance is an admission of the drawer's hand (as will be seen later), but not of the rest of the writing. Id.

by him gives him the right to charge the amount to the drawer as payment made upon the drawer's order;[1] he would not accept except upon that footing, or upon the undertaking of some one else to protect him. But where the bill is altered after it has left the drawer's hands, the acceptor cannot on payment make such charge; the drawer has not directed him to pay the altered bill. Acceptance, then, is not an admission of the genuineness of the *contents* of the bill, so as to work an estoppel against him in favor of a bona fide holder for value.

If, however, the drawer himself has altered the bill, or consented to the alteration of it, after drawing it, the case will be different, for he will then have directed the drawee to accept and pay the bill as altered. That distinction must be taken as the explanation of one or two cases which at first may seem to hold broadly that acceptance of an altered bill makes the acceptor liable upon the bill as altered. For example: The plaintiff is payee of a bill of exchange accepted by the defendant and now sued upon. The bill as originally drawn was payable three days after date, and in that condition was indorsed by the payee for the accommodation of the drawer, who now changes the word 'three' to 'thirty,' and passes the bill to A. The fact is afterwards discovered, and an arrangement made by which the bill is returned by A to the plaintiff; then it is accepted by the defendant without knowledge or notice of the alteration. The defendant is liable.[2]

---

[1] Compare the language of the court in Hortsman *v.* Henshaw, 11 How. 177.

[2] Ward *v.* Allen, 2 Met. 53. There were other complicating facts in this case, but they have no bearing upon the point now under consideration. The first head-note of the case is too broad. In Langton *v.* Lazarus, 5 Mees. & W. 629, also, the alteration was made by the drawer. That must be understood as the essential fact in reference to the acceptor's liability.

'By a party to it or by one in lawful possession of it.' An alteration made by a stranger has no effect upon the validity of the instrument if it is possible to show what its language was before the act; the alteration must be made by a party, or by one in lawful possession, — all others are strangers, — in order to destroy the instrument.[1] By a 'party' is meant any one who has placed his signature to it, or has been owner of or interested in the instrument; by 'one in lawful possession,' any one to whom the owner or other person interested in the instrument has intrusted it.[2]

If the blank has been wrongfully filled by one who has been intrusted with the instrument, with power to fill the blank or not in a certain contingency, the act will not constitute a material alteration, though the paper was delivered as complete. The case is one of agency, and the party whose confidence has been betrayed, that is, the principal, will be bound in favor of a bona fide holder for value.[3] That assumes, however, that no alteration of the written or printed language is made,[4] unless the facts indicate an authority to alter.[5]

The mere fact that one who has been acting as authorized agent of the defendant made the alteration will not bind the supposed principal, for agency confers no authority to commit a crime.[6] No relation of agency exists between co-signers as such of an instrument; and hence an alteration made by one co-maker of a promissory note, without the consent of the others, though before delivery, if the

---

[1] Langenberger v. Kroeger, 48 Cal. 147; Brooks v. Allen, 62 Ind. 401; Ætna Ins. Co. v. Winchester, 43 Conn. 391.

[2] See Brooks v. Allen and Ætna Ins. Co. v. Winchester, supra.

[3] Belknap v. National Bank, 100 Mass. 376, 381; Greenfield Bank v. Stowell, 123 Mass. 196, 203.

[4] Belknap v. National Bank, supra.

[5] Ætna Ins. Co. v. Winchester, 43 Conn. 391.

[6] Id.; Brooks v. Allen, 62 Ind. 401.

other makers have already signed, is a destruction of the instrument towards the latter.[1]

Thus far of the meaning of the term 'material alteration.' But suppose that the defendant, being maker of a promissory note, or drawer of a bill of exchange or a cheque, has facilitated the alteration, as for example, by leaving a blank space in the instrument, which has afterwards been fraudulently filled out, is he now estopped or barred from setting up the alteration? It must be understood that the case under consideration is one in which the instrument left the hands of the maker or drawer as a complete instrument; cases of entrusting one's blank signature, or one's signature to an uncompleted instrument stand upon a very different footing, as will be seen in another place.

It has sometimes been held that if the maker or the drawer, by leaving a blank, has made it easy for the wrongdoer to fill the blank and so alter the instrument, he, rather than the bona fide holder for value, must bear the loss. That is commonly put upon the ground of (supposed) negligence, sometimes upon the ground that of two innocent parties, he who occasioned the loss must bear the loss. The last is, at best, but a very imperfect statement of law, and cannot be taken as satisfactory in any such case; and the first, the ground of negligence, finds an answer in what has been said already in regard to delivery, — to wit, the negligence, if it be admitted that there is negligence, is not the legal, otherwise called the proximate cause, in ordinary cases, of the alteration. To be the legal cause of what was done, the negligence must have been in or in immediate connection with the alteration; the alteration must have been the natural or the probable result of the negligence.[2]

[1] Wood v. Steele, 6 Wall. 80; Greenfield Bank v. Stowell, 123 Mass. 196; Wood v. Draper, 112 Mass. 315.

[2] In a case of the fraudulent transfer of stock by the plaintiffs'

Though there are then cases to the contrary,[1] it may be safely stated that in principle, and by the weight of authority, a material alteration by a party, or by one in lawful possession, made in a note, bill, or cheque delivered as a completed instrument, by writing or printing words in a blank space, destroys the instrument so that no action can be maintained against the maker or drawer, or other non-consenting parties, even by a bona fide holder for value.[2] Nor does it make any difference whether the blank was left in the body or at the end of the instrument. For example: The plaintiff is a bona fide holder for value of a promissory note sued upon, purporting to have been signed by the defendant as maker, and containing at the end the words '10 per cent.' What the defendant did sign was the instrument in question without those words, delivering the same as a completed undertaking. The instrument signed closed with the words, 'with interest at,' after which there was a blank, which after delivery to the payee was filled in with the words above quoted, '10 per cent.' The defendant is not liable, the alteration having the effect to destroy the instrument.[3]

The contrary view, which has found favor in some of our

clerk, Bowen, L. J., said 'The proximate cause'—that is, the legal cause—'was the felony and crime' of the clerk, 'and it cannot be said that the felony was either the natural or likely or necessary or direct consequence of the carelessness of the plaintiffs.' Merchants of the Staple v. Bank of England, 21 Q. B. Div. 160. See also Bank of Ireland v. Evans Charities, 5 H. L. Cas. 389; Swan v. North British Co. 2 Hurl. & N. 175, 182, Arnold v. Cheque Bank, 1 C. P. Div. 578; Bigelow, Estoppel, 655, 656, 5th ed.

[1] Isnard v. Torres, 10 La. An. 103; Capital Bank v. Armstrong, 62 Mo. 59, Iron Mountain Bank v. Murdock, Id. 70; Ridington v Woods, 45 Cal. 406. See also Worrall v. Gheen, 39 Penn. St. 388.

[2] Holmes v. Trumper, 22 Mich. 427; L. C. 544; Greenfield Bank v. Stowell, 123 Mass. 196, and cases reviewed therein.

[3] Holmes v. Trumper, supra. See also McGrath v. Clark, 56 N. Y. 34. But see Redlich v Doll, 54 N. Y. 234, and quære.

courts, appears to have been based originally upon a misunderstanding of the effect of a decision of the English Common Pleas in relation to a blank space left in a cheque just before the amount for which the cheque had been made payable; the drawer's clerk, *by whom* the cheque was drawn, and to whom the cheque was then entrusted to obtain payment, having raised the sum payable by writing certain words in the blank.[1] But the contest there was between the drawer of the cheque and his banker, the drawee; no case arose of the claim of a bona fide holder for value, and though it was held that the drawer must under the circumstances bear the loss, nothing was said about estoppel. Moreover there was something approaching agency in the facts.[2] The case is, therefore, no authority for the position upon which some courts have acted, that the drawer of a cheque or bill, or the maker of a note, is estopped or barred from setting up the alteration in a suit by the holder of the instrument. The English courts, followed by some of the ablest of our own, have plainly repudiated the idea of any estoppel, and have declared that the decision must be understood as confined in its bearing to questions arising upon facts of the same nature.[3] The case, if to be regarded as rightly decided, is clearly distinguishable from cases such as we have been considering.[4]

---

[1] Young v. Grote, 4 Bing. 253.
[2] See Holmes v. Trumper, supra; Greenfield Bank v. Stowell, supra.
[3] Swan v. North British Co., 2 Hurl. & C., 175, 189, 190; Halifax Union v. Wheelwright, L. R. 10 Ex. 183, 192; Arnold v Cheque Bank, 1 C. P. Div. 578, 587, 588; Greenfield Bank v. Stowell, 123 Mass. 196, 200, 201; Holmes v. Trumper, 22 Mich. 427; L. C. 544, 551, 552.
[4] The cheque had been left in blank entirely, save signature, by the drawer with his wife for her use in his absence, and the wife *employed* the clerk to fill in the sum required. He did so, skilfully leaving the blank before 'fifty,' written with a small 'f;' and then, being entrusted with the cheque to draw the money, he wrote in the words mentioned.

It has well been questioned whether the leaving of blanks can ordinarily amount to negligence at all, not to say negligence the legal cause of the loss; for it is impracticable to execute an instrument, in ordinary business, without leaving blanks somewhere. There must be a blank at the beginning or at the end, unless, what not the most careful man ever does, a line is drawn before the first word and after the last, clean to the signature. Universal practice cannot be negligence.[1]

Marginal terms, such as conditions, stipulations, and the like, not being mere memoranda of facts, such as the consideration, — in other words, marginal terms which are intended to be part of the written contract, — are treated by the better authorities as inseparable from the main writing to which the signature is given. And it makes no difference whether such marginalia are signed or not. Accordingly, to remove such terms, by cutting them off or in any other way, without consent, will be fatal. There is no distinction, by the better authorities, for there are decisions to the contrary, between cases of that sort and cases of the alteration of language in the body of the signed instrument. The instrument signed has been destroyed, and no action upon it can be maintained either

---

That point is dwelt upon in Holmes *v*. Trumper, supra, as a 'very important circumstance.' The court there says 'The cheque was filled up by the plaintiff's clerk, the alteration made, and the money drawn by him in person, and the plaintiff, by *employing him* [italics by the court] as he did, as his clerk, and (through his wife) as his agent to fill the cheque, and in person to draw the money from the bankers, might well be held to have placed a confidence in him for which he should be responsible, or at least to have authorized the bankers to place confidence in him.' And so the court itself in Young *v*. Grote distinguish Hall *v*. Fuller. 5 Barn & C. 750, decided directly the other way. See also Greenfield Bank *v*. Stowell, supra.

[1] See the language of the court in Holmes *v*. Trumper, supra, and the quotation from it in Greenfield Bank *v*. Stowell, supra.

SECT. 3.] LEGAL OR ABSOLUTE DEFENCES. 195

in its present or in its original form.[1] And the same is plainly true of the cutting in two of instruments dextrously constructed, so that by cutting through them at a particular place one part will be left in form a perfect contract different in effect from the instrument uncut.[2] In cases such as these there is ordinarily not even the semblance of negligence, and it is difficult to conceive how the defendant can be treated as having assented, or how he can be barred from showing that he never assented, to the supposed contract.

Still another case of want of contract arises where between the plaintiff and the defendant there is a forged indorsement. Each person who signs a negotiable contract of the law merchant undertakes to pay to any one who acquires title according to the law merchant. That law requires, not that every intervening holder of the paper between the plaintiff and the defendant should have been owner of the instrument or even the lawful holder of it, but that every intervening indorsement should be genuine. The holder may have a good claim against later indorsers; back of the forged indorsement he cannot go, for want of legal assent on the part of the signers.[3] For example: The plaintiffs sue the defendants to recover the

---

[1] Gerrish v. Glines, 56 N. H. 9; Johnson v. Heagan, 23 Maine, 329; Shaw v. First Methodist Soc., 8 Met. 223; Fletcher v. Blodgett, 16 Vt. 26; Bay v. Shrader, 50 Miss. 326; Benedict v. Cowden, 49 N. Y. 396; Bank of America v. Woodworth, 18 Johns. 315; s. c. 19 Johns. 391; Brill v. Crick, 1 Mees. & W. 232. See also Franklin Sav. Inst. v. Reed, 125 Mass. 365; Benthall v. Hildreth, 2 Gray, 288; Heywood v. Perrin, 10 Pick. 228. But see Cornell v. Nebeker, 58 Ind. 425; Nebeker v. Cutsinger, 48 Ind. 436; Zimmerman v. Rote, 75 Penn. St. 108; Brown v. Reed, 79 Penn. St. 370.

[2] Brown v. Reed, supra.

[3] Canal Bank v. Bank of Albany, 1 Hill, 287; Hortsman v. Henshaw, 11 How. 177; L. C. 541; Arnold v. Cheque Bank, 1 C. P. D. 578.

amount paid by mistake by the plaintiffs as acceptors to the defendants as holders of a bill of exchange payable to A, whose indorsement had been forged. The defendants were bona fide holders for value. The plaintiffs are entitled to recover.[1]

There are one or two nominal exceptions to this rule. The maker of a note, or the drawer of a bill or a cheque, can make it payable to whomsoever he will; and if he makes it payable to a person having no interest in it, he may indorse that person's name, and put the instrument into circulation. So far as the question of liability upon the instrument is concerned, it would make no difference whether the maker or drawer had the authority of the payee to indorse his name or not; because having once used the payee's name for the purpose of putting the paper into circulation, he could not afterwards deny his right to do so. Indeed, it could not affect the case that the payee was a party in interest, so far as the liability of the maker or drawer, on the instrument, is concerned. The act might be unlawful for other purposes; but in a suit upon the instrument the defendant could not allege that he had forged the payee's name. For example: The plaintiff is suing to recover the amount of a bill of exchange paid by him as acceptor to the defendant, a bona fide holder for value, one of the drawers of the bill having forged the payee's name, and procured a discount of the bill. The plaintiff did not know of the forgery when he paid. He is not entitled to recover.[2]

The example, it will be observed, goes a step further

---

[1] Canal Bank v. Bank of Albany, supra.

[2] Coggill v. American Bank, 1 Comst. 113. See Hortsman v. Henshaw, supra. Where the paper is payable to a fictitious party, it may, it seems, be treated as payable to bearer. See Coggill v. American Bank, supra; Cooper v. Meyer, 10 Barn. & C 468; s. c 5 Man. & R. 387; Minet v. Gibson, 3 T. R. 81; s. c. 1 H. Black. 569; Bank of England v. Vagliano, 1891, A. C. 107; Bills of Ex. Act, 7, (3).

than the rule just stated. But the reason is obvious; the acceptor had paid according to the order of the drawer. Such payment entitled him to charge the sum to the drawer; and, as we have seen, where the acceptor (or drawee) can do that his act of acceptance (or payment) is binding. In such a case then the bona fide holder for value has a valid claim back of the forged indorsement, contrary to the rule in ordinary cases.

Forgery of the signature of the drawer of a bill of exchange stands upon a footing of its own. Were it not for a special rule of law, founded upon the natural effect of acceptance, the case would be in no wise peculiar, and the courts would therefore hold that no action could be maintained against the acceptor by any person. But the drawer and the drawee are, or they are generally assumed to be, correspondents; they are ordinarily in close business relations, the drawee usually holding funds of the drawer and often being his banker. The drawee is, therefore, presumably familiar with the hand of the drawer, and when he accepts a bill purporting to be the drawer's, he thereby asserts or admits that the signature is the genuine signature of the drawer. That may well have misled a purchaser of the bill; and the law therefore holds the acceptor, by reason of his acceptance, estopped to deny his liability to a purchaser who is a bona fide holder for value; the acceptance in such a case is binding, notwithstanding the fact that the drawer's signature is a forgery. For example: The plaintiff sues to recover the amount of a bill of exchange which as acceptor he has paid to the defendant, a bona fide holder for value who had discounted the bill after acceptance. The drawer's signature is forged, but the plaintiff did not know the fact when he accepted. The plaintiff is not entitled to recover; it was his duty to satisfy himself of the drawer's hand before acceptance, and his acceptance is a conclusive admission, in favor of the defendant, of the genuineness of the signature.[1]

The case from which the example is taken went still further. Another bill had been paid by the plaintiff, on presentment, without acceptance, the defendant having *already* taken it; and the same rule was applied, — the plaintiff was not allowed to show that the drawer's signature had been forged. The case, therefore, appears to go the length of holding the drawee bound by his act, whether of acceptance or payment, though that act could not have misled the holder into his purchase of the bill. The rule would then be unbending; acceptance or payment would in itself be binding in favor of a bona fide holder.

The later authorities appear to repudiate that doctrine, and to put the case on the ground which the example fairly implies, of estoppel. That is to say, acceptance binds the drawee in favor of a bona fide holder for value who took the bill after the acceptance, but not in favor of one who took it before acceptance.[2] That is probably the right view. Practice of the parties or usage may also affect the case. Thus it is laid down that the acceptor may allege the want of genuineness of the drawer's signature, if he can show that by a settled course of business between the parties, or by a general custom of the place, the holder took upon himself the duty of exercising some particular precaution to prevent the loss, and failed of performing that duty.[3] So also it has been held that if the holder himself indorsed the paper, as for collection, before it was presented to the drawee, the drawee will not be estopped from alleging that the drawer's signature was forged,

---

[1] Price *v.* Neal, 3 Burr. 1354. That is the leading case, and it has had a long following. See Bigelow, Estoppel, 481 et seq., 5th ed.

[2] McKleroy *v.* Southern Bank, 14 La. An. 458. See Bigelow, Estoppel, 491, 5th ed; Bills of Ex. Act, 54, (2).

[3] Ellis *v.* Ohio Ins. Co., 4 Ohio St. 628.

because now the holder is thought to have asserted the genuineness of the bill, and to have misled the drawee.[1] And again, if the owner of the bill, on presenting it to the drawee, withhold from him important information which the former has touching the question of genuineness, the acceptance will not be binding.[2]

It should be remembered that the estoppel goes no further than to cut off the acceptor's right to set up the want of genuineness of the drawer's signature, and that his acceptance does not preclude him from asserting that other signatures, with an exception above mentioned (where the drawer indorses the payee's name), are not genuine, or that the body of the bill has been altered.

Akin to cases of the kind is the effect of accepting a bill of exchange, or making a promissory note, in regard to the capacity of the payee to indorse the instrument if it is negotiable. The acceptor or the maker, as the case may be, is supposed to know whether the payee is, at the time of acceptance or making, competent to contract and so competent to indorse; and he is accordingly considered to have admitted the payee's present competency. The acceptance of a bill or the making of a note has sometimes been spoken of as a warranty of the payee's capacity, which would prevent the acceptor or maker from setting up the payee's want of capacity even against a holder who took the paper with knowledge that the payee was incompetent in law to pass the title to the instrument.[3] But it is safer to say that the act of acceptance or maker is only an admission of capacity, and therefore available only in favor of a holder without notice.[4] Whatever the true rule

---

[1] National Bank of N. A. v. Bangs, 106 Mass. 441.
[2] First National Bank v. Ricker, 71 Ill. 439.
[3] Compare Erwin v. Downs, 15 N. Y. 575.
[4] See Barlow v. Bishop, 1 East, 432, as explained by Lord Abinger

upon that point, the admission or the warranty is not prospective; the maker or acceptor cannot be supposed to know or to undertake that the payee shall *continue* to be competent.[1]

There are other cases also in which the defendant has become barred of the right to allege want of contract between himself and the holder of the paper. Thus, to acknowledge a signature as one's own will preclude one from asserting, against a bona fide holder for value, who takes the paper thereupon, that the signature is not genuine.[2] So also if it appear that there has been a regular course of dealing, in which bills have been accepted by a clerk or agent whose signature has been acted upon by all parties concerned as the signature of the employer or principal, the fact will afford very strong evidence against the latter that he has authorized the acceptance in the present case.[3] But a person is not bound as acceptor of a bill of exchange bearing a forged acceptance by the mere fact that he has previously paid one bill similarly forged, unless he has actually led the holder to believe in some other way that the present acceptance is genuine.[4]

§ 4. Incapacity: Corporations.

Incapacity, natural or legal, to contract, by way of making, accepting, drawing, or indorsing, is a defence in all

in Pitt *v.* Chappelow, 8 Mees. & W. 616, and quoted in Bigelow, Estoppel, 493, note, 5th ed.

[1] See Bigelow, Estoppel, 497, 5th ed.

[2] Goodell *v.* Bates, 14 R. I. 65; Cohen *v.* Teller, 93 Penn. St. 123; Rudd *v.* Matthews, 79 Ky. 479. See Bank of United States *v.* Bank of Georgia, 10 Wheat. 333, which goes still further. But see Koons *v.* Davis, 84 Ind. 387, 389, which may be doubted.

[3] Morris *v.* Bethell, L. R. 5 C. P. 47; Crout *v.* De Wolf, 1 R. I. 393.

[4] Morris *v.* Bethell, supra; Cohen *v.* Teller, supra.

cases in favor of the incompetent party, and, it may be added, as in contracts of the common law, in favor of him only. It matters not what false representations touching capacity may have been made, as, for instance, by an infant that he is of age;[1] it matters not that, besides false representations of the kind, the paper has passed for value and without notice into the hands of an indorsee. In some States a contrary rule obtains with regard to unauthorized contracts made by a partner in trade in the name of his partnership.[2]

It does not follow in law, however, from the fact that incapacity is a defence to an action upon the party's supposed contract, that he may not have capacity, when a holder, to transfer the paper to another. In regard to the power of transferring ownership of the instrument, some authorities appear to distinguish between mental or natural incapacity, and incapacity created by or due to some regulation of law merely, that is, legal incapacity. According to such authorities, if the party's incapacity is due to mental defect, he cannot, of his own will and act, transfer the title to the paper which he owns.[3] Other authorities hold that transfer in such a case would be voidable only, not void, and hence would be good until repudiated by the lawful guardian of the party.[4] However that may be, if the incapacity is merely legal, as in the case of an infant possessed of full mental capacity, the title may be passed

---

[1] Compare Baker v. Stone, 136 Mass. 405 ; Merriam v. Cunningham, 11 Cush. 40; Alvey v. Reed, 114 Ind. 148; Wieland v. Kobick, 110 Ill. 16; Burley v. Russell, 10 N. H. 184; Bartlett v. Wells, 1 Best & S. 836. But see Kilgore v. Jordan, 17 Texas, 341.

[2] See the cases cited in Farmers' Bank v. Butchers' Bank, 16 N. Y. 125, 135.

[3] Rogers v. Blackwell, 49 Mich. 192.

[4] Carrier v. Sears, 4 Allen, 336, explaining Peaslee v. Robbins, 3 Met. 164, seemingly contra ; Burke v. Allen, 29 N. H. 106; Ashcroft v. De Armond, 44 Iowa, 229; Riggan v. Green, 80 N. C. 236.

by him in favor of any subsequent holder against other parties than the infant; and that, too, whether the transfer is by indorsement or not.[1]

A few words should be said concerning corporations in this connection. A corporation created by statute has, by reason of its creation by statute, such powers only as the statute directly or by plain inference confers upon it, in other words, only the powers conferred and their incidents. Hence a corporation, as such, has no power to bind itself generally by making, accepting, drawing, or indorsing paper of the law merchant even in favor of a bona fide holder for value; power so to bind itself must be given to it by the legislature, either directly or by plain inference.[2] But in so far as the corporation has power to make a particular contract, it has power incidentally, that is, by plain inference, to make, accept, draw, or indorse in respect of such contract.[3] For example: A company is incorporated to construct a railway. The directors are empowered to do whatever they may consider incidental or conducive to the object. In furtherance of that object they accept a bill drawn upon them. The acceptance is binding.[4] Again: The same corporation accepts a bill drawn upon it in favor of the objects of *another* railway-construction company. The acceptance is not binding.[5]

---

[1] Burke v. Allen, 29 N. H. 106. That assumes of course that the party owns the paper (or has authority of the owner to transfer). At common law a married woman could not transfer paper made or indorsed to her when single; but the reason was, not because she was incompetent to *contract*, which is another thing, but because the paper, after her marriage, was no longer hers.

[2] Mott v. Hicks, 1 Cowen, 513; In re Peruvian Ry. Co., L. R. 2 Ch. 617.

[3] In re Peruvian Ry. Co., supra; Came v. Brigham, 39 Maine, 35; Curtis v. Leavitt, 15 N. Y. 9.

[4] In re Peruvian Ry. Co., L. R. 2 Ch. 617.

[5] Smead v. Indianapolis R. Co., 11 Ind. 104.

A corporation then may have power to make one kind of contract, and not have power to make a contract of another kind; and the result is, that accepting, making, or indorsing paper of the law merchant in the latter sort of case is not binding even in favor of a bona fide holder for value. Nor, by the better view, will the case be affected by the circumstance that the corporation may have made false representations of its powers.[1] But if, instead of being wholly without power to make the contract, it had power to make it, though not in the way or by the means employed, the corporation will be liable to bona fide holders for value.[2] It should further be observed, as was said of other cases above, that the incapacity of a corporation to contract in the particular case does not imply incapacity to transfer title.[3]

§ 5. Illegality: Void by Statute.

Illegality is not in itself a legal defence; it is only an equity. And that is true though the courts go so far as to say in a particular case that the contract is absolutely void for illegality, unless the statement is made upon authority of statute. If statute in terms declare a contract void without qualification, it cannot be enforceable even under the law merchant; whereas if a contract is declared void by the common law, or by construction of some statute which does not plainly declare it void, it will not necessarily be void in the law merchant. In other words, a contract which, by loose construction of statutes or under the operation of the common law, or between immediate parties under the operation of the law merchant, may be called void or even 'absolutely void,' —

---

[1] Northern Bank v. Porter, 110 U. S. 608.
[2] See upon this whole subject, Bigelow, Estoppel, 464–469, 5th ed.
[3] Brown v. Donnell, 49 Maine, 427.

a term sometimes used, but with doubtful fitness, — is not necessarily void when it takes the form of negotiable paper, and is found in the hands of a bona fide holder for value.

The difference between what we have called loose construction, and plain language of statute, may be shown by comparing the case of a promissory note made on Sunday, with that of a promissory note made under a statute like an old one in Massachusetts which declared that notes under $5.00 should be entirely in writing, otherwise they were to be 'utterly void,' or under the old usury statutes. The statutes in regard to Sunday observance do not declare that contracts made on Sunday shall be void, nor do they use language which necessarily or naturally bears such a meaning; it is only by 'loose construction' that Sunday contracts have been declared to be 'void' or 'absolutely void.' Now, no action could be maintained under the old statute in regard to notes under $5.00, or under any other statute using the like plain language, — not even a bona fide holder for value could maintain an action; whereas the contrary would be true of such a holder of a note made on Sunday. The statute in the one case creates a legal defence, in the other an equity. For example: The plaintiff is bona fide holder for value, and the defendant maker, of a large number of promissory notes sued upon, each under $5.00, and each bearing the impression of printing, and issued after April 1, 1805, though bearing an earlier date. They are antedated with a view to avoid a statute which declares notes of the kind, made or issued after said date, to be 'utterly void.' The plaintiff cannot recover.[1] Again: The plaintiff is holder for value bona fide, and the defendant is maker of a promissory note sued upon, made and payable in the State of New York upon a usurious consideration; the statutes of that State declaring con-

---

[1] Bayley v. Taber, 5 Mass. 286; L. C. 524.

tracts made upon usurious consideration to be void, without qualification. The plaintiff cannot recover.[1] Again (under Sunday laws): The plaintiff is a bona fide holder for value, and the defendant is maker of a promissory note sued upon, which note was made, dated, and delivered Sept. 4, 1892, which day was Sunday, and payable four months after day. The plaintiff discounted the note in the month of December following. He is entitled to recover.[2]

Sometimes statutes which declare that contracts made in violation of them shall be void, make an exception in favor of bona fide holders for value of negotiable instruments so made, as in the case of a prohibitory liquor law which declares paper made in violation of its provisions 'utterly null and void against all persons, and in all cases, excepting only as against the holders . . . who may have paid therefor a fair price . . . without notice or knowledge of such illegal consideration.' In such a case, again, the illegality becomes an equity, and by force of the statute itself the bona fide holder for value is entitled to recover payment of the paper.[3]

---

[1] See Holmes v. Williams, 10 Paige, 326; Mordecai v. Dawkins, 9 Rich. 262; Towne v. Rice, 122 Mass. 67, 71.

[2] See State Bank v. Thompson, 42 N. H. 369. And compare Horton v. Buffinton, 105 Mass. 399.

[3] Paton v. Coit, 5 Mich. 505.

CHAPTER XIV.

EQUITIES.

§ 1. Bona Fide Holder for Value.

Equities, as we have seen, imply the existence of a contract, the contract, because of such defences, being defeasible between the parties to the equities and all others standing 'in their shoes,' but binding in favor of bona fide holders for value. This is, indeed, the great field of bona fide holders for value, the field in which the rights of such holders stand out conspicuously as the most favored known to the law. It is here that the law merchant appears in its strongest colors and in its most striking contrast to the common law. It is negotiability that affords the coloring and the contrast.

The first thing to be grasped is the meaning of the term 'bona fide holder for value.' The term is one of deliberately chosen use, each part of it having a characteristic meaning, and each part being necessary to give the party the paramount rights above mentioned; though where it is not important to make any distinction, either part of the expression is often used for the whole. So other expressions, such as 'holder in due course of trade,' are used as the equivalent of bona fide holder for value. But to enable the holder to occupy the most favored position, he or some one before him must have been both a bona fide holder and a holder for value. What, then, constitutes one a bona fide holder, and what a holder for value?

§ 2. Bona Fide Holder: Notice: Negligence.

The term 'bona fide holder,' properly speaking, means a holder without knowledge or notice of any equities which could be set up against a prior holder of the instrument. Absence of knowledge or notice of the defence, when the paper was taken, is the essential thing in the matter of bona fides. Notice calls for very special explanation.

In other departments of law notice may be either absolute or constructive. The contrast to constructive notice is usually put as actual notice; but that is an objectionable designation; it naturally suggests, and indeed is commonly used and understood to mean, knowledge.[1] But that leaves too much for constructive notice; it leaves much to that kind of notice which is not 'constructive' at all, as, for example, notice by the public registry. And if notice by the registry be called actual notice, then actual notice is used in inconsistent senses: in one sense it means knowledge; in another, something short of knowledge.

The term 'absolute notice' creates no such confusion; it does not suggest or mean knowledge at all. It means the kind of notice which in and of itself is notice; the registry, for example, is notice in and of itself, — the statute makes it so, and it is, therefore, absolute notice; taking a negotiable bill or note after maturity is in and of itself notice (of equities, if any exist), — the law merchant makes it so, and hence it is absolute notice. Whether there is knowledge or not in these cases is immaterial.

'Constructive notice' is a very different thing both in manifestation and in effect. It arises from facts put-

---

[1] As a matter of fact, 'actual notice' in the law of bills and notes means knowledge; but it were better to say that the plaintiff had knowledge, than that he had actual notice.

ting one upon inquiry; a person has been put upon a trail. The trail must be followed, but if followed with proper diligence, there is an end of the notice altogether, whatever the result. The notice attaches, in other words, only when the trail is not taken up and diligently followed, that is, when there is negligence. In still other words, and dropping the figure, it is a case of knowledge of a preliminary fact or set of facts which would suggest to the average man the existence of some ulterior fact of importance; the preliminary fact puts him upon inquiry concerning the probable, ulterior fact. If he does not pursue the inquiry suggested, or if he pursues it faithlessly rather than faithfully, he is fixed with notice of it; he stands as if he knew it. Thus, a man about to buy a horse hears of a fact which would suggest to a man of average intelligence that possibly another may have a lien upon the animal. Now if that man buys the horse without making any inquiry in regard to the possible lien, he will buy it with notice if any lien in fact exists; on the other hand, if he makes diligent inquiry, and his suspicion is entirely removed, he takes title free from the defect though in point of fact there was a lien.

Absolute notice, as we have seen, is part of the law of bills, notes, and cheques; and it was at one time supposed that constructive notice — by putting upon inquiry and negligence — was also part of the same law, and in some States it is to this day. For example: The plaintiff, a banker, is indorsee of a bill of exchange, accepted by the defendant, and now sued upon. The bill, indorsed in blank, was offered to the plaintiff for discount by an entire stranger to him. The plaintiff makes no inquiry of the stranger concerning his title or right to the bill, and discounts it. The stranger had found the bill, and had no right to it except as finder. The plaintiff (by some authorities) cannot recover, having constructive notice that the stranger had no right to the bill; it was the plaintiff's duty, the bill being offered by a stranger, to make inquiry, and he was guilty of negligence in failing to make it.[1]

Such was the rule as laid down in England in the year 1824, and maintained there until the year 1836, when it was overturned. The rule of 1824 was never quite satisfactory, and it was finally declared, in 1836, in effect, that this doctrine of constructive notice, by way of negligence, being a bar to the demand of a holder who had paid value, and was not otherwise affected with notice, was unsuited to the law merchant as applied to bills and notes; and the contrary was now firmly and finally laid down. Negligence only, even though gross, was and still is in England held insufficient to defeat the claim of one whose right to recover is otherwise perfect; nothing short of bad faith will suffice to subject him to the equities which the defendant seeks to set up.[2] And that has long been the prevailing rule in this country, the most of our courts which had at first accepted the earlier doctrine, having, since 1836, abandoned that doctrine for the one just stated. For example: The plaintiff is an indorsee for value of a bill of exchange now sued upon, which was purchased by him in good faith, in point of fact, and the defendant is acceptor thereof. At the trial the following instruction was given to the jury: 'If such facts and circumstances were known to the plaintiff as caused him to suspect, or would have caused one of ordinary prudence to suspect, that the drawer had no interest in the bill, and no authority to use the same for his own benefit, and by ordinary diligence he could have ascertained these facts,' the plaintiff could not recover. The instruction was erroneous; nothing short of bad faith

---

[1] Gill v. Cubitt, 3 Barn. & C. 466; Sturgis v. Metropolitan Bank, 49 Ill. 220, 227; Merritt v. Duncan, 7 Heisk 156.

[2] Goodman v. Harvey, 4 Ad. & E. 870.

would overcome the plaintiff's demand, and the plaintiff need not show the absence of bad faith.[1]

Proof of bad faith will subject the plaintiff to equities, if such exist; and bad faith may be shown, for instance, by evidence that he had *suspicion* that the prior holder's title was somehow tainted or defective, and still went forward and purchased the instrument, closing his eyes to the facts and not making inquiry.[2] To that extent the doctrine of constructive notice, a term which may cover cases of bad faith as well as of negligence, obtains in the law of bills, notes, and cheques, and to that extent only, except in the few States in which the courts still adhere to the English doctrine of 1824.

Between knowledge and *absolute* notice of *equities*, there appears to be no difference having any legal significance;[3] either, of itself, will prevent one from being, in oneself, a bona fide holder. So far as it may be helpful to distinguish between the two, one may be said to have knowledge of that which one may testify to in court directly as a fact, including that of which one cannot so testify only because of some special reason of a personal or peculiar nature (e. g., what has passed between husband and wife or in any other confidential relation creating privilege); while absolute notice may be said to

---

[1] Goodman *v.* Simonds, 20 How. 343; L. C. 415. 'Putting upon inquiry' is a term still used occasionally, from force of habit; but the cases will generally be found to be cases of absolute notice or bad faith. What settles the incorrectness of it in relation to other cases is that negligence will not defeat the claim of one to being a bona fide holder.

[2] Jones *v.* Gordon, 2 App. Cas. 216, 228.

[3] 'Notice' is often used in the sense of knowledge, in connection with equities. Goodman *v.* Simonds, 20 How. 343, L. C. 415, 428. Secus of its use in connection with dishonor, knowledge there is not the same thing as notice. Ante, p. 110.

consist: (1) In specific information received of an equity itself; (2) In some statutory declaration; or (3) In some positive doctrine of the law merchant.

A few remarks will be helpful concerning these three modes of creating absolute notice. And first in regard to information of an equity. By 'information' is meant what is heard or read (as by direct communication), as distinguished from knowledge. Now, this information must be of the actual existence of an equity; anything short of such information could only put one upon inquiry, and that, as we have seen, is not enough. Clearly it will not be enough that information is given of facts involving a possible or potential equity. For example: The plaintiffs are indorsees, and the defendants acceptors, of a bill of exchange now sued upon. When the plaintiffs took the bill they were informed that it was accepted in part payment of the price of a brig, which by the bargain was to be put in repair and made seaworthy. This agreement had been broken, but of that fact the plaintiffs had no information or knowledge. The plaintiffs are entitled to recover; they were not bound to inquire whether the agreement for repairs had been performed.[1] Again: The plaintiff is indorsee, and the defendant acceptor, of a bill of exchange sued upon. The acceptance was in consideration of a promise by the drawer, made known to the plaintiff, to send to the acceptor six hundred bushels of wheat at the opening of navigation thereafter; which promise, performable before the bill became due, was not kept. The plaintiff is entitled to recover.[2]

If, however, in either of these cases the advice had been that the property was to be sold and the proceeds applied to the payment of the vendor and in discharge of the acceptances, there would have been specific information of

---

[1] Davis v. McCready, 17 N. Y. 230; L. C. 406.
[2] Cameron v. Chappell, 24 Wend. 94.

an equity.¹ The question, indeed, whether information is specific enough, and that too even though it appears upon the instrument itself, is to be determined by the natural import of its language; if there be any ground for doubt, it is a question for construction of language; and into the case may often enter the usage of the place or business.²

In regard to the second mode, 'statutory declaration,' all that need be said is that the legislature may make the performance of any act in a public way, such as the registration of an instrument, notice of its existence and contents.

In regard to the third mode, 'positive doctrine of the law merchant,' that refers to cases in which there has been, or may have been, no information of the existence of any particular equity or of any equity at all. The one typical case, if not the only case, of the kind is the taking of a negotiable instrument after maturity; that is positive notice of any equity whatever which may then exist. The only question, then, is whether the instrument was taken *after* its maturity. One or two points may be noticed. To take an instrument entitled to grace on the last day of grace is not to take it after maturity; at least, if it was taken within business hours of that day, being paper payable at a place having established hours of business.³ On the other hand, to take a cheque long after its date has well been held as taking it with prima facie indication that it has been dishonored; that is, that it is overdue.⁴ The date of paper, however, is only presumptive evidence of the time when it was issued; it may have been delivered long afterwards (or before), and it becomes a valid undertaking only from its delivery.⁵

[1] Holmes v. Kidd, 3 Hurl. & N. 891, Ex. Ch.
[2] Goodman v. Simonds, 20 How. 343; L. C. 415, 428.
[3] Farrell v. Lovett, 68 Maine, 326; Crosby v. Grant, 36 N. H. 273.
[4] Cowing v Altman, 71 N. Y. 435.
[5] Id. See Bills of Ex. Act, 21, (1).

§ 3. Holder for Value.

The term 'holder for value,' the complement of 'bona fide holder,' means, properly speaking, a holder who has taken the paper upon a valuable consideration, and has thereby acquired the title to it.

The term 'valuable consideration' is, of course, borrowed by the law merchant from the common law, or rather has been imposed upon the law merchant,[1] and has the same meaning which it bears in the law of contract generally; though its meaning has been pushed further in the law merchant than elsewhere. The consideration must be valuable; it is not enough that it is merely 'valid,' 'good,' or 'meritorious,' so as to convey the title, as in the case of gift. All the authorities agree in that proposition. It may be, indeed, that one to whom a negotiable instrument has been given can recover upon it; but that will be because the giver, or some prior holder, had a right of action upon it, and not because the present owner is himself a holder for value.

A valuable consideration consists in some right, interest, profit, or in a word *benefit*, accruing to the one party, or some forbearance, loss, or in a word *detriment* suffered by the other.[2] It is not necessary that there should be 'quid pro quo,' or benefit of any kind, to make one a holder for value; detriment is enough. That may be shown by the case of accommodation paper, already considered; the accommodation party has no benefit, or may have none, from the transaction, but he is bound towards one who takes the paper for value; that is, who parts with something of value, and so suffers detriment for the time. That that is a doctrine of contract in general may be shown by the following illustration: If A mortgage his

---

[1] See ante, p. 4.
[2] Currie v. Nind, L. R. 10 Ex. 162.

land to B, to secure B in lending money to C, B is a purchaser for valuable consideration, though A may have no benefit at all.[1]

While, however, the authorities agree upon the definition, they do not agree in its application. The courts of this country are divided upon the question of the effect of transfers of paper for security; and that makes about the only question touching valuable consideration which calls for special remark in a work like this; most other questions of consideration can be answered, in view of what has already been said, by the law of contracts in general. The particular point of difficulty is whether the mere taking of a negotiable instrument by a creditor from his debtor, as security for or in conditional payment of a pre-existing debt, but with full title, constitutes the taker a holder for value.

Such a case seems at first one merely of so-called 'valid' consideration, operative indeed between the debtor and his creditor, so as to enable the creditor to hold the instrument against his debtor, but wanting in value, and hence failing to make the creditor a holder for value. And so not a few courts in the United States, following the lead of the courts of New York, hold. For example: The plaintiff, suing in equity, being owner of a vessel, employs the defendants, A and B, to sell her on credit, taking good notes in payment to be transmitted to him. A and B sell the vessel and take notes of the purchasers, payable to certain persons, and duly indorsed. A and B now deliver the said notes to C and D, co-defendants in the case, who are under heavy responsibility for A and B as accommodation indorsers for them of paper not yet due, which paper C and D are at a later time obliged to pay. C and D know nothing of the circumstances under which A and B

[1] Ex parte Hearne, 1 Buck, 165; Marden *v.* Babcock, 2 Met. 99; 2 Bigelow, Fraud, 444.

became possessed of the notes, and believe them to be the rightful property of A and B; and they receive the notes as security for the responsibility which they had incurred, and three days afterwards dispose of some of them for cash, before becoming aware of the plaintiffs' rights. The plaintiffs are deemed entitled to the notes or their proceeds, the defendants not having taken them for valuable consideration.[1] Again: The plaintiff, suing in trover, alleges that the defendant has converted to his own use two promissory notes. The defendant came thus by the notes: A and B, being in debt to the defendant on a certain note which they could not pay, prevail upon the defendant to withdraw it from the hands of a collecting bank by delivering to him the two notes in question as security, in fraud of the rights of the plaintiff, the owner, the defendant promising to pay the overdue note in a short time. There has been no agreement, however, to forbear suit thereon. A and B stop payment and fail, without paying their debt to the defendant; and the defendant receives payment of the two notes. The plaintiff is deemed entitled to recover, the defendant not having taken the notes for value, the debt to secure which they were taken being wholly a pre-existing debt.[2]

Between the cases which make these two examples, a question similar in effect, at least as treated by the court,

[1] Bay v. Coddington, 5 Johns. Ch. 54; affirmed, 20 Johns. 637. This is the leading case on that side of the question, a case decided by Chancellor Kent.

[2] Stalker v. McDonald, 6 Hill, 93, affirming Bay v. Coddington, on review of the intervening authorities including Swift v. Tyson, 16 Peters, 1, to the contrary. See also Comstock v. Hier, 73 N. Y. 269; Royer v. Keystone Bank, 83 Penn. St. 248; Cummings v. Boyd, Id. 372; Bardsley v. Delp, 88 Penn. St. 420; Fenouille v. Hamilton, 35 Ala. 322; Lee v. Smead, 1 Met. (Ky.) 628; May v. Quimby, 3 Bush, 96; King v. Doolittle, 1 Head, 77; Bertrand v. Barkman, 13 Ark. 150; Roxborough v. Messick, 6 Ohio St. 448; Nutter v. Stover, 48 Maine, 163.

went to the Supreme Court of the United States, and that court took the contrary view; and the decision has had a large following, larger probably than that of the courts of New York. According to the Federal Court and its following, the creditor, taking full title though only as security or conditional payment, takes for value, notwithstanding the fact that the debt for which the paper was taken was a pre-existing debt in no respect then created. For example: The plaintiff is indorsee, and the defendant acceptor, of a bill of exchange sued upon. The plaintiff took the bill before it became due, in good faith, in payment of a promissory note due to him by A and B, drawers of the bill, the plaintiff fully believing the bill to be justly due. The bill had been accepted in part payment of lands sold by A and B under false and fraudulent representations by them. The plaintiff is a holder for value, though the debt was pre-existing entirely, and being also a bona fide holder he is entitled to recover; the case being treated by the court as if the plaintiff had taken the bill to *secure* payment of the pre-existing debt.[1] Again: The plaintiffs are indorsees, and the defendant is maker, of a promissory note now sued upon. The defendant made the note, without consideration, for the accommodation of the payee. The payee delivers the note indorsed by himself to A, without consideration, for the purpose of having it discounted for the payee's benefit. Instead of procuring the note to be discounted, A pledges it to the plaintiffs as collateral security for a (smaller) pre-existing debt due by

---

[1] Swift v. Tyson, 16 Peters, 1; L. C. 486. The report of the case states that the bill was taken in 'payment,' but the majority (there was a dissenting opinion) put the case on the footing of paper taken in security of a prior debt, and treat the taking in either way as a taking for value. Of course that was not necessary to the decision of the case, but the opinion was deliberately expressed, and it has been accordingly taken as authority for the doctrine expressed.

A to them. The plaintiffs take the note without knowledge of the facts here stated. They are holders for value, and are entitled to recover to the extent of the debt due to them by A.[1]

The doctrine thus laid down is the doctrine of the courts of England and of many of the courts of this country, and it appears to be sound. It does not follow from the fact that the debt to secure which the paper was taken was wholly pre-existing, and that there was no agreement for forbearance, or other factor in the case besides the transfer of title by the debtor to the creditor, that the creditor has not taken the paper for valuable consideration. Detriment to the creditor creates a valuable consideration; and detriment arises wherever the party assumes by the transaction burdens or duties not resting upon him before, the failing to bear or perform which will result in loss or in diminution of his debt. And such is the situation in question. The creditor takes from his debtor a negotiable security; perhaps there are parties to it liable conditionally only, on the taking of certain steps. The holder takes the security upon the implied condition or undertaking to perform the duties involved, on pain, in case of failure, of losing the debt secured or having it cut down to the extent of the loss caused to his debtor by

---

[1] Fisher v. Fisher, 98 Mass. 303. See also Merchants' Ins. Co. v. Abbott, 131 Mass. 397, 400; Stevens v. Blanchard, 3 Cush. 162, 169; Le Breton v. Pierce, 2 Allen, 8, 14; Railroad Co. v. National Bank, 102 U. S. 14, 58, 59; Bank of Republic v. Carrington, 5 R. I. 515; First Nat Bank v. McAllister, 46 Mich. 397; Dyer v. Rosenthal, 45 Mich. 588, Beuerman v. Van Buren, 44 Mich. 496; Reddick v. Jones, 6 Ired. 107; Gibson v. Connor, 3 Kelly, 47; Valette v Mason, 1 Smith (Ind.), 89; Turner v. Killian, 12 Neb. 580; Currie v. Misa, L. R. 10 Ex. 153; Percival v Frampton, 2 Cromp. M. & R. 180; Peacock v. Purcell, 14 C. B. N. S. 728; Taylor v. Blakelock, 32 Ch. Div 560. So by Bills of Ex Act, 27, (1), (b). Some of these are the still stronger cases of property transferred to the creditor. See 2 Bigelow, Fraud, 459, et seq.

his own failure of duty.[1] But it does not matter whether there are parties conditionally liable or not; in any event the holder takes the security upon the implied condition or undertaking that he will exercise diligence in collecting the money out of it and applying it upon the debt, on pain, in case of failure so to act, of discharging the debt to the extent of the loss sustained. All that involves, when the collateral is taken, — and that is the moment to be considered, — indefinite detriment, the possibility of having to sue with the trouble and expense incident, among other things. That clearly makes him a holder for value.

That would not be true where the security was passed to the creditor as a mere agent or bailee; such a distinction has well been taken.[2] The debtor himself in such a case is to be considered still as the real holder, for he can withdraw the security at will; the creditor, therefore, though having the security in his hands, is not in the legal sense the holder. Hence we have put the case as security transferred by the debtor to his creditor 'with full title,' though still as security. The situation of a trustee or assignee may also be excepted; such a person, though in virtue of his office a party with full title, and bound to perform certain duties, is by the current of authority treated as standing in the position of him from whom he received the instrument. He is not a holder for value in mere virtue of his office of trustee or assignee.[3]

---

[1] Peacock v. Purcell, 14 C. B. N. s. 728.

[2] See Austin v. Curtis, 31 Vt. 64; Oates v. First Nat Bank, 100 U. S 239; Bigelow's L C. Bills and Notes, 499, 500, 503.

[3] Swan v Crafts, 124 Mass. 453; Holland v Cruft, 20 Pick 321, 338; Palmer v. Thayer, 28 Conn. 238; Loos v. Wilkinson, 110 N Y. 195; s. c. 113 N. Y 485; Putnam v. Hubbell, 42 N Y 106, 114, Farrington v. Sexton, 43 Mich. 454; Main v. Lynch, 54 Md 658; Eigenbrun v. Smith, 98 N C 207. But see Sipe v. Earman, 26 Gratt. 563, Byrne v. Becker, 49 Mo. 548; Wilson v. Eifler, 7 Cold. 31 Of course an

It is admitted, even under the New York doctrine, that the holder of paper taken as collateral security for a pre-existing debt is a holder for value against an accommodation party to the security.[1] That appears to be a concession and yielding, so far, to the other doctrine.

The ground of the doctrine that transfer to a creditor imports value stands, it will be seen, without regard to the question whether there has been any undertaking, express or implied, for forbearance by the creditor; it stands, indeed, though it be plainly understood that there is no agreement for forbearance. If, however, there be an agreement, express or implied, to forbear, the case is by so much strengthened; and all the authorities, those of New York as well as the rest, agree that the creditor in such a case is a holder for value.[2] And such an agreement is deemed to be implied in a great many cases. Whether an implication of the kind arises depends somewhat upon the question whether the instrument taken as security is for the same amount as the original debt,[3] or for a different sum, more or less. If the new security is for the same sum as the original debt, and is payable on time, there is a strong implication that the creditor agrees to forbear suit until the maturity of such security. And a like implication springs up where the new security is for a larger sum than the old debt.[4]

---

assignee or a trustee *may* be a holder for value, for he may be a creditor or he may have parted with something of special value; but in his office merely he will take subject to equities, by the better rule. See 2 Bigelow, Fraud, pp. 450–456.

[1] Grocers' Bank *v.* Penfield, 69 N. Y. 502; Maitland *v.* Citizens' Bank, 40 Md. 540.

[2] See Pratt *v.* Conan, 37 N. Y. 440; Moore *v.* Ryder, 65 N. Y. 438, 442; Burns *v.* Rowland, 40 Barb. 368; Oates *v.* First Nat. Bank, 100 U. S. 239.

[3] Michigan Bank *v.* Leavenworth, 28 Vt. 209.

[4] Atkinson *v.* Brooks, 26 Vt. 569. It should be observed that it is

It is clear, too, that if the creditor parts in any other way with any valuable right, his claim as a holder for value is still further strengthened.[1] Thus, the plaintiff is everywhere a holder for value when he has parted with the defendant's note, upon receiving from him a new note, indorsed by a third person,[2] or where the new security is transferred to the creditor upon his giving up an overdue note,[3] or where the creditor receives the new security for the repayment of a loan of money upon another instrument,[4] or where he receives it on account of the discontinuance of proceedings in execution against one of the parties to it and as security for the payment of the judgment in that case.[5]

Thus far of receiving the instrument in conditional payment of, or as collateral security for, the pre-existing debt. Some authorities have professed to make a distinction between paper taken in conditional payment, and paper taken as collateral security, treating the holder as a holder for value, if he took in the first way, but not if he took in the second;[6] but the distinction is not well taken, and has not found much favor.

It is agreed that if the creditor received the paper in absolute payment or satisfaction of the debt, he is a holder for value.[7] But so unusual are cases of that kind

agreement for forbearance which is spoken, mere forbearance does not affect the case.

[1] Weaver v. Barden, 49 N. Y. 286, 293; Youngs v. Lee, 12 N. Y. 551; Essex Bank v. Russell, 29 N. Y. 673.

[2] Youngs v. Lee, supra.

[3] Brown v. Leavitt, 31 N. Y. 113.

[4] Bank of New York v. Vanderhorst, 32 N. Y. 553

[5] Boyd v. Cummings, 17 N. Y. 101.

[6] Fletcher v. Chase, 16 N. H. 38; Rice v. Raitt, 17 N. H. 116; Nutter v. Stover, 48 Maine, 163; Austin v. Curtis, 31 Vt. 64 (overruling Atkinson v. Brooks, 26 Vt. 569, and Michigan Bank v. Leavenworth, 28 Vt. 209); Ryan v. Chew, 13 Iowa, 589.

[7] Seymour v. Wilson, 19 N. Y. 417; Weaver v. Barden, 49 N. Y. 286, 294.

that it appears to be required in some States that an express agreement should be shown to establish the fact that the paper was so taken.[1] That, however, in so far as it means an agreement formulated in terms, is contrary to the analogies of the law, and the better authorities consider that sufficient evidence of any kind, otherwise proper, that the parties meant the transfer to operate as payment, may be received.[2]

As for paper taken to secure a debt created at the same time, there can be no place ordinarily for question; the creditor is a holder for value by all the authorities.[3] So, too, where any new credit or indulgence is given upon the faith of the new paper, that paper is held for value.[4] Still even in such cases the situation will be changed if the security is not passed at the time to the credit of the creditor, but is only to be applied by him when paid, he in the meantime holding it only as agent of the debtor; for then, as we have already said, the debtor is the real holder.[5]

§ 4. Mediate and Immediate Parties.

One further remark is necessary in regard to the whole term 'bona fide holder for value.' To make a man such, as

---

[1] Brown *v.* Olmsted, 50 Cal. 162; Tobey *v.* Barber, 5 Johns. 68; James *v.* Hackley, 16 Johns 273. See Peters *v* Beverly, 16 Peters, 532, 562.

[2] Thompson *v.* Briggs, 28 N. H. 40; Smith *v.* Smith, 27 N. H. 244; Johnson *v.* Cleaves, 15 N H. 332; Jaffrey *v.* Cornish, 10 N. H. 505; Gibson *c.* Tobey, 46 N. Y 637, 642.

[3] See Stotts *v.* Byers, 17 Iowa, 303; Curtis *v.* Mohr, 18 Wis. 615; Logan *v.* Smith, 62 Mo 455.

[4] Housum *v.* Rogers, 40 Penn. St 190; Washington Bank *v.* Krum 15 Iowa, 53.

[5] See Scott *v.* Ocean Bank, 23 N. Y. 289.

regards the defendant, with the *special* rights of the position, there must have intervened between the two at least one holder. And ordinarily such a holder is an indorsee; but the payee of a bill of exchange may be a bona fide holder for value against the acceptor, for one holder, to wit, the drawer, intervenes. Where there has been no intervening holder, the plaintiff and defendant are called immediate parties, and any defence is open which would be open to an action upon any ordinary simple contract in writing; the doctrine in regard to equities has no application to such a case.

§ 5. Equities: How Shown: Their Nature.

The cardinal rule we have now reached is that a bona fide holder for value takes free from equities, or as it is sometimes expressed, purchase for value without notice cuts off equities. It makes no difference from whom the paper was taken; it may have been taken from a thief; enough that the holder took it bona fide and for valuable consideration.

The existence of equities is to be shown by the defendant and fixed upon the plaintiff, after the plaintiff has made a presumptive case; and that the plaintiff makes by producing the paper in evidence, duly indorsed when indorsement is necessary, and proving the signatures.[1] In certain cases the defendant is helped out in his case by presumption; in others he is not.

If the defendant can show that the instrument was obtained from him by fraud or by duress, or if he can show that it was tainted in the hands of the party who took it from him, with illegality, he makes out his case by

---

[1] Statute in some States dispenses with the necessity of proving signatures the genuineness of which is not expressly denied.

presumption against the plaintiff; for the law presumes on such a state of facts that the plaintiff is not the true holder, that the true holder is the man affected by the taint of fraud, duress, or illegality, and that he has merely turned the paper over to the plaintiff colorably for the purpose of suit. In other words, the law presumes that the plaintiff is at least not a holder for value; and the plaintiff is now put to his proofs to sustain his claim. For example: The plaintiff is indorsee of a promissory note made by the defendants, and now sued upon. The defendants offer to show that the payee of the note illegally arrested them, and that this note was given to procure their release from duress, upon the promise of the payee to set them at liberty, which was accordingly done. They offer no other evidence; nor does the plaintiff offer any evidence to meet it, and a verdict is taken for the defendant by consent, subject to the opinion of the court. The defendant's evidence is sufficient; proof of duress by the payee would be a good defence against him; and the presumption is that the payee, being guilty of illegal conduct, has placed the note in the hands of the plaintiff to sue upon it for him.[1] Again: The plaintiff is indorsee, and the defendants are acceptors, of a bill of exchange now sued upon. The defendants offer to prove that the bill was accepted by them in payment of intoxicating liquor sold to them by the payees in violation of statute, and offer no other evidence. The plaintiff objects to the admissibility of the evidence, and the objection is sustained, and judgment rendered for the plaintiff. The ruling against receiving the evidence offered by the defendants is wrong; the evidence is proper and is sufficient to raise a presumption that the payees have put the bill into the hands of the plaintiff to sue upon it for them.[2]

[1] Clark v. Pease, 41 N. H. 414; L. C. 507.
[2] Paton v. Coit. 5 Mich. 505; L. C. 529.

How far the plaintiff indorsee should go in the way of meeting the presumption is not quite clear. He must at least show that he took the instrument for value, and it seems that he must also give in evidence the circumstances under which he took it. If that evidence does not indicate that he took the instrument with notice of the equity, and is believed, he will then be entitled to recover. In other words, it appears not to be required of the plaintiff, in answer to the evidence of fraud, duress, or illegality, that he should give evidence directly to the purpose of showing that he took without notice.[1]

In the case of other equities, such as want or failure of consideration, proof of their existence raises no presumption against an indorsee claiming to be a bona fide holder for value.[2] The evidence would, therefore, be insufficient to meet the plaintiff's case; though his own case is only presumptive, for he has thus far given no actual evidence, other than by the production of the paper, that he is a bona fide holder for value. The defendant must accordingly go further, and give evidence either that the plaintiff took with notice of the equity in question or that he is not a holder for value.[3]

Taking paper with notice, or without valuable consideration, subjects the taker, however, only to such equities as existed at the time he took it; if none then existed, his title will be good. It is then no defence that the holder

[1] See Paton v. Coit, 5 Mich. 505; L. C. 529, 531; Sullivan v. Langley, 120 Mass. 437. Compare 2 Bigelow, Fraud, 487, and notes.

[2] A fortiori of evidence that the defendant signed for accommodation, for that is not of itself an equity. Duncan v. Gilbert, 5 Dutch. 521; Grant v. Ellicott, 7 Wend. 227; L. C. 448; Knight v. Pugh, 4 Watts & S. 445.

[3] See Paton v. Coit, supra; Clark v. Pease, 41 N. H. 414; L. C. 507.

took the paper after its maturity; the effect of so taking the paper is to subject him to existing equities, and if none exist he is entitled to recover. Negotiable paper does not lose its property of negotiability on passing its maturity.[1] An exception is made, in this country, in the case of accommodation paper; to take such paper after maturity is treated as taking it with notice of an equity, to wit, that the defendant loaned his credit only until the paper became due.[2]

It should also be observed that if the holder was a holder for value bona fide when he took the paper, he will remain such, though afterwards he may become aware of some equity which might have been set up against a prior holder. Indeed, as we have seen, it is no defence that the holder knew, when he took the paper, of the existence of an agreement between the defendant and the party next after him, under which equities have since arisen, if none such existed when the holder took the paper.[3] If, however, the holder made but part payment of the purchase price of the instrument, and before completing payment received notice of an equity, he cannot become a bona fide holder for value except in respect of his part payment.[4]

It remains to consider what is meant by equities. The answer in general is plain enough; any facts which would be a defence to an ordinary simple contract of the common law, not being what we have denominated Legal or

---

[1] Leavitt v. Putnam, 3 Comst. 494; L. C. 129.

[2] Chester v. Dorr, 41 N. Y. 279; Bower v. Hastings, 36 Penn. St. 285; Kellogg v. Barton, 12 Allen, 527. Contra, Charles v. Marden, 1 Taunt. 224; Sturtevant v. Forde, 4 Man. & G. 101; Caruthers v. West, 12 Q. B. 143; Jewell v. Parr, 13 C. B. 909; Story, Notes, § 194.

[3] Patten v. Gleason, 106 Mass. 439.

[4] Dresser v. Missouri Const. Co., 93 U. S. 92.

Absolute Defences, may be and commonly are called equities, — with one or two exceptions.

The exceptions are made by accommodation contracts of the law merchant. It is no defence to a suit upon a bill, note, or cheque, that the plaintiff took the paper with notice or even with direct knowledge that the defendant signed the same for accommodation, not doing so for the accommodation of the plaintiff; for he gave the use of his name and credit for the express purpose of enabling the party accommodated to get credit.[1] The case is as if the defendant had said to the plaintiff, 'If you will let this man have money I will see that you are paid;' the accommodation, unlike want or failure of consideration in the ordinary sense, is not an equity.

If, however, the instrument was used in violation of the terms, if any, upon which the accommodation was given, that will make a different case; a fraudulent diversion, and such use would be a fraudulent diversion, would constitute an equity, in the face of which the plaintiff could recover only upon the footing that he was a bona fide holder for value. For example: The plaintiffs are indorsees for value, and the defendant is accommodation indorser, of a promissory note now sued upon. The maker of the note was indebted to the plaintiffs, and in adjusting the debt the plaintiffs said that they would accept the defendant as surety. The defendant finally indorses the note for the accommodation of the maker upon condition that a third person, who then held a note made by the defendant, deposited that note with another to be held by him until the defendant should be discharged from the indorsement. The condition was not complied with, and the facts were known to the plaintiff when he took the note. The plaintiff is not entitled to recover.[2]

[1] Grant v. Ellicott, 7 Wend. 227; L. C. 448.
[2] Small v. Smith, 1 Denio, 583; L. C. 449.

The distinction between legal or absolute defences and equities, after what has been said in the preceding chapter, will generally be plain. One case, however, already alluded to, should be stated with clearness here. Alteration of the instrument makes an absolute defence; to fill a blank space left in a *completed* instrument being an example. But to fill a blank space in an *uncompleted* instrument, — such as a promissory note signed in blank, — which has been put into the hands of a person who betrays the signer's confidence by filling the blank and delivering the instrument in violation of instructions, is not an alteration. It is or may be a fraudulent act, but it is not criminal. It is simply a case of agency in which the principal's confidence has been abused, but the act, notwithstanding its wrongfulness, binds the principal in favor of bona fide holders for value.[1] It is only an equity.

The rule of law upon this point may be thus stated: One who writes his name as maker, acceptor, drawer, or indorser, and intrusts the paper to another to fill up the contract and make him party to a negotiable instrument, thereby confers upon the person so intrusted, in favor of bona fide holders for value, the right to complete the contract at pleasure, so far as consistent with the instrument as written or printed at the time it is delivered to the person intrusted with it.[2]

By the law merchant equities can arise only out of the transaction itself in which the defendant became a party to the paper. Statute may, indeed, enable a defendant to

---

[1] Angle *v* Northwestern Ins. Co., 92 U. S. 330.

[2] Angle *v.* Northwestern Ins Co., supra; Whitmore *v.* Nickerson, 125 Mass. 496; Greenfield Bank *v.* Stowell, 123 Mass. 196, 199, 203; Blakey *v.* Johnson, 13 Bush, 197; Sittig *v.* Birkestack, 38 Md. 158; Ledwick *v.* McKim, 53 N. Y. 307; Burson *v.* Huntington, 21 Mich 415; Van Etta *v* Evenson, 28 Wis. 33; Yocum *v.* Smith, 63 Ill. 321.

avail himself of other claims against the immediate party thereto, by way of set-off; but unless the statute go further, these will not be equities, and will not be available against a later party, even though he took the paper (for value) with knowledge of the right of set-off,[1] at least if the paper was taken by him before maturity. If it was taken after maturity, the contrary appears to be true, under some statutes.[2]

Finally an indorsee may recover in the face of equities known to him when he took the paper, and further though he took it without valuable consideration, if between him and the defendant there is one who was a bona fide holder for value. The defendant would be liable to such prior holder, and the plaintiff only stands in his place. For example: The plaintiffs are joint indorsees, and the defendant is maker, of a promissory note sued upon. There was no consideration between the original parties, and the note was not made for accommodation. One of the plaintiffs is a bona fide holder for value, the other took the note with notice of the want of consideration; but title is derived through others who were bona fide holders for value. The plaintiffs are entitled to recover.[3]

---

[1] See Whitehead v. Walker, 10 Mees. & W. 696; In re Overend, L. R. 6 Eq 344; Chandler v. Drew, 6 N. H. 469; Arnot v Woodburn, 35 Mo 99; Way v Lamb, 15 Iowa, 79.

[2] Baxter v. Little, 6 Met. 7.

[3] Hascall v. Whitmore, 19 Maine, 102; L. C. 404 See also Cromwell v Sac, 96 U. S. 51; Marion v. Clark, 94 U. S. 278; Mornyer v. Cooper, 35 Iowa, 257; Boyd v. McCann, 10 Md. 118; Prentice v Zane, 2 Gratt. 262; Bassett v. Avery, 15 Ohio St. 299; Woodworth v. Huntoon, 40 Ill. 131; Robinson v. Reynolds, 2 Q. B. 196, 211

§ 6. Amount of Recovery.

The question often arises where the holder, being a bona fide holder for value, has not paid the face value of the bill, note, or cheque, whether he is entitled to recover the face value or must be content with less, and if with less, then with how much less, assuming the existence of equities available against a prior holder. The question will depend upon the consideration whether the instrument was (1) bought outright or taken in absolute payment of debt, or (2) taken to secure or in conditional payment of debt.

If the holder took the instrument in the first of these modes, he is entitled, by the decided weight of authority, to claim the face value, though he may have paid much less for it, assuming, of course, that he is a bona fide holder for value.[1] The holder is entitled to recover the face of the instrument not only when he has bought the paper in the ordinary sense, as by discounting it, but also when he has taken it in payment of property then sold, or in the course of a barter, or has given his negotiable security for it, provided it was received in absolute payment.[2] It matters not whether the defendant's contract was entered into for actual or supposed valuable consideration or for accommodation.[3]

Some authorities, however, hold that where the plaintiff

---

[1] Fowler v. Strickland, 107 Mass. 552; Cromwell v. Sac, 96 U. S. 51; Dresser v. Missouri Ry. Co., 93 U. S. 92; Moore v. Baird, 30 Penn. St. 138; Bange v. Flint, 25 Wis. 544; Lay v. Wissman, 36 Iowa, 305; Bailey v. Smith, 14 Ohio St. 396; Jones v. Gordon, 2 App. Cas. 616, 622; In re Gomersall, L. R. 1 Ch. 137, 142.

[2] Dresser v. Missouri Ry. Co., supra; Woodruff v. Hill, 116 Mass. 310.

[3] Allaire v. Hartshorne, 1 Zabr. 665; Williams v. Smith, 2 Hill, 301; Edwards v. Jones, 2 Mees. & W. 414.

paid less than the face value, he can recover no more, against one in whose favor equities exist which would be available against a prior holder, than he or some holder before him paid for the paper.[1]

If the holder took the paper to secure or in conditional payment of a debt, precedent or then newly created, obviously his claim, between him and his debtor, cannot be greater than the amount due on the debt;[2] but it may be that the debtor himself had a claim for the full amount of the paper, notwithstanding the equities, and in that case his creditor, the holder, would be entitled to recover the face value, holding the excess above the debt in trust for the debtor.[3] But the debtor might probably stop him in claiming for anything more than the debt, as by a release to the defendant. Or it may be that some other holder might claim the face value of the instrument. In such cases the defendant owes the amount to some one, and it cannot matter to him who demands it, provided the person can give him a discharge.[4]

[1] Holcomb v. Wyckoff, 35 N. J. 35; Holman v. Hobson, 8 Humph. 127.

[2] See Park Bank v. Watson, 42 N. Y. 490.

[3] Lay v. Wissman, 36 Iowa, 305; Allaire v. Hartshorne, 1 Zabr. 665; Chicopee Bank v. Chapin, 8 Met. 40, 44.

[4] Allaire v. Hartshorne, supra.

CHAPTER XV.

DISCHARGE OF SURETY: DEALINGS WITH PRINCIPAL DEBTOR.

§ 1. Indorser as Surety.

If the doctrines of the law pertaining to the contracts of guaranty and suretyship in regard to dealings with the principal debtor were confined to those two subjects, this chapter would be unnecessary; at any rate, it would only be necessary to say that dealings with the principal debtor have the same effect upon the contract of a guarantor or a surety in contracts of the law merchant as elsewhere in the law. But those doctrines are not confined to guaranty and suretyship; they apply to indorsement as well, indorsement itself being in reality a contract of assurance, though in a sense of its own; indeed, for the purposes in question, indorsement is often called a contract of suretyship. It is obvious that each indorser is then a surety, not merely for the maker or acceptor, but also for all parties before him; all prior parties, in other words, are principal debtors in relation to any particular indorser, and so the matter must be understood in this chapter.

The fact should, therefore, be stated that dealings with the principal debtor which would have the effect to discharge a surety in the ordinary sense will have a like effect upon an indorser. The chief cases of the kind may be stated in order to a clear understanding of the matter.

§ 2. Surrender of Securities.

One of the chief rules of suretyship is that the creditor must not surrender to the principal debtor securities placed in his hands to assure performance of the contract or payment of the debt, on the ground that the surety, in virtue of a doctrine of equity called subrogation, would be entitled to such securities for the same purpose in case he should be compelled to pay, or being bound to pay should pay voluntarily. The surrender of such securities, without the surety's consent, would, therefore, be a violation of the surety's rights, and hence would discharge him. That rule applies as well in favor of an indorser in the case of dealings of the kind between the holder of the paper and any party before the indorser.

§ 3. Agreement for Time : Compositions : Reservation of Rights.

Another of the chief rules of suretyship is this: The creditor must not discharge the principal debtor, or make any binding agreement with him to extend the time of performance agreed upon in the contract with the surety, without the surety's consent, unless (in cases where he may) he plainly reserves his rights against the surety. To give such a discharge, or to make such an agreement, without the reservation of rights, would discharge the surety. That rule also applies to indorsers; binding agreements of the kind, without consent of the indorser and without a reservation of rights against him, operate as a discharge of the indorser's liability.

In regard to discharges, the rule is that a discharge of any party to a bill, note, or cheque is a discharge of all subsequent non-consenting parties, not merely where the discharge granted in favor of the earlier party is effected by payment of the paper by him, but presumptively where it arises from mere agreement to compound or release liability. Payment of the paper extinguishes it, and hence the liability of all parties to it; agreement to compound discharges the party towards the holder, and so may well be treated as a presumptive discharge of all who follow as sureties for him. For example: The defendant is second indorser, with liability once duly fixed, and the plaintiff is holder of a promissory note. The plaintiff gives a discharge, without the defendant's consent, to the first indorser of the note, by contract under seal; that party's liability also having been duly fixed. The defendant is discharged.[1]

It is true that in such a case the defendant, if compelled to pay, would have recourse over against the prior party discharged; but the practical result of such recourse in most cases would be that the party who gave the discharge would have to defend the suit, or would be liable for the amount of the judgment obtained. To hold, then, that that party cannot sue the later indorser prevents needless circuity of action.[2] Still the resulting discharge of the later party is deemed presumptive only, and the presumptive intention may in some cases be rebutted. That may be accomplished by the holder's reserving his rights, so far as he may, against the subsequent parties, as where the indorser himself is a party to the discharge granted to the earlier party. For example: The defendant is indorser with liability once fixed, and the plaintiff is holder, of a promissory note payable to A, who indorses it to the defendant, who indorses it to the plaintiff. The maker and A make a composition deed with their creditors, conveying all their estate to trustees, among them the

---

[1] Newcomb v. Raynor, 21 Wend. 108, L. C. 597.
[2] Id.

defendant, and are discharged, the deed, however, containing a proviso that 'it shall not operate in favor of or be construed to release any persons or person who may be bound' for the maker or A, 'or who may have indorsed any note or notes drawn or indorsed by' both or either of them. The defendant, being a party to the composition deed, is not discharged.[1]

A like case would be made where the discharge arises from a merely personal agreement by the holder not to sue the party in whose favor the discharge runs; for in such a case the person so agreeing would not incur any liability if *another* should sue, and hence he would not have to defend suit brought by the later party against the one discharged by agreement, nor would he be affected in any way by judgment obtained by the plaintiff in such suit. True, the party discharged might not gain much by the agreement, as would be the case where the later party, compelled to pay, should sue him upon his indorsement or other contract; but that would be his own affair, and would not affect the case. The presumptive intention to discharge the later party would be duly rebutted.[2]

It must be understood, however, that the composition deed, or other agreement of discharge, does not amount to a release in the technical sense of the common law. A release in that sense is a conveyance (by deed) of all the releasor's interest, as is shown by the English common law mode of conveying land by lease and release; and if a man has once conveyed away all his rights, there is nothing left for him to reserve. The attempted reservation

---

[1] Pannell *v.* McMechen, 4 Har. & J. 474; L. C. 598. See also Sohier *v.* Loring, 6 Cush. 537; Morse *v.* Huntington, 40 Vt. 488; Hagey *v.* Hill, 75 Penn. St. 108; Overend *v.* Oriental Corp., L. R. 7 H. L. 348.

[2] Compare Sohier *v.* Loring, supra; Kearsley *v.* Cole, 16 Mees. & W. 128.

would be repugnant to the deed, and hence would be void. If, however, the instrument, though in general form a release, can be construed an agreement not to sue, the reservation may be good.¹

In regard to indulgence, there must be a plain agreement to extend the time of payment; it is not enough that there is a delay to sue, however long, within the period of limitation, even though the indorser suffer damage by reason of the delay.² And the agreement must, of course, be valid.³ But an express agreement is not necessary, and difficulty is encountered in some cases in determining whether the facts amount to an agreement for extension. That is apt to be the case where an additional security is taken from the principal debtor without any express understanding on the point of time. The effect of such a transaction is reached in certain cases by presumption.

How the courts have treated the taking of security may be shown by a few brief statements and one or two examples. Where the holder, at maturity of the paper in question, takes a further security due thereafter, a presumption arises that it was understood that the time of payment of the paper already due was to be extended, at least where the security was, as it usually is, to be considered in satisfaction, if paid, of the paper thus secured. And the result will be that non-consenting indorsers are discharged, rights against them not having been reserved. For example: The defendant is indorser, and the plaintiff holder, of a promissory note now sued upon, upon which the usual steps to fix the indorser's liability have been taken. At the maturity of the note the holder takes from the maker a cheque on others payable six days thereafter,

---

¹ Sohier v Loring and Kearsley v. Cole, supra, explaining some of the cases.
² Allen v. Brown, 124 Mass. 77.
³ Infra, p. 237.

to be in satisfaction of the note if paid. The cheque is not paid when it comes due. The defendant is discharged from his liability on his indorsement, on the ground that presumptively the plaintiff agreed to extend the time of payment by the maker of the note for six days, and that there is nothing in the facts to overcome the presumption.[1] Again: The defendant is indorser, and the plaintiff holder, of a bill of exchange overdue, upon which the usual steps have been taken. After the bill becomes due the plaintiff takes part payment of the acceptor, and agrees to take a new acceptance from him payable at a future day for the rest, meantime keeping the bill in suit as security. This is presumptively an agreement to give time, and there being no evidence to rebut the presumption the defendant is discharged.[2]

As we have seen in the preceding chapter, the presumption appears to arise, if the collateral taken is due at a time subsequent to that of the paper so secured, whether the amount due in the collateral is as great as, or greater than, that of the paper secured. But the presumption is probably stronger where the amount is the same.[3] Where the sum payable in the collateral is less than in the other, or where the new security is of a different character, as where the holder takes a mortgage for the payment of the sum thereafter, it is doubtful if any presumption for extension of time of the note or bill arises.[4] So where the new security is not given in place or on account of the paper in suit, but as a mere pledge, the title being retained by the

---

[1] Okie v. Spencer, 2 Whart. 253; L. C. 584.

[2] Gould v. Robson, 8 East, 576. The later case of Pring v. Clarkson, 1 B. & C. 14, apparently contra, was not well decided, and has generally been repudiated. See Kendrick v. Lomax, 2 Cromp. & J. 405; Okie v. Spencer, supra.

[3] See Michigan Bank v. Leavenworth, 28 Vt. 209; Atkinson v. Brooks, 26 Vt. 569.

[4] See United States v. Hodge, 6 How. 279.

debtor, so that the creditor in taking the security is a mere trustee or agent of the debtor for collecting it and applying the money on the note or bill in suit, the presumption, it seems, does not arise.[1]

Again, it is not enough that there is an agreement for extension of time (or for discharge); the agreement must, as has already been stated, have been valid, in order to work a discharge of the indorser. For example: The defendant is indorser and the plaintiffs are holders of a bill of exchange, the steps for fixing liability having been duly taken. Afterwards one of the plaintiffs applies to the drawer of the bill for payment, and threatens to sue immediately if an arrangement is not made to pay the bill. The drawer then proposes to the plaintiff that if the plaintiff will indulge him four or five weeks, he himself will certainly pay the bill. The plaintiff agrees, and does not inform the defendant, but the drawer does not pay the bill, though the time of indulgence has passed. The defendant is not discharged, the agreement being without consideration.[2]

Indeed it seems that the indorser is not discharged by an agreement for delay, though the agreement is valid, if still the indorser could not have had recourse against the party to whom the indulgence was given, for between those two the situation is not one of principal and surety. Such would be the case where the party granted indulgence was a bankrupt in law at the time. For example: The defendant is indorser, and the plaintiff holder, of a promissory note, steps being duly taken. At the maturity of the note the plaintiff enters into a valid, binding agreement with the maker, then a discharged bankrupt, without the defendant's knowledge, by which the plaintiff agrees not to sue the maker for two months. The defendant is not dis-

---

[1] Austin v. Curtis, 31 Vt. 64.
[2] McLemore v. Powell, 12 Wheat. 554; L. C. 589.

charged, because the indulgence could not prejudice him, the defendant having no recourse under the bankruptcy laws against the maker.[1]

Where the agreement, of whatever nature, made with the principal debtor is in writing, as usually it is, the reservation of rights must be in writing also, by reason of the rule which excludes parol evidence to vary a written contract.[2] There appears to be no reason, however, why the whole agreement for discharge or giving time, together with the reservation of rights, where permissible, may not be oral.

There can be no reservation of rights either in the cases already referred to, where there has been a payment, or where the party attempting to reserve would be liable over to the party discharged or indulged if that one were sued by the later party; or in any case in which the rights of the indorser might be prejudiced if he were to be held as still liable. A case of the kind would occur where the holder surrendered securities to which the indorser would be entitled on payment, a case already referred to.[3]

§ 4. Request to Sue.

Another important rule of suretyship prevails in many States, but not in all, to wit, that the surety may request the creditor, when the time of performance comes on, to bring suit; failing to heed which request will have the effect to discharge the surety to the extent of any detriment he might thereby sustain, as where there was property of the debtor within reach at the time, which afterwards disappeared. That rule, it seems, applies to

---

[1] Tiernan v Woodruff, 5 McLean, 350; L. C. 593.
[2] Hagey v. Hill, 75 Penn. St. 108.
[3] Id.; Mayhew v. Boyd, 5 Md. 102.

indorsers; that is, an indorser whose liability has been fixed, or who had waived the taking of the usual steps, may, where the rule just stated prevails, require the holder to sue any prior party bound to pay, on pain of discharging such indorser to the extent of any loss he may sustain by failing to sue as requested.

§ 5. Accommodation Contracts.

The foregoing doctrines govern not only indorsement, but all other engagements which are on their face, or are known to be, secondary, such as accommodation undertakings. For example: The defendant is one of two joint makers of a promissory note, having joined for accommodation, of which fact the plaintiff, holder of the note, was aware when he took it. Without the defendant's consent he has made a binding agreement with the principal joint maker for an extension of time. The defendant is discharged.[1]

Formerly, indeed, the situation of an accommodation party to a note, bill, or cheque was likened in general to that of an ordinary surety. But the later authorities show that the likeness is not general; they declare that an accommodation acceptor or maker will not be discharged by any agreement, however valid, to extend the time of payment or to give a discharge from liability to the party for whom the accommodation was given, where that party is liable under a distinct and different kind of contract, such as an indorsement. It makes no difference that the agreement was made with knowledge of the accommodation, at least if the holder had no notice of the fact when he took the paper. For example: The defendant accepts a bill of exchange for the accommodation of the

---

[1] Barron v. Cady, 40 Mich. 259.

drawer, and the plaintiff becomes holder of the bill in due course, for value, and without notice of the accommodation. Afterwards he is informed of the nature of the acceptance, and later still enters into a valid agreement not to sue the drawer, discharging him from liability. That does not discharge the defendant.[1]

That proceeds upon the ground that the holder is entitled to treat the parties as liable according to the contract which they have actually made. The plaintiff, in such a case as that of the example, has presumably bought the paper in reliance upon the contracts as they appear thereon, and that has given to him a right which cannot be taken away without his consent. Consent he has not given. Indeed the case would appear to be the same in principle, though he had had knowledge of the accommodation when he bought the paper, for it would still be presumable that he bought it relying upon the several contracts as they stand on the paper. And so the modern authorities hold.[2]

§ 6. Agreement for Time with Stranger.

An agreement for time or the like, if made with one not a party to the paper, and not with the person in whose favor it is made, would not in any case, it is held, have the effect to discharge later parties. The holder has, indeed, in such a case bound himself not to sue the particular party; but that party could not enforce the agreement or set it up in bar of an action against him.[3]

---

[1] Farmers' Bank v. Rathbone, 26 Vt. 19, L. C. 622. See note, p. 158

[2] Id.; Fentum v. Pocock, 5 Taunt. 192 (overruling Laxton v Peat, 2 Camp. 185, and Collott v. Haigh, 3 Camp. 281); Price v. Edmonds, 10 B. & C. 578, 584, Nichols v. Norris, 3 B. & Ad. 41; Harrison v. Courtauld, Id. 36; 3 Kent, 104.

[3] Frazer v. Jordan, 8 El. & B. 303.

§ 7. Ground of Doctrine.

The doctrines above presented do not rest upon the ground that there was any agreement, express or implied, in the original contract, whereby the indorser or other party was to be discharged, in case the holder should do any of the things mentioned. They rest upon grounds of equity or of statute, or, it may be, in some instances of special though doubtful views of the common law. And, let it be repeated, they apply in favor of all persons secondarily liable, within the limitations stated.

CHAPTER XVI.

PAYMENT.

§ 1. General Rule: Presumptive Payment: Surrender.

Payment and surrender of a negotiable bill of exchange, promissory note, or cheque, made at the right time, to the right person, by the right person, will extinguish the liability of all parties to the instrument. Payment of an unnegotiable bill, note, or cheque made at any time, and proper in other respects, has the same effect. It will not be necessary to say anything more on the subject in regard to unnegotiable instruments.

Payment may, in certain cases, be shown by prima facie presumption. Thus, possession of paper after maturity raises a presumption of the kind, especially if the paper is then found in the hands of the maker or acceptor, or even of the drawee of a bill who had not accepted it.[1] But the presumption, being prima facie, may be rebutted. Indeed the drawee of a bill of exchange or a cheque may prove to be the holder of it, and as such entitled to maintain an action upon it; for, instead of accepting, he may have discounted the bill. For example: The plaintiffs, being drawees of a bill of exchange now sued upon, and bearing the indorsement of the defendants, *discount* it in favor of the payees (defendants) before it becomes due, not being bound to accept it. At its maturity the drawer has

---

[1] McGee *v.* Prouty, 9 Met. 547; Eckert *v.* Cameron, 43 Penn. St. 122.

no funds in their hands, the bill is dishonored, and the usual steps are taken to fix the liability of the defendants. The plaintiffs are entitled to recover; their act of discounting the bill being proper, and not amounting to a payment of it.[1]

Unexplained, however, an act of that kind would be treated in some States as payment, and would consequently extinguish the liability of all the parties; though, as will be noticed, the case put is one of possession obtained *before* maturity. It is considered, where that rule obtains, that the paper must have been in the hands of the party, in the ordinary course of business, either for acceptance or after payment.[2] Hence, until the transaction was explained, neither such drawee nor any subsequent holder with notice could sue upon it. The like rule would apply to the maker of a note or the acceptor of a bill. But that view is repudiated in other States, and the position taken that, though the party primarily liable, for example, the maker of a note, offers the paper indorsed for discount, there is no presumption, from the fact that the paper is in his hands, that it has been paid. The proper inference, it is thought, is that the paper was indorsed for the accommodation of the one offering it, and was left in his hands to enable him to raise money by it; at any rate there would be nothing to fix upon the purchaser notice of payment.[3] And that appears to be the true view.

While the paper remains in the hands of the maker or acceptor, however, such party cannot sue upon it obviously; for if he were to recover on the footing of an indorsee suing an indorser, the latter could at once maintain an action against him in turn as maker or

---

[1] Swope *v.* Ross, 40 Penn. St. 186; L. C. 618.

[2] Central Bank *v.* Hammett, 50 N. Y. 158. But see Witte *v.* Williams, 8 Rich. N. S. 290, 305.

[3] Eckert *v.* Cameron, 43 Penn. St. 120; Witte *v.* Williams, supra; Morley *v.* Culverwell, 7 Mees. & W. 174; Harmer *v.* Steele, 4 Ex. 1.

acceptor. But the drawee of a bill, not having accepted, is not in such a position; *he* might either transfer the paper, or, as we have seen, sue upon it, after having duly discounted it. The distinction then should be noticed between the purchase of paper and the payment of it.

In certain cases it appears to be necessary that the payment should be accompanied or directly followed by surrender of the instrument, even in cases in which there could be no danger from a further transfer. That is, even though payment has been made at or after maturity; it appears to be necessary sometimes that the maker or acceptor should actually take up the paper; only by so doing is he acting 'in due course,' or according to the law merchant. Such action is treated as necessary where payment is made, at whatever time, to one who, having an apparent title, is not in fact the true owner, or authorized to act for the true owner.

If in such a case as that payment is made in good faith at or after maturity, and the instrument is surrendered accordingly, the party paying, that is, the maker or acceptor, will be discharged, and with him all other parties to the instrument. That proceeds upon the ground that, the instrument being payable to bearer originally, or afterwards indorsed in blank, any one in possession of it is presumptively the owner; but as it is possible that the person in possession may have no right to the instrument, the party paying should require the paper to be delivered up to him as the final assurance of his discharge. If he should fail to do so, taking instead, for instance, a receipt for the money, with an undertaking for the return of the instrument thereafter, the true owner, any time before such return, could enforce another payment.[1]

---

[1] Upon this whole subject see Wheeler *v.* Guild, 20 Pick. 545; L. C. 609. In that case the payment was made *before* maturity, and the deci-

§ 2. At the Right Time.

Payment then, in and of itself, operates to discharge all parties only when made at the right time, which means at or after maturity. Payment may indeed be made before maturity, and will operate as a discharge against all who have notice of the fact; or if the paper is taken up, as it should be, and destroyed, or not afterwards put into circulation again, payment before maturity will operate as a discharge. But the paper, if not taken up, may be put into circulation again after such payment, and then if it should fall into the hands of a bona fide holder for value *his* claim would not be affected by the payment.[1] This supposes that payment is made to the real owner of the paper, or to one authorized to receive it for him.

sion, therefore, is not in strictness an authority in respect of payment made at or after maturity. There may then be some doubt upon the point. But the language of the court is intended to cover both cases. 'If a bill,' said Shaw, C. J., ' be paid at maturity, in full, by the acceptor, or other party liable, to a person having a legal title in himself by indorsement, and having the custody and possession of the bill ready to surrender, and the party paying has no notice of any defect of title or authority to receive, the payment will be good. But in both cases faith is given to the holder mainly on the ground of his possession of the bill ready to be surrendered or delivered, and the actual surrender and delivery of it upon the payment or transfer. If, therefore, upon such payment the holder has not the actual possession of the bill ready to be delivered, and does not in fact surrender it, but gives a receipt or other evidence of the payment, and if it turns out that the party thus receiving had not a good right and lawful authority to receive and collect the money, but that another person had such right, the payment will not discharge the party paying, but will be in his own wrong; he must pay the bill again to the right owner, and must seek his redress against the party receiving his money. . . .'

[1] See Wheeler *v.* Guild, 20 Pick. 545; L. C. 609.

§ 3. To the Right Person.

In the next place, the payment, to be effectual against another demand, must be made to the right person. All that that means, however, is that, if it is in other respects according to law, it should be made to one apparently entitled to receive the money, not that it must be made to the true owner. It may be that the person receiving the money is not entitled to it; he may even have stolen the instrument; that will be the misfortune of the owner, and he must lose his money, provided that the payment is made, in good faith, at or after maturity, and is accompanied by a surrender of the paper, as we have seen.[1] But if the maker, acceptor, or drawee has notice that the person calling for payment is not entitled to receive it, he will pay at his peril. Payment made to the true owner, at or after maturity, extinguishes all liability without any surrender of the instrument.

§ 4. By the Right Person.

Lastly, payment must be made by the right person, or on the right person's behalf. The meaning of the statement is, that it should be made by, or on behalf of, him who is primarily, or in another sense ultimately, bound to pay and take up the paper. Hence 'payment,' so-called, by the drawer of a bill, or by an indorser, to obtain his own discharge, is not payment at all, in the proper sense of extinguishing the paper, unless it is further made on behalf of the maker, acceptor, or drawee. Thus an acceptor sued for payment cannot set up, by way either of full or of partial defence, that payment, of what-

---

[1] Wheeler v. Guild, supra.

ever amount, has been made by the drawer, unless he can further show that the payment was made in satisfaction and extinguishment of the bill.[1] To discharge the drawer or any other party is not to discharge the acceptor.

That, however, supposes that the acceptance was not for the drawer's accommodation. An accommodation party is not the one ultimately bound to take up the paper; the party accommodated must do that. Hence an acceptor (or maker) for accommodation could set up payment made by the party accommodated, whether it was made professedly on behalf of the accommodation party or not.[2] That proceeds upon the ground that the accommodation party is only a surety for the party for whose accommodation he signed, and that payment by the principal debtor is payment by the surety and all others concerned.

If the whole sum due was paid by the party accommodated, it matters not, according to English authority,[3] whether the holder had notice of his relation to the maker or acceptor or not; not more than nominal damages at any rate could, thereafter, be recovered against such party. If, however, the accommodated party made but part payment of the sum due, the rest could be recovered in any case against the maker or acceptor, assuming that such payment was not made in satisfaction and discharge of the paper.[4]

Payment in such cases, it should be added, includes release from liability. Thus, to release the drawer of a bill for whose accommodation it had been accepted would release the

---

[1] Jones *v.* Broadhurst, 9 C. B. 173; Randall *v.* Moon, 12 C. B. 261.

[2] Cook *v.* Lister, 13 C. B. N. S. 543.

[3] Id. But see Farmers' Bank *v.* Rathbone, 26 Vt. 19; L. C. 622; Ante, pp. 158, 229, 230.

[4] Id.; Thornton *v.* Maynard, L. R. 10 C. P. 695. Further see Bigelow's L. C. Bills and Notes, 664, et seq.

acceptor; absolutely, if it was made on behalf of the acceptor or for the purpose of extinguishing the bill, or to the extent of the sum paid for the release, if it was not, and the holder had notice of the accommodation.[1]

[1] See Farmers' Bank v. Rathbone, 26 Vt. 19; L. C. 622.

CHAPTER XVII.

CONFLICT OF LAWS.

§ 1. General Doctrine.

Questions of the conflicting laws of different States and countries are common enough to require attention in a concluding chapter of this book. Such questions relate to the liability (1) of maker or acceptor, (2) of drawer or indorser; and they will be considered in that order.

There is, however, a general doctrine of the conflict of law, applicable in one way or another to all the contracts of paper of the law merchant, which may be thus stated: If the contract is good by the law which the parties had in contemplation in entering into the particular contract, it is, generally speaking, good everywhere; if not good by such law, it is not good anywhere. It should be understood, at the same time, that that is a very modern way of stating the general doctrine, a way reached only after much doubt and tentative effort. The student must, therefore, expect to find statements of the law, in the older books and possibly now and then in the more recent ones, at variance. It has been common in the past to say that the law which governs is the lex loci contractus; but that the law of the place where the contract was made, or where it is to be performed, does not always prevail is now well settled. That, in reality, is the meaning in part of the separation of the subject into the two branches above designated; different rules prevail, by the better authorities, in regard to questions of liability of parties primarily liable and of parties secondarily liable.

§ 2. Maker or Acceptor.

First, then, of the conflict of laws touching the liability of maker or acceptor.

Let us in the first place suppose that a promissory note is made and indorsed abroad, or in some other State than that in which the holder and plaintiff resides and sues. Now the plaintiff, in order to recover, must of course show that he holds the paper by a valid title or right, and supposing that the laws of the two States or countries differ in what is required to make a good title in the holder, the question will be, what law governs, the domestic law or the foreign. The answer in this case is, the law of the State or country in which the indorsement was made; if it was not good by that law, though it would be good by the domestic law, the plaintiff will not be entitled to recover.[1]

In the next place, let us suppose that a promissory note was made in the State or country of the holder and of the forum, and that it is payable there, but that it has been indorsed abroad, there being the same conflict of laws as that last mentioned. Now, the title of the plaintiff, according to recent and well-considered authority, will depend upon the question whether the indorsement would pass a title by the *domestic* law.[2] That law must naturally have been the one contemplated by the parties; there is nothing on the face of such an instrument to indicate that the parties contemplated that it might come under the operation of foreign law; it is made and payable at home.

---

[1] Trimbey *v.* Vignier, 1 Bing. N. C. 151. Long after this case was decided it was found out that the foreign law had been mistaken. Bradlaugh *v.* De Rin, L. C. 3 C. P. 538; s. c. 5 C. P. 473. But the principle applied was correct.

[2] Lebel *v.* Tucker, L. R. 3 Q. B. 77.

The fact that it happens to be in circulation in a foreign State cannot affect the question of the plaintiff's title.[1]

Suppose in the next place that the note is made abroad, that it is payable in the State of the holder, and that it is indorsed by the payee abroad. In that case it is plain that the parties contemplated that the note would be indorsed abroad, where it was made; and hence the holder must have acquired title by the foreign law. Here, in principle then, the law of the place of contract governs.

Next, let it be supposed that the subject of litigation is a bill of exchange, that the bill was drawn abroad, accepted and payable in the State of the holder, and then indorsed where drawn. That makes a somewhat more complex question, and to solve it correctly this fact must be remembered, that the liability of the drawer and that of the acceptor go hand in hand; if the drawer cannot be made liable, the acceptor could not on payment charge the sum against him. The question then should be, whether the drawer is liable by the indorsement, or rather whether the holder has acquired a title which is good against the drawer of the bill; and that question, it is clear, must be decided by the law of the State or country in which the bill was drawn, unless it appears that the law of some other country was contemplated. There is nothing to indicate that any foreign law was in mind. The bill will probably be indorsed where it is drawn; hence the law of the State or country, in regard to the validity of the indorsement will govern in the suit against the acceptor.[2]

In regard to questions of interest, usury, and damages, in an action against the maker or the acceptor, the law of the State or country in which the note or bill is payable governs, unless there is indication that some other law

---

[1] Lebel v. Tucker, L. R. 3 Q. B. 77, Lush, J.
[2] Bradlaugh v. De Rin, supra.

was contemplated.[1] The mere fact then that the contract would, for example, be usurious by the law of the State in which it was made, would not necessarily require the courts, even of that State, to treat it as usurious; the question would everywhere be whether it was usurious by the law of the State in which it was made payable. However, if it should turn out that the making the instrument payable in some other State than that in which it was made was a mere subterfuge of the parties, to evade the usury laws of their own State, the contract would be treated as usurious.[2] And it has been held that the same would be true in case such contracts were declared absolutely void by the laws of the State in which they were made.[3]

§ 3. Drawer or Indorser.

Next, of the conflict of laws touching the liability of drawer or indorser.

In regard to presentment and demand, the law of the place of performance governs the question of time;[4] and that because the drawer and the indorsers are sureties, in a broad sense, for the acceptor and the maker. But

---

[1] Railroad Co. v. Ashland, 12 Wall. 226; Dickinson v. Edwards, 77 N. Y. 573; Hibernia Bank v. Lacombe, 84 N. Y. 367, 377; Hunt v. Hall, 37 Ala. 702. In Massachusetts, non-stipulated interest and damages are treated as matters of the remedy, and are accordingly governed by the law of the place of suit, the lex fori. Ayer v. Tilden, 15 Gray, 178. But that is plainly wrong. Ex parte Heidelback, 2 Lowell, 526.

[2] Story, Confl. Laws, pp. 442, 443, 8th ed.

[3] Akers v. Demond, 103 Mass. 318.

[4] Aymar v. Sheldon, 12 Wend. 439; Chatham Bank v. Allison, 15 Iowa, 357; Rouquette v. Overmann, L. R. 10 Q. B. 525. But see Hatcher v. McMorine, 4 Dev. 122, 124.

whether presentment and demand are necessary, in the absence of waiver, and whether the steps taken, if taken at the right time, were properly taken, the law of the place of indorsement governs.[1]

In regard to protest and notice, the place of the drawing or the indorsement furnishes the governing law upon a question of the necessity of these steps; while the law of the place of payment probably governs upon a question of the mode and time of taking them. Thus, in regard to the first of these questions, suppose a bill of exchange payable after date, drawn in Pennsylvania to the order of a citizen of New York, payable in the latter State, and indorsed by the payee, were dishonored on presentment for *acceptance*. In such a case it would not be necessary to notify the drawer, and it would be useless to do so, because of the local law of Pennsylvania;[2] while the contrary would be true in regard to the payee-indorser, residing in New York, because of the general law merchant. In regard to the second question it will be enough to say, for instance, that if a deputy of a notary public were authorized to act by the law of the place of payment, he might so act, though it should appear that by the law of the place of indorsement the notary must act in person; and if by the law of the place of payment four days of grace were allowed, presentment must be made on the fourth day, to be followed by the other steps accordingly, whatever the law of the place of indorsement, for the liability of the drawer and indorsers depends upon that of the acceptor or maker. But the time when notice of dis-

---

[1] Aymar *v.* Sheldon, supra; Allen *v.* Merchants' Bank, 22 Wend. 215; Thorp *v.* Craig, 10 Iowa, 461; Short *v.* Trabue, 4 Met. (Ky.) 299; Hunt *v.* Standart, 15 Ind. 33 (overruling Shanklin *v.* Cooper, 8 Blackf. 41); Huse *v.* Hamblin, 29 Iowa, 501. But see Dunn *v.* Adams, 1 Ala. 527, as to protest and quære.

[2] Read *v.* Adams, 6 Serg. & R. 356. See also Horne *v.* Rouquette, 3 Q. B. Div. 514.

honor should be given or sent is governed, it seems, by the law of the place of indorsement.[1]

Where indorsement is made in a State or a country in which the law merchant has been changed or does not prevail, the question of the liability of the indorser, otherwise than as above considered, will be governed by the law of such State or country. Thus, in some States indorsers are not liable merely upon the taking of the steps required by the law merchant; the holder must first bring suit against the maker or acceptor, and endeavor to obtain payment from him, unless such suit would be useless. The law of the place of indorsement would govern in such cases.[2]

In regard to the amount recoverable from a drawer or an indorser, the fact that they are looked upon as sureties of the acceptor or maker indicates the extent of their liability and the governing law. The surety is liable for the sum which the principal debtor fails to pay, no more and no less; and hence, in principle and by the weight of authority, the governing law is the law of the place governing the contract of the acceptor or maker.[3] The statement and rulings sometimes made that the law of the place of indorsement governs in such a case is believed to be incorrect.[4] Payment by the principal debtor, that is,

---

[1] Horne v. Rouquette, 3 Q. B. Div. 514, casting doubt upon Rothschild v. Currie, 1 Q. B. 43, 49, a case much cited.

[2] Williams v. Wade, 1 Met. 82; Short v. Trabue, 4 Met. (Ky.) 299; Trabue v. Short, 18 La. An. 257; Trabue v. Short, 5 Cold. 293; Dundas v. Bowler, 3 McLean, 397, 400. But see Coffman v. Bank of Kentucky, 41 Miss. 212.

[3] Jewell v. Wright, 30 N. Y. 259; Dickinson v. Edwards, 77 N. Y. 573. See Rouquette v. Overmann, L. R. 10 Q. B. 525; Wayne Bank v. Low, 81 N. Y. 566, 570; Hildreth v. Shepard, 55 Barb. 269. Several cases contra in New York have been overruled.

[4] There are several such decisions, mostly however by intermediate courts. They are founded more or less upon Gibbs v. Fremont, 9 Ex.

of the sum due by the law governing his own contract, will always discharge the surety.

25, Allen *v.* Kemble, 6 Moore, P. C. 314, 321, and Cooper *v.* Waldegrave, 2 Beav. 282, 285. Concerning the last named case see the remarks of Cockburn, C. J., in Rouquette *v.* Overmann, supra. And further see Story, Confl. Laws, pp. 442, 443, note, 8th ed.; Bills of Ex. Act, 72.

CHAPTER XVIII.

ENGLISH BILLS OF EXCHANGE ACT.

An Act to codify the law relating to Bills of Exchange, Cheques, and Promissory Notes. (18th August, 1882.)[1]

Part I.

PRELIMINARY.

1. This Act may be cited as the Bills of Exchange Act, 1882.

2. In this Act, unless the context otherwise requires:

'Acceptance' means an acceptance completed by delivery or notification.

'Action' includes counterclaim and set-off.

'Banker' includes a body of persons whether incorporated or not, who carry on the business of banking.

'Bankrupt' includes any person whose estate is vested in a trustee or assignee under the law for the time being in force relating to bankruptcy.

'Bearer' means the person in possession of a bill or note which is payable to bearer.

'Bill' means bill of exchange, and 'note' means promissory note.

'Delivery' means transfer of possession, actual or constructive, from one person to another.

---

[1] 45 & 46 Vict. c. 61.

'Holder' means the payee or indorsee of a bill or note who is in possession of it, or the bearer thereof.

'Indorsement' means an indorsement completed by delivery.

'Issue' means the first delivery of a bill or note, complete in form, to a person who takes it as a holder.

'Person' includes a body of persons whether incorporated or not.

'Value' means valuable consideration.

'Written' includes printed, and 'writing' includes print.

Part II.

Bills of Exchange.

Form and Interpretation.[1]

3. (1) A bill of exchange is an unconditional order in writing, addressed by one person to another, signed by the person giving it, requiring the person to whom it is addressed to pay on demand or at a fixed or determinable future time a sum certain in money to or to the order of a specified person, or to bearer.

(2) An instrument which does not comply with these conditions, or which orders any act to be done in addition to the payment of money, is not a bill of exchange.

(3) An order to pay out of a particular fund is not unconditional within the meaning of this section;[2] but an unqualified order to pay, coupled with (*a*) an indication of a particular fund out of which the drawee is to re-imburse himself, or a particular account to be debited with the amount, or (*b*) a statement of the transaction which gives rise to the bill, is unconditional.[3]

---

[1] Compare Chaps. I., II.   [2] Ante, p. 19.
[3] Ante, p. 20.

(4) A bill is not invalid by reason:—

(*a*) That it is not dated;

(*b*) That it does not specify the value given, or that any value has been given therefor;

(*c*) That it does not specify the place where it is drawn or the place where it is payable.

4. (1) An inland bill is a bill which is or on the face of it purports to be (*a*) both drawn and payable within the British Islands, or (*b*) drawn within the British Islands upon some person resident therein. Any other bill is a foreign bill.

For the purposes of this Act 'British Islands' mean any part of the United Kingdom of Great Britain and Ireland, the islands of Man, Guernsey, Jersey, Alderney, and Sark, and the islands adjacent to any of them being part of the dominions of Her Majesty.

(2) Unless the contrary appear on the face of the bill, the holder may treat it as an inland bill.

5. (1) A bill may be drawn payable to, or to the order of, the drawer; or it may be drawn payable to, or to the order of, the drawee.

(2) Where in a bill drawer and drawee are the same person, or where the drawee is a fictitious person or a person not having capacity to contract, the holder may treat the instrument, at his option, either as a bill of exchange or as a promissory note.

6. (1) The drawee must be named or otherwise indicated in a bill with reasonable certainty.

(2) A bill may be addressed to two or more drawees whether they are partners or not, but an order addressed to two drawees in the alternative, or to two or more drawees in succession, is not a bill of exchange.

7.[1] (1) Where a bill is not payable to bearer, the payee must be named or otherwise indicated therein with reasonable certainty.

(2) A bill may be made payable to two or more payees jointly, or it may be made payable in the alternative to one of two, or one or some of several payees. A bill may also be made payable to the holder of an office for the time being.

(3) Where the payee is a fictitious or non-existing person the bill may be treated as payable to bearer.

8. (1) When a bill contains words prohibiting transfer, or indicating an intention that it should not be transferable, it is valid as between the parties thereto, but is not negotiable.

(2) A negotiable bill may be payable either to order or to bearer.

(3) A bill is payable to bearer which is expressed to be so payable, or on which the only or last indorsement is an indorsement in blank.

(4) A bill is payable to order which is expressed to be so payable, or which is expressed to be payable to a particular person, and does not contain words prohibiting transfer or indicating an intention that it should not be transferable.

(5) Where a bill, either originally or by indorsement, is expressed to be payable to the order of a specified person, and to him or his order, it is nevertheless payable to him or his order at his option.

9. (1) The sum payable by a bill is a sum certain within the meaning of this Act, although it is required to be paid,[2]—

(a) With interest.

---

[1] Ante, pp. 13, 14.   [2] Ante, pp. 16-19.

(b) By stated instalments.

(c) By stated instalments, with a provision that upon default in payment of any instalment the whole shall become due.

(d) According to an indicated rate of exchange, or according to a rate of exchange to be ascertained as directed by the bill.

(2) Where the sum payable is expressed in words and also in figures, and there is a discrepancy between the two, the sum denoted by the words is the amount payable.

(3) Where a bill is expressed to be payable with interest, unless the instrument otherwise provides, interest runs from the date of the bill, and if the bill is undated, from the issue thereof.

10. (1) A bill is payable on demand, —

(a) Which is expressed to be payable on demand, or at sight,[1] or on presentation; or,

(b) In which no time for payment is expressed.

(2) Where a bill is accepted or indorsed when it is overdue, it shall, as regards the acceptor who so accepts, or any indorser who so indorses it, be deemed a bill payable on demand.[2]

11. A bill is payable at a determinable future time within the meaning of this Act which is expressed to be payable, —

(1) At a fixed period after date or sight.

(2) On or at a fixed period after the occurrence of a specified event which is certain to happen, though the time of happening may be uncertain.

An instrument expressed to be payable on a contingency is not a bill, and the happening of the event does not cure the defect.[3]

---

[1] Compare ante, p. 90.   [2] Ante, pp. 91, 92.
[3] Ante, pp. 19, 20.

12. Where a bill expressed to be payable at a fixed period after date is issued undated, or where the acceptance of a bill payable at a fixed period after sight is undated, any holder may insert therein the true date of issue or acceptance, and the bill shall be payable accordingly.

Provided that (1) where the holder in good faith and by mistake inserts a wrong date, and (2) in every case where a wrong date is inserted, if the bill subsequently comes into the hands of a holder in due course, the bill shall not be avoided thereby, but shall operate and be payable as if the date so inserted had been the true date.

13. (1) Where a bill or an acceptance or any indorsement on a bill is dated, the date shall, unless the contrary be proved, be deemed to be the true date of the drawing, acceptance, or indorsement, as the case may be.

(2) A bill is not invalid by reason only that it is antedated or post-dated, or that it bears date on a Sunday.

14. Where a bill is not payable on demand, the day on which it falls due is determined as follows:[1]—

(1) Three days, called days of grace, are, in every case where the bill itself does not otherwise provide, added to the time of payment as fixed by the bill, and the bill is due and payable on the last day of grace: Provided that—

(*a*) When the last day of grace falls on Sunday, Christmas Day, Good Friday, or a day appointed by Royal proclamation as a public fast or thanksgiving day, the bill is, except in the case hereinafter provided for, due and payable on the preceding business day.

(*b*) When the last day of grace is a bank holiday (other than Christmas Day or Good Friday) under the Bank Holidays Act, 1871, and Acts amending or extending it,

---

[1] Ante, pp. 92–94.

or when the last day of grace is a Sunday and the second day of grace is a Bank Holiday, the bill is due and payable on the succeeding business day.

(2) Where a bill is payable at a fixed period after date, after sight, or after the happening of a specified event, the time of payment is determined by excluding the day from which the time is to begin to run, and by including the day of payment.

(3) Where a bill is payable at a fixed period after sight, the time begins to run from the date of the acceptance, if the bill be accepted, and from the date of noting or protest, if the bill be noted or protested for non-acceptance, or for non-delivery.

(4) The term 'month' in a bill means calendar month.

15. The drawer of a bill and any indorser may insert therein the name of a person to whom the holder may resort in case of need, that is to say, in case the bill is dishonoured by non-acceptance or non-payment. Such person is called the referee in case of need. It is in the option of the holder to resort to the referee in case of need or not as he may think fit.

16. The drawer of a bill, and any indorser, may insert therein an express stipulation, —

(1) Negativing or limiting his own liability to the holder;

(2) Waiving as regards himself some or all of the holder's duties.

17. (1) The acceptance of a bill is the signification by the drawee of his assent to the order of the drawer.

(2) An acceptance is invalid unless it complies with the following conditions, namely: —

(*a*) It must be written on the bill and be signed by the drawee.[1] The mere signature of the drawee without additional words is sufficient.[2]

(*b*) It must not express that the drawee will perform his promise by any other means than the payment of money.

18. A bill may be accepted, —

(1) Before it has been signed by the drawer, or while otherwise incomplete;

(2) When it is overdue, or after it has been dishonoured by a previous refusal to accept, or by non-payment;

(3) When a bill payable after sight is dishonoured by non-acceptance, and the drawee subsequently accepts it, the holder, in the absence of any different agreement, is entitled to have the bill accepted as of the date of first presentment to the drawee for acceptance.

19. (1) An acceptance is either (*a*) general or (*b*) qualified.

(2) A general acceptance assents without qualification to the order of the drawer. A qualified acceptance in express terms varies the effect of the bill as drawn.

In particular, an acceptance is qualified which is, —

(*a*) Conditional, that is to say, which makes payment by the acceptor dependent on the fulfilment of a condition therein stated;[3]

(*b*) Partial, that is to say, an acceptance to pay part only of the amount for which the bill is drawn;

(*c*) Local, that is to say, an acceptance to pay only at a particular specified place.

An acceptance to pay at a particular place is a general

---

[1] Compare ante, p. 37. [2] Id.
[3] Ante, pp. 40, 41.

acceptance, unless it expressly states that the bill is to be paid there only and not elsewhere: —

(d) Qualified as to time;

(e) The acceptance of some one or more of the drawees, but not of all.

20. (1) Where a simple signature on a blank stamped paper is delivered by the signer in order that it may be converted into a bill, it operates as a prima facie authority to fill it up as a complete bill for any amount the stamp will cover, using the signature for that of the drawer, or the acceptor, or an indorser; and, in like manner, when a bill is wanting in any material particular, the person in possession of it has a prima facie authority to fill up the omission in any way he thinks fit.

(2) In order that any such instrument when completed may be enforceable against any person who became a party thereto prior to its completion, it must be filled up within a reasonable time, and strictly in accordance with the authority given. Reasonable time for this purpose is a question of fact.

Provided that if any such instrument after completion is negotiated to a holder in due course, it shall be valid and effectual for all purposes in his hands, and he may enforce it as if it had been filled up within a reasonable time and strictly in accordance with the authority given.

21. (1) Every contract on a bill, whether it be the drawer's, the acceptor's, or an indorser's, is incomplete and revocable, until delivery of the instrument in order to give effect thereto.[1]

Provided that where an acceptance is written on a bill, and the drawee gives notice to or according to the direc-

---

[1] Ante, pp. 174–179.

tions of the person entitled to the bill that he has accepted it, the acceptance then becomes complete and irrevocable.

(2) As between immediate parties, and as regards a remote party other than a holder in due course, the delivery,—

(*a*) In order to be effectual must be made either by or under the authority of the party drawing, accepting, or indorsing, as the case may be;[1]

(*b*) May be shown to have been conditional or for a special purpose only, and not for the purpose of transferring the property in the bill.

But if the bill be in the hands of a holder in due course, a valid delivery of the bill by all parties prior to him so as to make them liable to him is conclusively presumed.

(3) Where a bill is no longer in the possession of a party who has signed it as drawer, acceptor, or indorser, a valid and unconditional delivery by him is presumed until the contrary is proved.

Capacity and Authority of Parties.[2]

22. (1) Capacity to incur liability as a party to a bill is co-extensive with capacity to contract.

Provided that nothing in this section shall enable a corporation to make itself liable as drawer, acceptor, or indorser of a bill unless it is competent to it so to do under the law for the time being in force relating to corporations.

(2) Where a bill is drawn or indorsed by an infant, minor, or corporation having no capacity or power to incur liability on a bill, the drawing or indorsement entitles the holder to receive payment of the bill, and to inforce it against any other party thereto.[3]

23. No person is liable as drawer, indorser, or acceptor of a bill who has not signed it as such: Provided that

---

[1] Ante, pp. 175, 176. [2] Ante, pp. 200-203. [3] Ante, pp. 201, 202.

(1) Where a person signs a bill in a trade or assumed name, he is liable thereon as if he had signed it in his own name;

(2) The signature of the name of a firm is equivalent to the signature by the person so signing of the names of all persons liable as partners in that firm.

24. Subject to the provisions of this Act, where a signature on a bill is forged or placed thereon without the authority of the person whose signature it purports to be, the forged or unauthorized signature is wholly inoperative, and no right to retain the bill, or to give a discharge therefor, or to enforce payment thereof against any party thereto, can be acquired through or under that signature, unless the party against whom it is sought to retain or enforce payment of the bill is precluded from setting up the forgery or want of authority.[1]

Provided that nothing in this section shall affect the ratification of an unauthorised signature not amounting to a forgery.

25. A signature by procuration operates as notice that the agent has but a limited authority to sign, and the principal is only bound by such signature if the agent in so signing was acting within the actual limits of his authority.

26. (1) Where a person signs a bill as drawer, indorser, or acceptor, and adds words to his signature, indicating that he signs for or on behalf of a principal, or in a representative character, he is not personally liable thereon; but the mere addition to his signature of words describing him as an agent, or as filling a representative character, does not exempt him from personal liability.[2]

---

[1] Ante, pp. 195–200. [2] Ante, pp. 30–32.

(2) In determining whether a signature on a bill is that of the principal or that of the agent by whose hand it is written, the construction most favourable to the validity of the instrument shall be adopted.

The Consideration for a Bill.

27. (1) Valuable consideration for a bill may be constituted by,[1]—

(*a*) Any consideration sufficient to support a simple contract;

(*b*) An antecedent debt or liability.[2] Such a debt or liability is deemed valuable consideration whether the bill is payable on demand or at a future time.

(2) Where value has at any time been given for a bill, the holder is deemed to be a holder for value as regards the acceptor and all parties to the bill who became parties prior to such time.

(3) Where the holder of a bill has a lien on it arising either from contract or by implication of law, he is deemed to be a holder for value to the extent of the sum for which he has a lien.

28. (1) An accommodation party to a bill is a person who has signed a bill as drawer, acceptor, or indorser, without receiving value therefor, and for the purpose of lending his name to some other person.[3]

(2) An accommodation party is liable on the bill to a holder for value; and it is immaterial whether, when such holder took the bill, he knew such party to be an accommodation party or not.[4]

---

[1] Ante, pp. 213–221.
[2] Ante, pp. 214–219.
[3] Ante, p. 157.
[4] Ante, pp. 159, 160.

29. (1) A *holder in due course*[1] is a holder who has taken a bill, complete and regular on the face of it, under the following conditions, namely,—

(*a*) That he became the holder of it before it was overdue, and without notice that it had been previously dishonoured, if such was the fact;

(*b*) That he took the bill in good faith and for value, and that at the time the bill was negotiated to him he had no notice of any defect in the title of the person who negotiated it.

(2) In particular, the title of a person who negotiates a bill is defective within the meaning of this Act when he obtained the bill, or the acceptance thereof, by fraud, duress, or force and fear, or other unlawful means, or for an illegal consideration, or when he negotiates it in breach of faith, or under such circumstances as amount to a fraud.[2]

(3) A holder (whether for value or not), who derives his title to a bill through a holder in due course, and who is not himself a party to any fraud or illegality affecting it, has all the rights of that holder in due course as regards the acceptor and all parties to the bill prior to that holder.[3]

30. (1) Every party whose signature appears on a bill is prima facie deemed to have become a party thereto for value.

(2) Every holder of a bill is prima facie deemed to be a holder in due course;[4] but if in an action on a bill it is admitted or proved that the acceptance, issue, or subsequent negotiation of the bill is affected with fraud, duress, or force and fear, or illegality, the burden of proof is shifted, unless and until the holder proves that, subsequent to the alleged fraud or illegality, value has in good faith been given for the bill.[5]

---

[1] Ante, p. 206.
[2] Ante, pp. 222, 223.
[3] Ante, p. 228.
[4] Ante, pp. 170, 171.
[5] Ante, pp. 222–224.

Negotiation of Bills.

31. (1) A bill is negotiated when it is transferred from one person to another in such a manner as to constitute the transferee the holder of the bill.

(2) A bill payable to bearer is negotiated by delivery.[1]

(3) A bill payable to order is negotiated by the indorsement of the holder completed by delivery.

(4) Where the holder of a bill payable to his order transfers it for value without indorsing it, the transfer gives the transferee such title as the transferrer had in the bill,[2] and the transferee in addition acquires the right to have the indorsement of the transferrer.[3]

(5) Where any person is under obligation to indorse a bill in a representative capacity, he may indorse the bill in such terms as to negative personal liability.[4]

32. An indorsement in order to operate as a negotiation must comply with the following conditions, namely,—

(1) It must be written on the bill itself and be signed by the indorser. The simple signature of the indorser on the bill, without additional words, is sufficient.[5]

An indorsement written on an allonge, or on a 'copy' of a bill issued or negotiated in a country where 'copies' are recognised, is deemed to be written on the bill itself.[6]

(2) It must be an indorsement of the entire bill. A partial indorsement, that is to say, an indorsement which purports to transfer to the indorsee a part only of the amount payable, or which purports to transfer the bill to two or more indorsees severally, does not operate as a negotiation of the bill.

(3) Where a bill is payable to the order of two or more

---

[1] Ante, p. 62.
[2] Id.
[3] Id. note.
[4] Ante, p. 63, note 3.
[5] Ante, pp. 61, 63.
[6] Ante, p. 61.

payees or indorsees who are not partners all must indorse, unless the one indorsing has authority to indorse for the others.

(4) Where, in a bill payable to order, the payee or indorsee is wrongly designated, or his name is mis-spelt, he may indorse the bill as therein described, adding, if he think fit, his proper signature.[1]

(5) Where there are two or more indorsements on a bill, each indorsement is deemed to have been made in the order in which it appears on the bill, until the contrary is proved.

(6) An indorsement may be made in blank or special. It may also contain terms making it restrictive.

33. Where a bill purports to be indorsed conditionally, the condition may be disregarded by the payer, and payment to the indorsee is valid whether the condition has been fulfilled or not.

34. (1) An indorsement in blank specifies no indorsee, and a bill so indorsed becomes payable to bearer.

(2) A special indorsement specifies the person to whom, or to whose order, the bill is to be payable.

(3) The provisions of this Act relating to a payee apply with the necessary modifications to an indorsee under a special indorsement.

(4) When a bill has been indorsed in blank, any holder may convert the blank indorsement into a special indorsement by writing above the indorser's signature a direction to pay the bill to, or to the order of, himself or some other person.

35. (1) An indorsement is restrictive which prohibits the further negotiation of the bill, or which expresses that it is a mere authority to deal with the bill as thereby

---

[1] Compare, p. 63.

directed and not a transfer of the ownership thereof, as, for example, if a bill be indorsed, 'Pay D. only,' or, 'Pay D. for the account of X,' or, 'Pay D. or order for collection.'

(2) A restrictive indorsement gives the indorsee the right to receive payment of the bill and to sue any party thereto that his indorser could have sued, but gives him no power to transfer his rights as indorsee unless it expressly authorise him to do so.

(3) Where a restrictive indorsement authorises further transfer, all subsequent indorsees take the bill with the same rights and subject to the same liabilities as the first indorsee under the restrictive indorsement.

36. (1) Where a bill is negotiable in its origin, it continues to be negotiable until it has been (*a*) restrictively indorsed or (*b*) discharged by payment or otherwise.

(2) Where an overdue bill is negotiated, it can only be negotiated subject to any defect of title affecting it at its maturity, and thenceforward no person who takes it can acquire or give a better title than that which the person from whom he took it had.

(3) A bill payable on demand is deemed to be overdue within the meaning and for the purposes of this section, when it appears on the face of it to have been in circulation for an unreasonable length of time. What is an unreasonable length of time for this purpose is a question of fact.

(4) Except where an indorsement bears date after the maturity of the bill, every negotiation is prima facie deemed to have been effected before the bill was overdue.

(5) Where a bill which is not overdue has been dishonoured, any person who takes it with notice of the dishonour takes it subject to any defect of title attaching thereto

at the time of dishonour, but nothing in this sub-section shall affect the rights of a holder in due course.

37. Where a bill is negotiated back to the drawer, or to a prior indorser, or to the acceptor, such party may, subject to the provisions of this Act, re-issue and further negotiate the bill, but he is not entitled to enforce payment of the bill against any intervening party to whom he was previously liable.

38. The rights and powers of the holder of a bill are as follows:—

(1) He may sue on the bill in his own name;

(2) Where he is a holder in due course, he holds the bill free from any defect of title of prior parties, as well as from mere personal defences available to prior parties among themselves, and may enforce payment against all parties liable on the bill;

(3) Where his title is defective (*a*) if he negotiates the bill to a holder in due course, that holder obtains a good and complete title to the bill, and (*b*) if he obtains payment of the bill the person who pays him in due course gets a valid discharge for the bill.

General Duties of the Holder.

39. (1) Where a bill is payable after sight, presentment for acceptance is necessary in order to fix the maturity of the instrument.

(2) Where a bill expressly stipulates that it shall be presented for acceptance, or where a bill is drawn payable elsewhere than at the residence or place of business of the drawee, it must be presented for acceptance before it can be presented for payment.

(3) In no other case is presentment for acceptance necessary in order to render liable any party to the bill.

(4) Where the holder of a bill, drawn payable elsewhere than at the place of business or residence of the drawee, has not time, with the exercise of reasonable diligence, to present the bill for acceptance before presenting it for payment on the day that it falls due, the delay caused by presenting the bill for acceptance before presenting it for payment is excused, and does not discharge the drawer and indorsers.

40. (1) Subject to the provisions of this Act, when a bill payable after sight is negotiated, the holder must either present it for acceptance or negotiate it within a reasonable time.[1]

(2) If he do not do so, the drawer and all indorsers prior to that holder are discharged.

(3) In determining what is a reasonable time within the meaning of this section, regard shall be had to the nature of the bill, the usage of trade with respect to similar bills, and the facts of the particular case.[2]

41. (1) A bill is duly presented for acceptance which is presented in accordance with the following rules:—

(*a*) The presentment must be made by or on behalf of the holder[3] to the drawee or to some person authorised to accept or refuse acceptance on his behalf at a reasonable hour on a business day and before the bill is overdue.

(*b*) Where a bill is addressed to two or more drawees, who are not partners, presentment must be made to them all, unless one has authority to accept for all, when presentment may be made to him only.[4]

(*c*) Where the drawee is dead, presentment may be made to his personal representative.[5]

---

[1] Ante, pp. 90, 91.
[2] Ante, p. 91.
[3] Ante, p. 100.
[4] Ante, pp. 103–104.
[5] Ante, p. 103.

(d) Where the drawee is bankrupt, presentment may be made to him or to his trustee.[1]

(e) Where authorised by agreement or usage, a presentment through the post-office is sufficient.

(2) Presentment in accordance with these rules is excused, and a bill may be treated as dishonoured by non-acceptance,—

(a) Where the drawee is dead or bankrupt,[2] or is a fictitious person or a person not having capacity to contract by bill;

(b) Where, after the exercise of reasonable diligence, such presentment cannot be effected;[3]

(c) Where, although the presentment has been irregular, acceptance has been refused on some other ground.

(3) The fact that the holder has reason to believe that the bill, on presentment, will be dishonoured does not excuse presentment.

42. (1) When a bill is duly presented for acceptance and is not accepted within the customary time, the person presenting it must treat it as dishonoured by non-acceptance. If he do not, the holder shall lose his right of recourse against the drawer and indorsers.[4]

43. (1) A bill is dishonoured by non-acceptance:—

(a) When it is duly presented for acceptance, and such an acceptance as is prescribed by this Act is refused or cannot be obtained; or,

(b) When it is duly presented for acceptance, and such an acceptance as is prescribed by this Act is refused or cannot be obtained; or,

---

[1] Ante, p. 103.
[2] But compare ante, p. 152.
[3] Ante, p. 142.
[4] But compare ante, pp. 39, 40.

(*c*) When presentment for acceptance is excused, and the bill is not accepted.

(2) Subject to the provisions of this Act when a bill is dishonoured by non-acceptance, an immediate right of recourse against the drawer and indorsers accrues to the holder, and no presentment for payment is necessary.[1]

44. (1) The holder of a bill may refuse to take a qualified acceptance, and if he does not obtain an unqualified acceptance may treat the bill as dishonoured by non-acceptance.

(2) Where a qualified acceptance is taken, and the drawer or an indorser has not expressly or impliedly authorised the holder to take a qualified acceptance, or does not subsequently assent thereto, such drawer or indorser is discharged from his liability on the bill.

The provisions of this sub-section do not apply to a partial acceptance whereof due notice has been given. Where a foreign bill has been accepted as to part, it must be protested as to the balance.

(3) When the drawer or indorser of a bill receives notice of a qualified acceptance, and does not within a reasonable time express his dissent to the holder, he shall be deemed to have assented thereto.

45. Subject to the provisions of this Act a bill must be duly presented for payment. If it be not so presented the drawer and indorsers shall be discharged.

A bill is duly presented for payment which is presented in accordance with the following rules:—

(1) Where the bill is not payable on demand, presentment must be made on the day it falls due.[2]

(2) Where the bill is payable on demand, then, subject to the provisions of this Act, presentment must be made

---

[1] Ante, p. 89. [2] Ante, p. 92.

within a reasonable time after its issue in order to render the drawer liable, and within a reasonable time after its indorsement, in order to render the indorser liable.[1]

In determining what is a reasonable time, regard shall be had to the nature of the bill, the usage of trade with regard to similar bills, and the facts of the particular case.

(3) Presentment must be made by the holder or by some person authorised to receive payment on his behalf at a reasonable hour on a business day, at the proper place as hereinafter defined, either to the person designated by the bill as payer, or to some person authorised to pay or refuse payment on his behalf, if with the exercise of reasonable diligence such person can there be found.

(4) A bill is presented at the proper place:[2] —

(*a*) Where a place of payment is specified in the bill, and the bill is there presented.

(*b*) Where no place of payment is specified, but the address of the drawee or acceptor is given in the bill, and the bill is there presented.

(*c*) Where no place of payment is specified and no address given, and the bill is presented at the drawee's or acceptor's place of business if known, and if not, at his ordinary residence if known.[3]

(*d*) In any other case, if presented to the drawee or acceptor wherever he can be found, or if presented at his last known place of business or residence.

(5) Where a bill is presented at the proper place, and after the exercise of reasonable diligence no person authorised to pay or refuse payment can be found there, no further presentment to the drawee or acceptor is required.

(6) Where a bill is drawn upon, or accepted by, two or more persons who are not partners, and no place of pay-

---

[1] Ante, p. 92.
[2] Ante, pp. 84–89.
[3] Ante, pp. 85–87.

ment is specified, presentment must be made to them all.¹

(7) Where the drawee or acceptor of a bill is dead, and no place of payment is specified, presentment must be made to a personal representative, if such there be, and with the exercise of reasonable diligence he can be found.²

(8) Where authorised by agreement or usage, a presentment through the post-office is sufficient.³

46. (1) Delay in making presentment for payment is excused when the delay is caused by circumstances beyond the control of the holder, and not imputable to his default, misconduct, or negligence. When the cause of delay ceases to operate, presentment must be made with reasonable diligence.⁴

(2) Presentment for payment is dispensed with:⁵ —

(*a*) Where, after the exercise of reasonable diligence, presentment, as required by this Act, cannot be effected.

The fact that the holder has reason to believe that the bill will, on presentment, be dishonoured does not dispense with the necessity for presentment.

(*b*) Where the drawee is a fictitious person.

(*c*) As regards the drawer, where the drawee or acceptor is not bound, as between himself and the drawer, to accept or pay the bill, and the drawer has no reason to believe that the bill would be paid if presented.⁶

(*d*) As regards an indorser, where the bill was accepted or made for the accommodation of that indorser, and he has no reason to expect that the bill would be paid if presented.

(*e*) By waiver of presentment, express or implied.⁷

---

¹ Ante, pp. 104, 105.
² Ante, p. 103.
³ Compare, ante, p. 83.
⁴ Ante, p. 143.
⁵ Ante, pp. 149–153.
⁶ Ante, p. 48.
⁷ Ante, pp. 143–146.

47. (1) A bill is dishonoured by non-payment (*a*) when it is duly presented for payment, and payment is refused or cannot be obtained, or (*b*) when presentment is excused and the bill is overdue and unpaid.

(2) Subject to the provisions of this Act, when a bill is dishonoured by non-payment, an immediate right of recourse against the drawer and indorsers accrues to the holder.

48. Subject to the provisions of this Act, when a bill has been dishonoured by non-acceptance or by non-payment, notice of dishonour must be given to the drawer and each indorser, and any drawer or indorser to whom such notice is not given is discharged; Provided that, —

(1) Where a bill is dishonoured by non-acceptance, and notice of dishonour is not given, the rights of a holder in due course, subsequent to the omission, shall not be prejudiced by the omission.

(2) Where a bill is dishonoured by non-acceptance, and due notice of dishonour is given, it shall not be necessary to give notice of a subsequent dishonour by non-payment, unless the bill shall in the mean time have been accepted.

49. Notice of dishonour in order to be valid and effectual must be given in accordance with the following rules, —

(1) The notice must be given by or on behalf of the holder, or by or on behalf of an indorser who, at the time of giving it, is himself liable on the bill.[1]

(2) Notice of dishonour may be given by an agent either in his own name, or in the name of any party entitled to give notice, whether that party be his principal or not.

(3) Where the notice is given by or on behalf of the

---

[1] Ante, p. 119.

holder, it enures for the benefit of all subsequent holders and all prior indorsers who have a right of recourse against the party to whom it is given.[1]

(4) Where notice is given by or on behalf of an indorser entitled to give notice as hereinbefore provided, it enures for the benefit of the holder and all indorsers subsequent to the party to whom notice is given.[2]

(5) The notice may be given in writing or by personal communication, and may be given in any terms which sufficiently identify the bill, and intimate that the bill has been dishonoured by non-acceptance or non-payment.[3]

(6) The return of a dishonoured bill to the drawer or an indorser is, in point of form, deemed a sufficient notice of dishonour.

(7) A written notice need not be signed, and an insufficient written notice may be supplemented and validated by verbal communication. A misdescription of the bill shall not vitiate the notice, unless the party to whom the notice is given is in fact misled thereby.[4]

(8) Where notice of dishonour is required to be given to any person, it may be given either to the party himself, or to his agent in that behalf.[5]

(9) Where the drawer or indorser is dead, and the party giving notice knows it, the notice must be given to a personal representative, if such there be and with the exercise of reasonable diligence he can be found.[6]

(10) Where the drawer or indorser is bankrupt, notice may be given either to the party himself or to the trustee.[7]

(11) Where there are two or more drawers or indorsers who are not partners, notice must be given to each of them,

---

[1] Ante, pp. 120, 121.
[2] Id.
[3] Ante, pp. 110–115.
[4] Ante, pp. 110, 111
[5] Ante, p 122.
[6] Ante, pp. 122, 123.
[7] But compare, Ante, p. 155.

unless one of them has authority to receive such notice for the others.[1]

(12) The notice may be given as soon as the bill is dishonoured, and must be given within a reasonable time thereafter.

In the absence of special circumstances, notice is not deemed to have been given within a reasonable time, unless,[2] —

(*a*) Where the person giving, and the person to receive, notice reside in the same place, the notice is given or sent off in time to reach the latter on the day after the dishonour of the bill.

(*b*) Where the person giving, and the person to receive, notice reside in different places, the notice is sent off on the day after the dishonour of the bill, if there be a post at a convenient hour on that day, and if there be no such post on that day, then by the next post thereafter.

(13) Where a bill when dishonoured is in the hands of an agent, he may either himself give notice to the parties liable on the bill, or he may give notice to his principal. If he give notice to his principal, he must do so within the same time as if he were the holder, and the principal upon receipt of such notice has himself the same time for giving notice as if the agent had been an independent holder.[3]

(14) Where a party to a bill receives due notice of dishonour, he has after the receipt of such notice the same period of time for giving notice to antecedent parties that the holder has after the dishonour.[4]

(15) Where a notice of dishonour is duly addressed and posted, the sender is deemed to have given due notice of dishonour, notwithstanding any miscarriage by the post-office.

---

[1] Ante, p. 122.
[2] Ante, pp. 128–134.
[3] Ante, pp. 133, 134.
[4] Ante, pp. 132, 133.

50. (1) Delay in giving notice of dishonour is excused where delay is caused by circumstances beyond the control of the party giving notice, and not imputable to his default, misconduct, or negligence. When the cause of delay ceases to operate, the notice must be given with reasonable diligence.[1]

(2) Notice of dishonour is dispensed with,[2] —

(*a*) When, after the exercise of reasonable diligence,[3] notice as required by this Act cannot be given to, or does not reach, the drawer or indorser sought to be charged:

(*b*) By waiver express or implied. Notice of dishonour may be waived before the time of giving notice has arrived, or after the omission to give due notice;

(*c*) As regards the drawer in the following cases, namely, (1) where drawer and drawee are the same person, (2) where the drawee is a fictitious person or a person not having capacity to contract, (3) where the drawer is the person to whom the bill is presented for payment, (4) where the drawee or acceptor is as between himself and the drawer under no obligation to accept or pay the bill, (5) where the drawer has countermanded payment;

(*d*) As regards the indorser in the following cases, namely, (1) where the drawee is a fictitious person or a person not having capacity to contract, and the indorser was aware of the fact at the time he indorsed the bill, (2) where the indorser is the person to whom the bill is presented for payment, (3) where the bill was accepted or made for his accommodation.

51. (1) Where an inland bill has been dishonoured, it may, if the holder think fit, be noted for non-acceptance or non-payment, as the case may be; but it shall not be necessary to note or protest any such bill in order to preserve the recourse against the drawer or indorser.[4]

[1] Ante, p. 143.
[2] Ante, pp. 154–156.
[3] Ante, p. 142.
[4] Ante, pp. 106, 108, 109.

(2) Where a foreign bill, appearing on the face of it to be such, has been dishonoured by non-acceptance, it must be duly protested for non-acceptance, and where such a bill, which has not been previously dishonoured by non-acceptance, is dishonoured by non-payment, it must be duly protested for non-payment. If it be not so protested, the drawer and indorsers are discharged.[1] Where a bill does not appear on the face of it to be a foreign bill, protest thereof in case of dishonour is unnecessary.

(3) A bill which has been protested for non-acceptance may be subsequently protested for non-payment.

(4) Subject to the provisions of this Act, when a bill is noted or protested, it must be noted on the day of its dishonour. When a bill has been duly noted, the protest may be subsequently extended as of the date of the noting.[2]

(5) Where the acceptor of a bill becomes bankrupt or insolvent, or suspends payment before it matures, the holder may cause the bill to be protested for better security against the drawer and indorsers.

(6) A bill must be protested at the place where it is dishonoured: Provided that,—

(*a*) When a bill is presented through the post-office and returned by post dishonoured, it may be protested at the place to which it is returned and on the day of its return, if received during business hours, and if not received during business hours, then not later than the next business day;

(*b*) When a bill drawn payable at the place of business or residence of some person other than the drawee, has been dishonoured by non-acceptance, it must be protested for non-payment at the place where it is expressed to be payable, and no further presentment for payment to, or demand on, the drawee is necessary.

---

[1] Ante, pp. 106–108.   [2] Ante, p. 109.

(7) A protest must contain a copy of the bill, and must be signed by the notary making it, and must specify,[1]—

(*a*) The person at whose request the bill is protested;

(*b*) The place and date of protest, the cause or reason for protesting the bill, the demand made, and the answer given, if any, or the fact that the drawee or acceptor could not be found.

(8) Where a bill is lost or destroyed, or is wrongly detained from the person entitled to hold it, protest may be made on a copy or written particulars thereof.[2]

(9) Protest is dispensed with by any circumstance which would dispense with notice of dishonour. Delay in noting or protesting is excused when the delay is caused by circumstances beyond the control of the holder, and not imputable to his default, misconduct, or negligence. When the cause of delay ceases to operate, the bill must be noted or protested with reasonable diligence.

52. (1) When a bill is accepted generally presentment for payment is not necessary in order to render the acceptor liable.

(2) When by the terms of a qualified acceptance presentment for payment is required, the acceptor, in the absence of an express stipulation to that effect, is not discharged by the omission to present the bill for payment on the day that it matures.

(3) In order to render the acceptor of a bill liable, it is not necessary to protest it, or that notice of dishonour should be given to him.[3]

(4) Where the holder of a bill presents it for payment, he shall exhibit the bill to the person from whom he demands payment,[4] and when a bill is paid, the holder shall forthwith deliver it up to the party paying it.

---

[1] Ante, pp. 106, 107.
[2] Compare ante, p. 149.
[3] See p. 36.
[4] Ante, p. 82.

Liabilities of Parties.

53. (1) A bill, of itself, does not operate as an assignment of funds in the hands of the drawee available for the payment thereof,[1] and the drawee of a bill who does not accept as required by this Act is not liable on the instrument.[2] This sub-section shall not extend to Scotland.

(2) In Scotland, where the drawee of a bill has in his hands funds available for the payment thereof, the bill operates as an assignment of the sum for which it is drawn in favor of the holder, from the time when the bill is presented to the drawee.

54. The acceptor of a bill, by accepting it,—

(1) Engages that he will pay it according to the tenor of his acceptance;[3]

(2) Is precluded from denying to a holder in due course:

(a) The existence of the drawer, the genuineness of his signature, and his capacity and authority to draw the bill;[4]

(b) In the case of a bill payable to drawer's order, the then capacity of the drawer to indorse, but not the genuineness or validity of his indorsement;

(c) In the case of a bill payable to the order of a third person, the existence of the payee and his then capacity to indorse, but not the genuineness or validity of his indorsement.[5]

55. (1) The drawer of a bill by drawing it,[7]—

(a) Engages that on due presentment it shall be accepted and paid according to its tenor, and that if it be dishonoured he will compensate the holder or any indorser

---

[1] Ante, p. 20.
[2] Ante, p. 36.
[3] Id.
[4] See ante, pp. 197–200.
[5] Ante, pp. 132, 134.
[6] Ante, pp. 199, 200.
[7] Ante, p. 47.

who is compelled to pay it, provided that the requisite proceedings on dishonour be duly taken;

(*b*) Is precluded from denying to a holder in due course the existence of the payee and his then capacity to indorse.

(2) The indorser of a bill by indorsing it,[1] —

(*a*) Engages that on due presentment it shall be accepted and paid according to its tenor, and that if it be dishonoured he will compensate the holder or a subsequent indorser who is compelled to pay it, provided that the requisite proceedings on dishonour be duly taken;

(*b*) Is precluded from denying to a holder in due course the genuineness and regularity in all respects of the drawer's signature and all previous indorsements;[2]

(*c*) Is precluded from denying to his immediate or a subsequent indorsee that the bill was at the time of his indorsement a valid and subsisting bill, and that he had then a good title thereto.

56. Where a person signs a bill otherwise than as drawer or acceptor, he thereby incurs the liabilities of an indorser to a holder in due course.[3]

57. Where a bill is dishonoured, the measure of damages, which shall be deemed to be liquidated damages, shall be as follows: —

(1) The holder may recover from any party liable on the bill, and the drawer who has been compelled to pay the bill may recover from the acceptor, and an indorser who has been compelled to pay the bill may recover from the acceptor or from the drawer or from a prior indorser, —

(*a*) The amount of the bill;

(*b*) Interest thereon from the time of presentment for

---

[1] Ante, p. 74.
[2] Ante, pp. 76-79.
[3] Compare ante, pp. 33-35.

payment, if the bill is payable on demand, and from the maturity of the bill in any other case;

(c) The expenses of noting, or when protest is necessary, and the protest has been extended, the expenses of protest.

(2) In the case of a bill which has been dishonoured abroad, in lieu of the above damages, the holder may recover from the drawer or an indorser, and the drawer or an indorser who has been compelled to pay the bill may recover from any party liable to him, the amount of the re-exchange with interest thereon until the time of payment.

(3) Where by this Act interest may be recovered as damages, such interest may, if justice require it, be withheld wholly or in part, and where a bill is expressed to be payable with interest at a given rate, interest as damages may or may not be given at the same rate as interest proper.

58. (1) Where the holder of a bill payable to bearer negotiates it by delivery without indorsing it, he is called a 'transferrer by delivery.'

(2) A transferrer by delivery is not liable on the instrument.

(3) A transferrer by delivery who negotiates a bill, thereby warrants to his immediate transferee, being a holder for value, that the bill is what it purports to be, that he has a right to transfer it, and that at the time of transfer he is not aware of any fact which renders it valueless.

Discharge of Bill.

59. (1) A bill is discharged by payment in due course by, or on behalf of, the drawee or acceptor.[1]

[1] Ante, pp. 242-248.

'Payment in due course' means payment made at or after the maturity of the bill to the holder thereof in good faith and without notice that his title to the bill is defective.

(2) Subject to the provisions hereinafter contained, when a bill is paid by the drawer or an indorser it is not discharged;[1] but,

(*a*) Where a bill payable to, or to the order of, a third party is paid by the drawer, the drawer may enforce payment thereof against the acceptor, but may not re-issue the bill.

(*b*) Where a bill is paid by an indorser, or where a bill payable to drawer's order is paid by the drawer, the party paying it is remitted to his former rights as regards the acceptor or antecedent parties, and he may, if he thinks fit, strike out his own and subsequent indorsements, and again negotiate the bill.

(3) Where an accommodation bill is paid in due course by the party accommodated the bill is discharged.[2]

60. When a bill payable to order on demand is drawn on a banker, and the banker on whom it is drawn pays the bill in good faith and in the ordinary course of business, it is not incumbent on the banker to show that the indorsement of the payee or any subsequent indorsement was made by or under the authority of the person whose indorsement it purports to be, and the banker is deemed to have paid the bill in due course, although such indorsement has been forged or made without authority.

61. When the acceptor of a bill is or becomes the holder of it at or after its maturity, in his own right, the bill is discharged.

[1] Ante, pp. 246, 247.
[2] Ante, p. 247.

62. (1) When the holder of a bill at or after its maturity absolutely and unconditionally renounces his rights against the acceptor, the bill is discharged.

The renunciation must be in writing, unless the bill is delivered up to the acceptor.

(2) The liabilities of any party to a bill may, in like manner, be renounced by the holder before, at, or after its maturity; but nothing in this section shall affect the rights of a holder in due course without notice of the renunciation.

63. (1) Where a bill is intentionally cancelled by the holder or his agent, and the cancellation is apparent thereon, the bill is discharged.

(2) In like manner any party liable on a bill may be discharged by the intentional cancellation of his signature by the holder or his agent. In such case any indorser who would have had a right of recourse against the party whose signature is cancelled, is also discharged.

(3) A cancellation made unintentionally, or under a mistake, or without the authority of the holder, is inoperative; but where a bill or any signature thereon appears to have been cancelled, the burden of proof lies on the party who alleges that the cancellation was made unintentionally, or under a mistake, or without authority.

64. (1) Where a bill of acceptance is materially altered without the assent of all parties liable on the bill, the bill is avoided except as against a party who has himself made, authorised, or assented to the alteration, and subsequent indorsers.[1]

Provided that,—

Where a bill has been materially altered, but the alteration is not apparent, and the bill is in the hands of a

---

[1] Ante, pp. 181–191.

holder in due course, such holder may avail himself of the bill as if it had not been altered, and may enforce payment of it according to its original tenor.[1]

(2) In particular, the following alterations are material: namely, any alteration of the date, the sum payable, the time of payment, the place of payment, and, where a bill has been accepted generally, the addition of a place of payment without the acceptor's assent.

Acceptance and Payment for Honour.[2]

65. (1) Where a bill of exchange has been protested for dishonour by non-acceptance, or protested for better security, and is not overdue, any person, not being a party already liable thereon, may, with the consent of the holder, intervene and accept the bill supra protest, for the honour of any party liable thereon, or for the honour of the person for whose account the bill is drawn.

(2) A bill may be accepted for honour for part only of the sum for which it is drawn.

(3) An acceptance for honour supra protest in order to be valid must —

(*a*) Be written on the bill, and indicate that it is an acceptance for honour;

(*b*) Be signed by the acceptor for honour.

(4) Where an acceptance for honour does not expressly state for whose honour it is made, it is deemed to be an acceptance for the honour of the drawer.

(5) Where a bill payable after sight is accepted for honour, its maturity is calculated from the date of the noting for non-acceptance, and not from the date of the acceptance for honour.

66. (1) The acceptor for honour of a bill by accepting it engages that he will, on due presentment, pay the bill

[1] See ante, p. 187, note.   [2] See ante, pp. 41, 42.

according to the tenor of his acceptance, if it is not paid by the drawee, provided it has been duly presented for payment, and protested for non-payment, and that he receives notice of these facts.

(2) The acceptor for honour is liable to the holder and to all parties to the bill subsequent to the party for whose honour he has accepted.

67. (1) Where a dishonoured bill has been accepted for honour supra protest, or contains a reference in case of need, it must be protested for non-payment before it is presented for payment to the acceptor for honour, or referee in case of need.[1]

(2) Where the address of the acceptor for honour is in the same place where the bill is protested for non-payment, the bill must be presented to him not later than the day following its maturity; and where the address of the acceptor for honour is in some place other than the place where it was protested for non-payment, the bill must be forwarded not later than the day following its maturity for presentment to him.

(3) Delay in presentment or non-presentment is excused by any circumstance which would excuse delay in presentment for payment or non-presentment for payment.

(4) When a bill of exchange is dishonoured by the acceptor for honour it must be protested for non-payment by him.

68. (1) Where a bill has been protested for non-payment, any person may intervene and pay it supra protest for the honour of any party liable thereon, or for the honour of the person for whose account the bill is drawn.

(2) Where two or more persons offer to pay a bill for the

---

[1] Ante, p. 42. Must there be a protest for non-acceptance, to make the acceptor 'in case of need' liable?

honour of different parties, the person whose payment will discharge most parties to the bill shall have the preference.

(3) Payment for honour supra protest, in order to operate as such and not as a mere voluntary payment, must be attested by a notarial act of honour, which may be appended to the protest or form an extension of it.

(4) The notarial act of honour must be founded on a declaration made by the payer for honour, or his agent in that behalf, declaring his intention to pay the bill for honour, and for whose honour he pays.

(5) Where a bill has been paid for honour, all parties subsequent to the party for whose honour it is paid are discharged, but the payer for honour is subrogated for, and succeeds to both the rights and duties of, the holder as regards the party for whose honour he pays, and all parties liable to that party.

(6) The payer for honour, on paying to the holder the amount of the bill and the notarial expenses incidental to its dishonour, is entitled to receive both the bill itself and the protest. If the holder do not on demand deliver them up, he shall be liable to the payer for honour in damages.

(7) Where the holder of a bill refuses to receive payment supra protest he shall lose his right of recourse against any party who would have been discharged by such payment.

Lost Instruments.

69. Where a bill has been lost before it is overdue, the person who was the holder of it may apply to the drawer to give him another bill of the same tenor, giving security to the drawer if required to indemnify him against all persons whatever in case the bill alleged to have been lost shall be found again.

If the drawer on request as aforesaid refuses to give such duplicate bill he may be compelled to do so.

70. In any action or proceeding upon a bill, the court or a judge may order that the loss of the instrument shall not be set up, provided an indemnity be given to the satisfaction of the court or judge against the claims of any other person upon the instrument in question.

Bill in a Set.

71. (1) Where a bill is drawn in a set, each part of the set being numbered, and containing a reference to the other parts, the whole of the parts constitutes one bill.

(2) Where the holder of a set indorses two or more parts to different persons, he is liable on every such part, and every indorser subsequent to him is liable on the part he has himself indorsed as if the said parts were separate bills.

(3) Where two or more parts of a set are negotiated to different holders in due course, the holder whose title first accrues is as between such holders deemed the true owner of the bill; but nothing in this sub-section shall affect the rights of a person who in due course accepts or pays the part first presented to him.

(4) The acceptance may be written on any part, and it must be written on one part only.

If the drawee accepts more than one part, and such accepted parts get into the hands of different holders in due course, he is liable on every such part as if it were a separate bill.

(5) When the acceptor of a bill drawn in a set pays it without requiring the part bearing his acceptance to be delivered up to him, and that part at maturity is outstanding in the hands of a holder in due course, he is liable to the holder thereof.

(6) Subject to the preceding rules, where any one part of a bill drawn in a set is discharged by payment or otherwise, the whole bill is discharged.

Conflict of Laws.[1]

72. Where a bill drawn in one country is negotiated, accepted, or payable in another, the rights, duties, and liabilities of the parties thereto are determined as follows: —

(1) The validity of a bill as regards requisites in form is determined by the law of the place of issue, and the validity as regards requisites in form of the supervening contracts, such as acceptance, or indorsement, or acceptance supra protest, is determined by the law of the place where such contract was made.

Provided that —

(a) Where a bill is issued out of the United Kingdom it is not invalid by reason only that it is not stamped in accordance with the law of the place of issue;

(b) Where a bill, issued out of the United Kingdom, conforms, as regards requisites in form, to the law of the United Kingdom, it may, for the purpose of enforcing payment thereof, be treated as valid as between all persons who negotiate, hold, or become parties to it in the United Kingdom.

(2) Subject to the provisions of this Act, the interpretation of the drawing, indorsement, acceptance, or acceptance supra protest of a bill is determined by the law of the place where such contract is made.

Provided that where an inland bill is indorsed in a foreign country the indorsement shall, as regards the payer, be interpreted according to the law of the United Kingdom.

---

[1] Ante, pp. 249-255

(3) The duties of the holder with respect to presentment for acceptance or payment, and the necessity for or sufficiency of a protest or notice of dishonour, or otherwise, are determined by the law of the place where the act is done or the bill is dishonoured.

(4) Where a bill is drawn out of but payable in the United Kingdom, and the sum payable is not expressed in the currency of the United Kingdom, the amount shall, in the absence of some express stipulation, be calculated according to the rate of exchange for sight drafts at the place of payment on the day the bill is payable.

(5) Where a bill is drawn in one country and is payable in another, the due date thereof is determined according to the law of the place where it is payable.

Part III.

CHEQUES ON A BANKER.

73. A cheque is a bill of exchange drawn on a banker payable on demand.[1]

Except as otherwise provided in this Part, the provisions of this Act applicable to a bill of exchange payable on demand apply to a cheque.

[1] May not a bill of exchange proper be drawn upon a banker and payable on demand, e. g., a draft drawn in sets in New York on a banker in London? To call a cheque a bill of exchange of a special kind is likely to mislead. The two differ almost as much as a cheque and a promissory note. See ante, pp. 52–57. The title itself to the Bills of Exchange Act ('An Act to codify the Law relating to Bills of Exchange, *Cheques*, and Promissory Notes') implies that a cheque is something different from and not merely a species of bill of exchange. It is doubtful whether even a foreign cheque should be called a species of (foreign) bill; protest would not be necessary, it seems, in order to hold the drawer.

74. Subject to the provisions of this Act,—

(1) Where a cheque is not presented for payment within a reasonable time of its issue, and the drawer or the person on whose account it is drawn, had the right at the time of such presentment, as between him and the banker, to have the cheque paid, and suffers actual damage through the delay, he is discharged to the extent of such damage, that is to say, to the extent to which such drawer or person is a creditor of such banker to a larger amount than he would have been had such cheque been paid.[1]

(2) In determining what is a reasonable time, regard shall be had to the nature of the instrument, the usage of trade and of bankers, and the facts of the particular case.

(3) The holder of such cheque as to which such drawer or person is discharged shall be a creditor, in lieu of such drawer or person, of such banker to the extent of such discharge, and entitled to recover the amount from him.

75. The duty and authority of a banker to pay a cheque drawn on him by his customer are determined by,—

(1) Countermand of payment;

(2) Notice of the customer's death.

Crossed Cheques.[2]

76. (1) Where a cheque bears across its face an addition of,—

(*a*) The words 'and company,' or any abbreviation thereof between two parallel transverse lines, either with or without the words 'not negotiable;' or,

(*b*) Two parallel transverse lines simply either with or without the words 'not negotiable;'

---

[1] Ante, pp. 53, 54.
[2] See Bellamy *v.* Marjoribanks, 7 Exch. 402; Scrutton, Mercantile Law, 81–84.

that addition constitutes a crossing, and the cheque is crossed generally.

(2) Where a cheque bears across its face an addition of the name of the banker, either with or without the words 'not negotiable,' that addition constitutes a crossing, and the cheque is crossed specially and to that banker.

77. (1) A cheque may be crossed generally or specially by the drawer.

(2) Where a cheque is uncrossed, the holder may cross it generally or specially.

(3) Where a cheque is crossed generally, the holder may cross it specially.

(4) Where a cheque is crossed generally or specially, the holder may add the words 'not negotiable.'

(5) Where a cheque is crossed specially, the banker to whom it is crossed may again cross it specially to another banker for collection.

(6) Where an uncrossed cheque, or a cheque crossed generally, is sent to a banker for collection, he may cross it specially to himself.

78. A crossing authorised by this Act is a material part of the cheque; it shall not be lawful for any person to obliterate or, except as authorised by this Act, to add to or alter the crossing.

79. (1) Where a cheque is crossed specially to more than one banker, except when crossed to an agent for collection being a banker, the banker on whom it is drawn shall refuse payment thereof.

(2) Where the banker on whom a cheque is drawn which is so crossed, nevertheless pays the same, or pays a cheque crossed generally otherwise than to a banker, or if crossed specially otherwise than to the banker to whom it is crossed, or his agent for collection being a banker, he is

liable to the true owner of the cheque for any loss he may sustain owing to the cheque having been so paid.

Provided that where a cheque is presented for payment which does not at the time of presentment appear to be crossed, or to have had a crossing which has been obliterated, or to have been added to or altered otherwise than as authorised by this Act, the banker paying the cheque in good faith and without negligence shall not be responsible or incur any liability, nor shall the payment be questioned by reason of the cheque having been crossed, or of the crossing having been obliterated or having been added to or altered otherwise than as authorised by this Act, and of payment having been made otherwise than to a banker or to the banker to whom the cheque is or was crossed, or to his agent for collection, being a banker, as the case may be.

80. Where the banker on whom a crossed cheque is drawn, in good faith and without negligence, pays it, if crossed generally, to a banker, and if crossed specially, to the banker to whom it is crossed, or his agent for collection being a banker, the banker paying the cheque, and, if the cheque has come into the hands of the payee, the drawer shall respectively be entitled to the same rights and be placed in the same position as if payment of the cheque had been made to the true owner thereof.

81. Where a person takes a crossed cheque which bears on it the words 'not negotiable,' he shall not have, and shall not be capable of giving, a better title to the cheque than that which the person from whom he took it had.

82. Where a banker in good faith and without negligence receives payment for a customer of a cheque crossed generally or specially to himself, and the customer has no title, or a defective title, thereto, the banker shall not incur any liability to the true owner of the cheque by reason only of having received such payment.

Part IV.

PROMISSORY NOTES.

83. (1) A promissory note is an unconditional promise in writing made by one person to another, signed by the maker, engaging to pay, on demand or at a fixed or determinable future time, a sum certain in money, to, or to the order of, a specified person, or to bearer.

(2) An instrument in the form of a note payable to maker's order is not a note within the meaning of this section unless and until it is indorsed by the maker.

(3) A note is not invalid by reason only that it contains also a pledge of collateral security with authority to sell or dispose thereof.

(4) A note which is, or on the face of it purports to be, both made and payable within the British Islands is an inland note. Any other note is a foreign note.

84. A promissory note is inchoate and incomplete until delivery thereof to the payee or bearer.

85. (1) A promissory note may be made by two or more makers, and they may be liable thereon jointly, or jointly and severally, according to its tenor.

(2) Where a note runs 'I promise to pay,' and is signed by two or more persons, it is deemed to be their joint and several note.

86. (1) Where a note payable on demand has been indorsed, it must be presented for payment within a reasonable time of the indorsement. If it be not so presented, the indorser is discharged.

(2) In determining what is a reasonable time, regard

shall be had to the nature of the instrument, the usage of trade, and the facts of the particular case.

(3) Where a note payable on demand is negotiated, it is not deemed to be overdue, for the purpose of affecting the holder with defects of title of which he had no notice, by reason that it appears that a reasonable time for presenting it for payment has elapsed since its issue.

87. (1) Where a promissory note is in the body of it made payable at a particular place, it must be presented for payment at that place in order to render the maker liable. In any other case presentment for payment is not necessary in order to render the maker liable.[1]

(2) Presentment for payment is necessary in order to render the indorser of a note liable.

(3) Where a note is in the body of it made payable at a particular place, presentment at that place is necessary in order to render an indorser liable; but when a place of payment is indicated by way of memorandum only, presentment at that place is sufficient to render the indorser liable, but a presentment to the maker elsewhere, if sufficient in other respects, shall also suffice.

88. The maker of a promissory note by making it, —

(1) Engages that he will pay it according to its tenor;

(2) Is precluded from denying to a holder in due course the existence of the payee and his then capacity to indorse.

89. (1) Subject to the provisions in this part, and except as by this section provided, the provisions of this Act relating to bills of exchange apply, with the necessary modifications, to promissory notes.

(2) In applying those provisions the maker of a note

---

[1] Compare ante, p. 22.

shall be deemed to correspond with the acceptor of a bill, and the first indorser of a note shall be deemed to correspond with the drawer of an accepted bill payable to drawer's order.

(3) The following provisions as to bills do not apply to notes; namely, provisions relating to, —

(*a*) Presentment for acceptance;
(*b*) Acceptance;
(*c*) Acceptance supra protest;
(*d*) Bills in a set.

(4) Where a foreign note is dishonoured, protest thereof is unnecessary.

Part V.

SUPPLEMENTARY.

90. A thing is deemed to be done in good faith, within the meaning of this Act, where it is in fact done honestly, whether it is done negligently or not.

91. (1) Where, by this Act, any instrument or writing is required to be signed by any person, it is not necessary that he should sign it with his own hand, but it is sufficient if his signature is written thereon by some other person by or under his authority.

(2) In the case of a corporation, where, by this Act, any instrument or writing is required to be signed, it is sufficient if the instrument or writing be sealed with the corporate seal.

But nothing in this section shall be construed as requiring the bill or note of a corporation to be under seal.

92. Where, by this Act, the time limited for doing any act or thing is less than three days, in reckoning time, non-business days are excluded.

'Non-business days,' for the purposes of this Act, means,—

(*a*) Sunday, Good Friday, Christmas Day;

(*b*) A bank holiday under the Bank Holidays Act, 1871, or Acts amending it;

(*c*) A day appointed by Royal proclamation as a public fast or thanksgiving day.

Any other day is a business day.

93. For the purposes of this Act, where a bill or note is required to be protested within a specified time or before some further proceeding is taken, it is sufficient that the bill has been noted for protest before the expiration of the specified time or the taking of the proceeding; and the formal protest may be extended at any time thereafter as of the date of the noting.

94. Where a dishonoured bill or note is authorised or required to be protested, and the services of a notary cannot be obtained at the place where the bill is dishonoured, any householder or substantial resident of the place may, in the presence of two witnesses, give a certificate, signed by them, attesting the dishonour of the bill, and the certificate shall in all respects operate as if it were a formal protest of the bill.

The form given in Schedule I.[1] to this Act may be used with necessary modifications, and if used shall be sufficient.

95. The provisions of this Act as to crossed cheques shall apply to a warrant for payment of dividend.

96. The enactments mentioned in the second schedule to this Act are hereby repealed as from the commencement of this Act to the extent in that schedule mentioned.[2]

[1] Schedules omitted here.   [2] Unimportant here.

Provided that such repeal shall not affect anything done or suffered, or any right, title, or interest acquired or accrued before the commencement of this Act, or any legal proceeding or remedy in respect of any such thing, right, title, or interest.

97. (1) The rules in bankruptcy relating to bills of exchange, promissory notes, and cheques shall continue to apply thereto notwithstanding anything in this Act contained.

(2) The rules of common law, including the law merchant, save in so far as they are inconsistent with the express provisions of this Act, shall continue to apply to bills of exchange, promissory notes, and cheques.

(3) Nothing in this Act or in any repeal effected thereby shall affect —

(*a*) The provisions of the Stamp Act, 1870, or Acts amending it, or any law or enactment for the time being in force relating to the revenue;

(*b*) The provisions of the Companies Act, 1862, or Acts amending it, or any Act relating to joint stock banks or companies;

(*c*) The provisions of any Act relating to or confirming the privileges of the Bank of England or the Bank of Ireland respectively;

(*d*) The validity of any usage relating to dividend warrants, or the indorsements thereof.

98. Nothing in this Act, or in any repeal effected thereby, shall extend or restrict, or in any way alter or affect the law and practice in Scotland in regard to summary diligence.

99. Where any Act or document refers to any enactment repealed by this Act, the Act or document shall be construed, and shall operate, as if it referred to the corresponding provisions of this Act.

100. In any judicial proceeding in Scotland, any fact relating to a bill of exchange, bank cheque, or promissory note, which is relevant to any question of liability thereon, may be proved by parol evidence. Provided that this enactment shall not in any way affect the existing law and practice whereby the party who is, according to the tenor of any bill of exchange, bank cheque, or promissory note, debtor to the holder in the amount thereof, may be required, as a condition of obtaining a sist of diligence, or suspension of a charge, or threatened charge, to make such consignation, or to find such caution as the court or judge before whom the cause is depending may require.

This section shall not apply to any case where the bill of exchange, bank cheque, or promissory note, has undergone the sesennial prescription.

INDEX.

INDEX.

A.

ABSCONDING,
    as excuse of presentment, 151, 152.
ABSOLUTE DEFENCES, 172, 174–205.
        (*See* LEGAL OR ABSOLUTE DEFENCES.)
ABSOLUTE NOTICE, 207, 208, 210–212.
        (*See* NOTICE OF EQUITIES.)
ACCEPTANCE,
    presentment for, 57–60.
    in case of bills payable after date, 58–60.
    in case of bills payable at or after sight, 59.
    as admission of drawer's signature, 197–199.
    extent of admission, 198, 199.
    as admission or warranty of capacity, 199.
    conditional, 40, 41.
        (*See* ACCEPTOR'S CONTRACT; PROMISE TO ACCEPT.)
ACCEPTOR'S CONTRACT,
    acceptance proper, 36–39.
    drawee before acceptance under no liability, 36.
    what acceptance is, 36.
    how acceptor contracts, 36, 37.
    how acceptance made, 37, 38.
    statutes, 37.
    modes of acceptance, 38.
    'accepted,' 38.
    name of drawee, 38.
    'presented' or 'seen,' 38.
    oral acceptance, 38.
    such acceptance not within Statute of Frauds, 38, 39.
    quasi-acceptance, 39–45.
    'by giving credit,' 39, 40.
    conditional acceptance, 40, 41.
    acceptance supra protest, 41, 42.
    acceptance 'in case of need,' 42.
    'virtual acceptance' or promise to accept, 42–45.
    certification of cheque, 45, 56, 57.
        (*See* CERTIFICATION OF CHEQUE.)

ACCEPTOR'S CONTRACT,—*continued*.
    admission of genuineness, 197–199.
    admission of capacity, 199.
                (*See* ACCEPTANCE; FORGERY.)

ACCIDENT,
    as an excuse of presentment, 94, 95.
    alteration of paper by, 184–187.

ACCOMMODATION CONTRACTS,
    what are, 157.
    consideration, 157, 158.
    accommodation party a surety sub modo, 158, 159.
    taking accommodation paper with notice, 159.
    taking accommodation paper for pre-existing debt, 219.
    fraudulent diversion, 226.

AGENCY,
    signing as 'agent,' 30–32.
    mere description of signer, 30, 31.
    exempting oneself from liability, 31, 32.
    notice of dishonor by agent, 119.
    notice of dishonor to agent, 122.
    agent treated as owner as to time of notice of dishonor, 133, 134.
    creditor taking paper as agent, 218.

ALTERATION,
    definition of term, 181.
    changing legal effect, 181.
    by accident or mistake, 184–187.
    without consent, 186–189.
    by stranger, 190.
    by custodian or agent, 190.
    facilitated by last holder, 191–194.
    doctrine of estoppel in such cases, 193.
    removing marginal terms, 194, 195.
    cutting instrument in two, 195.
    forgery, 196–199.
                (*See* FORGERY.)

ANOMALOUS SIGNATURE,
    a kind of indorsement, 33.
    different doctrines as to, 33, 34.
    not for security of payee, 34, 35.

ATTORNEY FEES, 17, 18.

B.

BANK,
    presence of paper in, 83.
    branches of, 89.
    paper payable at, 116, 117.
    power of officers of, to certify cheques, 45.

INDEX.

BANKRUPT,
    agreement with, for time, 237, 238.
BANKRUPTCY,
    as excuse of presentment, 103, 104.
BILL OF EXCHANGE,
    defined, 6.
BLANK SPACES,
    leaving, in completed paper, 191–194, 227.
    in uncompleted paper, 227.
        (*See* LEGAL OR ABSOLUTE DEFENCES.)

C.

'CANADA MONEY,'
    paper payable in, 15.
CAPACITY,
    of parties in general, 8, 200–203.
    admission or warranty of, 199.
    of corporations, 202, 203.
CASHIER OF BANK,
    power of, to certify cheques, 45.
CERTAINTY OF PARTIES, 13, 14.
CERTAINTY OF SUM,
    necessity of, 16.
    alternate sums, 17.
    attorney fees, 17, 18.
    payment 'on or before' a certain time, 18.
    payment with current exchange, 18.
    accelerating time of payment, 18, 19.
CERTAINTY OF TIME,
    necessity of, 19.
    condition or contingency, 19, 22.
    payment out of particular fund, 19.
    additional language, 20, 21.
    definiteness of time, 23.
    payment 'on or before' a certain time, 24.
    no time stated, 24.
    'when convenient,' 24.
    reasonable time, 24.
    'at such times as' the holder may require, 25.
    time in alternative, 25.
CERTIFICATE OF PROTEST.
        (*See* PROTEST.)
CERTIFICATION OF CHEQUE,
    distinguished from acceptance, 45.

CERTIFICATION OF CHEQUE, — *continued*.
    how made, 45.
    effect of, 45, 46, 56, 57.
    authority of teller of bank, 45.
        of cashier, president, or vice-president, 45.
    in certain cases discharges drawer, 56, 57.
    ground of same, 57.
CHEQUE,
    defined, 6.
    certification of, 45, 46, 56, 57. (*See* CERTIFICATION OF CHEQUE.)
    liability of drawer of, 52–57.
    not properly a bill of exchange, 52. (*See* DRAWER'S CONTRACT.)
CIPHER,
    signature in, 25.
COLLATERAL SECURITY,
    paper taken as, 214–219.
COMPETENCY,
    of parties in general, 8, 200–203.
    of indorser to impeach paper, for another, 79, 80.
    warranty of payee's, to indorse, 199.
    of corporations, 202, 203.
COMPOSITION AND RELEASE, 232–234.
CONDITION,
    fatal to bill, note, or cheque, 19–25.
CONDITIONAL ACCEPTANCE, 40, 41.
CONDITIONAL PAYMENT,
    paper taken in, 213–219.
CONFLICT OF LAWS,
    general doctrine of, 249.
    as to liability of maker or acceptor, 250–252.
    in regard to amount recoverable against maker or acceptor, 251, 252.
    as to liability of drawer or indorser, 252–255.
    in regard to presentment and demand, 252, 253.
    in regard to protest and notice, 253, 254.
    in regard to amount recoverable, 254, 255.
CONSENT,
    to alteration, 186–189.
CONSIDERATION,
    imposed upon the custom of merchants, 4, 5.
    valuable, 157, 158, 213–219.
CONTRACT,
    consideration, 8, 157, 158, 213–219.
    union of minds, 8, 174–203.
    competency of parties, 8, 199–203.
        (*See* LEGAL OR ABSOLUTE DEFENCES.)

CORPORATIONS,
    capacity of, 202, 203.
'CURRENCY,'
    paper payable in, 15.
'CURRENT EXCHANGE,'
    paper payable with, 18.
'CURRENT FUNDS,'
    paper payable in, 15.
CUSTOM OF MERCHANTS,
    as origin of law of bills and notes, 1.
    a foreign product, 2.
    what foreign merchants brought to England, 2.
    how the custom became law, 2–4.
    knew nothing of consideration, 4.
    consideration imposed by the common law courts, 4, 5.
    custom of merchants becomes law merchant, 8.
CUTTING IN TWO, 195.

D.

DAMAGES,
    in case of equities, 229, 230.
    conflict of laws as to, 250–255.
DEATH,
    as excuse of presentment, 96, 97, 101, 105.
    as excuse of notice, 122, 123.
DEFINITIONS,
    'negotiability,' 2.
    'promissory note,' 6.
    'cheque,' 6.
    'bill of exchange,' 6.
    'foreign bill,' 6.
    'inland bill,' 6.
    'maker,' 6, 7.
    'drawer,' 7.
    'payee,' 7.
    'drawee,' 7.
    'indorsee,' 7.
    'holder,' 7.
    'alteration,' 181.
    'bona fide holder for value,' 206–212, 213–221.
DELIVERY,
    fraud in, 174, 179.
DEMAND.
        (*See* PRESENTMENT AND DEMAND.)
DILIGENCE,
    in fixing indorser's liability, 129, 131, 132, 142.

DISCHARGE.
(*See* PAYMENT.)

DISCHARGE OF SURETY,
dealings with principal debtor, 231.
indorser as surety, 231.
surrender of securities, 232.
agreement for time, 232–234.
compositions, 232–234.
reserving rights, 233, 234, 238.
'release' a term of double meaning, 234, 235.
agreement to forbear necessary, 235–238.
taking further security, 235, 236.
agreement must be valid, 235, 237.
    made with bankrupt, 237, 238.
request to sue, 238.
accommodation contracts distinguished, 239, 240.
doctrine of suretyship not fully applied to such, 239, 240.
agreement with stranger, 240.
ground of doctrine as to dealings with principal debtor, 241.

DRAWER'S CONTRACT,
distinguished from maker's, 47.
drawer, in position of first indorser, 47.
right to draw, 47–52.
drawing without funds, 48, 49.
reasonable ground for drawing, 49–51.
drawing on oneself, 52.
corporation or partnership drawing on itself, 52.
drawer of cheque, 52–57.
cheque not properly a bill of exchange, 52.
differences between the two as to drawer, 52, 53.
drawer of cheque not receiving notice of dishonor, 53, 54.
diligence of holder, 55.
keeping cheque in circulation, 55, 56.
certification of cheque discharges drawer in certain cases, 56, 57.
presentment for acceptance of bills payable after date, 58–60.
conflict of laws as to drawer's contract, 252–255.

DRAWER'S SIGNATURE,
admission of, 197–199. (*See* ACCEPTANCE.)

DURESS, 222.

E.

EPIDEMIC,
as excuse of presentment, 96.

EQUITIES,
distinguished from absolute defences, 172, 173, 227.
imply contract, 206.

EQUITIES, — *continued.*
    domain of bona fide holders for value, 206.
    term 'bona fide holder for value,' 206.
    term 'bona fide holder,' 206-212.
    notice, 207-212.
    confusion of terms of notice, 207.
    absolute notice, 207, 208, 210-212.
    constructive notice, 207-210.
    putting upon inquiry, 208-210.
    negligence not bad faith, 209, 210.
    suspicion of wrong-doing, 210.
    knowledge of equities, 210.
    notice in sense of knowledge, 210, note.
    forms of absolute notice, 211, 212.
    term 'holder for value,' 213-221.
    complement of 'bona fide holder,' 213.
    valuable consideration explained, 213-218.
    conflict of authority in regard to taking for pre-existing debt, 214-219.
    'valid' consideration, 214.
    New York doctrine, 214, 215.
    doctrine of federal courts, 215-217.
        of English courts, 217.
    subject considered in principle, 217, 218.
    creditor taking as agent or bailee, 218.
    taking accommodation paper for pre-existing debt, 219.
    forbearance, 219.
    implication of agreement to forbear, 219.
    parting with rights, 220.
    conditional payment and collateral security, 220.
    paper taken in absolute payment, 220, 221.
    newly-created debt, 221.
    mediate and immediate parties, 221, 222.
    existence of equities, how shown, 222-224.
    fraud, duress, and illegality, 222-224.
    these a presumptive defence, 223, 224.
    other equities, 224.
    subsequent notice, 224, 225.
    what meant by equities, 225, 226.
    accommodation paper, 226.
    fraudulent diversion thereof, 226.
    filling blank spaces in instrument, 227.
    set-off, 228.
    holder with notice or without value taking from bona fide holder for value, 228.
    amount of recovery, 229, 230.

EQUITIES, — *continued*.
    buying paper outright, 229.
    taking paper as security, 230.

ESTOPPEL,
    in cases of negligent delivery, 178.
    in cases of alteration, 193.
    acceptor's estoppel, 197–199.

EVIDENCE,
    certificate of protest as, 107–109.
    as to liability of indorser, 71–73.
    indorser's competency as witness for another party, to impeach paper, 79, 80.

EXCUSE OF NOTICE,
    temporary, 94–97, 143.
    waiver or excuse of presentment, 154.
    notice not lightly dispensed with, 155.
    express waiver of notice, 155, 156.
    drawing a bill without reason, 156.
    drawing on oneself, 156.

EXCUSE OF PRESENTMENT,
    temporary, 94–97, 143.
    waivers, 143–147.
    promise to pay, 144.
    requesting the holder to give time, 144, 145.
    waiver of protest of inland bill or promissory note, 145, 146.
    waiver may be before or after maturity, 146, 147.
    ignorance of facts, 146.
    ignorance of law, 146, 147.
    fund put into indorser's hands, 147, 148.
    indorser as primary debtor, 148, 149.
    excuse of presentment alone, 149, 150.
    excuse of demand, 150.
    excuse of both presentment and demand, 150–153.
    removal, 150, 151.
    absconding, 151, 152.
    insolvency, 152.
    waiving notice of dishonor, 152.
    death of maker or acceptor, 152, 153.

EXCUSE OF PROTEST,
    as to foreign bills, 153, 154.
    as to inland bills, 154.

F.

FORBEARANCE,
    agreement for, 219.

FOREIGN BILL,
    defined, 6.
    protest of, 106–108.
FOREIGN MERCHANTS,
    introduce custom of merchants, 2–8.
FORGERY,
    of indorsement, 195–197.
    of drawer's signature, 197–199.
    acceptor's estoppel, 197, 199.
FRAUD,
    as an equity, 222, 226. (*See* EQUITIES.)
    as an absolute defence, 179, 180. (*See* LEGAL OR ABSOLUTE DEFENCES.)
    in form of misrepresentation, 179, 180.
FUNDS,
    drawing on particular, 19.
    drawing without, 48, 49.

G.

GENUINENESS,
    warranty of 197–199.
GRACE,
    a foreign product, 2.
    originally mere indulgence, 3.
    in case of guaranty and suretyship, 168.
        (*See* PRESENTMENT AND DEMAND.)
GUARANTY AND SURETYSHIP,
    accommodation party a surety sub modo, 158, 159.
    distinction between guaranty and suretyship, 161, 162.
    guaranty in specific sense, 162–169.
    consideration, 162–165.
    guaranty at time of principal contract, 162.
    guaranty afterwards, 163, 164.
    Statute of Frauds, 164, 165.
    negotiability of guaranty, 165–168.
    grace, 168.
    presentment and notice, 168, 169.
    suretyship in specific sense, 169.

H.

HOLDER'S POSITION,
    right to sue mediate party, 170, 171.
    presumptive right of holder, 171.
    legal or absolute defences distinguished from equities, 172, 173.

I.

IGNORANCE OF FACT,
 in waiver, 146.
IGNORANCE OF LAW,
 in waiver, 146.
ILLEGALITY,
  (*See* LEGAL OR ABSOLUTE DEFENCES.)
INDORSER'S CONTRACT,
 nature of, 61, 74.
 who may indorse, 61, 62.
 when indorsement necessary, 62.
 transfer without indorsement of paper payable to order, 62.
 in what form, 63.
 by him who has the legal title, 63.
 indorsement by late holder's personal representative, 63.
 partnership indorsement, 63, 64.
 indorsement by partners, 64.
 to one of the partnership, 64.
 death of partner, 64.
 partnership holders of paper payable to bearer or indorsed in blank, 64, 65.
 dissolution of partnership otherwise than by death, 65.
 right of survivors to indorse, 65.
 paper payable to agent requires no indorsement to principal, 65.
 no part indorsement allowed, 65, 66.
 different forms of indorsement, 66.
 indorsement in blank, 67.
  in full, 67.
  in full restrictive, 67, 68.
  without recourse, 68.
  for collection, 68.
 other cases of indorsement, 69.
 conditional indorsement, 69, 70.
 joint indorsement, 70.
 indorsement on separate paper, 70.
 apparent indorsement, 71–73.
 evidence to control the same, 71–73.
 conditions of indorser's liability, 74.
 legal effects of indorsement, 74–80.
 an order to pay, 74, 75.
 compared to drawing a bill, 75, 76.
 extent of the equivalency, 75, 76.
 indorsement admits validity of the paper, 76, 77.
 whether a warranty of validity, 77–79.
 warranty of capacity, 78.

INDEX. 317

INDORSER'S CONTRACT, — *continued.*
    whether indorser a competent witness to dispute validity, 79, 80.
    conflict of authority upon the subject, 79, 80.
    presentment and demand distinguished, 81–84.
        (*See* PRESENTMENT AND DEMAND.)
    modus of these steps, 81–84 (*See* id.)
    place of presentment, 84–89. (*See* id.)
    time of presentment, 89–100. (*See* id.)
    presentment, by whom, 100–103. (*See* id.)
    presentment, to whom, 103–105. (*See* id.)
    protest, 106–110. (*See* PROTEST.)
    notice of dishonor, 110–142. (*See* NOTICE OF DISHONOR.)
    excuse of presentment and notice, 143–153, 154–156. (*See* EXCUSE OF SAME.)
    excuse of protest, 153, 154. (*See* EXCUSE OF PROTEST.)
    conflict of laws as to indorser, 252–255. (*See* CONFLICT OF LAWS.)

INEVITABLE ACCIDENT,
    as excuse of presentment, 94, 95.

INLAND BILL,
    defined, 6.
    protest of, 108–110.

INSOLVENCY,
    as excuse for presentment, 152.

INUREMENT,
    notice of dishonor by, 127, 128.

K.

KNOWLEDGE OF DISHONOR,
    distinguished from notice, 110, 210, note.

KNOWLEDGE OF EQUITIES,
    distinguished from notice, 210.

L.

LAW MERCHANT,
    distinguished from common law, 8, 9.
    custom of merchants becomes law merchant, 8.

LAWS, CONFLICT OF.
        (*See* CONFLICT OF LAWS.)

LEGAL OR ABSOLUTE DEFENCES,
    distinguished from equities, 172, 173, 227.
    want of contract, 174–203.
    delivery, 174–179.
    may be made by intention or by negligence, 175.

LEGAL OR ABSOLUTE DEFENCES, — *continued.*
   delivery by intention, 175, 176.
      by a custodian, 175, 176.
   delivery by negligence, 176, 177.
   paper stolen or obtained by fraud in delivery, 177, 178.
   estoppel in relation to cases of theft through negligence, 178.
   doctrine of two innocent persons as to such cases, 178, 179.
   fraud in esse contractus, 179, 180.
   distinguished from case of misrepresentation, 179.
   what this kind of fraud consists in, 179, 180.
   doctrine of two innocent persons as to such cases, 180.
   alteration, 181-194.
   definition of the term, 181.
   changing legal effect of paper, 181-183.
   alteration by accident, or mistake, 184-187.
   without consent, 186-189.
   alteration by stranger, 190.
      by a custodian or agent, 190.
   alteration facilitated by last holder, 191-194.
   doctrine of estoppel in such cases, 193.
   leaving blanks not necessarily negligent, 194.
   removing marginal terms, 194, 195.
   cutting instruments in two, 195.
   forged indorsement, 195-197.
   forgery of payee's name by drawer, 196.
   forgery of drawer's signature, 197-199.
   acceptance as admission of drawer's signature, 197-199.
   competency of payee to indorse, 199.
   acknowledging signature, 200.
   incapacity, 200-203.
   incapacity to contract distinguished from incapacity to transfer, 201.
   incapacity of corporations, 202, 203.
   illegality of contract, 203-205.
   paper void by statute, 204, 205.
      exception of bona fide holders for value, 205.

M.

MAIL,
   notice by, 124-127, 135.
MAKER'S CONTRACT,
   signature, 27, 28.
   joint and several note, 28-30.
   nature of joint promise, 28, 29.
   nature of several promise, 29.

MAKER'S CONTRACT, — *continued.*
    promise by partners, 29.
    promise of surety, 29, 30.
    signing as 'agent' and the like, 30–32.
    anomalous undertaking of stranger, 33–35.
    conflict of laws as to, 250–252.

MARGINAL TERMS,
    removal of, 194, 195.

MARK,
    signing by, 25.

MATURITY OF PAPER, 91, 92, 128–134.
    (See NOTICE OF DISHONOR.)

MESSENGER,
    notice of dishonor by, 127.

MISTAKE,
    as excuse of presentment, 94, 95.
    alteration of paper by, 184–187.

MONEY,
    payment in, 14.
    statute of Anne, 14.
    what meant by money, 15.
    'in cotton,' 15.
    'in good East India bonds,' 15.
    'in carpenter's work,' 15.
    'in current funds,' 15.
    'in Canada money,' 15.
    'in current bank notes,' 15, note.
    'in good current money,' 15, note.
    'in Arkansas money,' 15, note.
    what the courts will know as equivalent to money, 16.
    exceptional rule as to consideration, 16.

N.

'NEED' ACCEPTANCE,
    in case of, 42.

NEGLIGENCE,
    in delivery, 176–178.
    facilitating alteration, 191–194.
    (See LEGAL OR ABSOLUTE DEFENCES.)

NEGOTIABILITY,
    meaning of, 2, 3.
    a foreign product, 2.
    of guaranty, 165–168.

NOTARY,
    protest by, 102, 103.
    deputy of, 102, 103.
    absence of, 103.

NOTICE OF DISHONOR,
> form of, 110–119.
>> no form of words prescribed, 110.
>> of what indorser should be apprised, 110, 111.
>> notice of non-payment merely, 111–119.
>> course of English authority as to such notice, 112–115.
>> course of American authority, 115–119.
>> paper payable at bank distinguished, 116, 117.
>> purpose of notice, 118.
>> notification that indorser is looked to for payment, 119.
> notice, by whom, 119.
>> by holder or agent, or by indorser bound to pay, 119, 120.
>> notice by stranger, 119, 120.
>> notice by indorser, 120, 121.
>> notice by acceptor or maker, 121, 122.
> notice to whom, 122, 123.
>> to indorser or agent, 122.
>> death of indorser, 122, 123.
>> death of partner indorser, 123.
> notice, how, 123–128.
>> direct and expeditious mode, 123, 124.
>> by mail, 124–127, 135.
>> personal notice, 127, 135.
>> messenger, 127.
>> successive notices, 127.
>> inurement, 127, 128.
> notice, when, 128–134.
>> on day of dishonor or day after, 128.
>> diligence, 129, 131, 132, 142.
>> non-secular days, 129.
>> departure of mail, 129, 130.
>> several successive indorsements, 129, 130.
>> whether holder has entire day, 130, 131.
>> notice by indorser, time of, 132, 133.
>> notice on Sunday, 133.
>> agent, 133, 134.
>> paper indorsed after maturity, 134.
> notice, where, 135–141.
>> personal notice, 135.
>> by mail, 135.
>> several post-offices in indorser's town, 135, 136.
>> post-office address, 137.
>> no post-office in indorser's town, 137.
>> removal of indorser, 137, 138.
>> absence from home, 138, 139.
>> making inquiry, 139–141.

NOTICE OF DISHONOR, — *continued.*
    place of date, 141.
    diligence, 142.
    excuse of notice, 154–156.
    conflict of laws as to notice of dishonor, 254.
NOTICE OF EQUITIES,
    taking accommodation paper with notice, 159.
              (*See* EQUITIES.)
'NOTING,' 109, 110.

O.

ORDER,
    need of, for bill of exchange or cheque, 12, 13.
    word 'order' not required, 12.

P.

PARTICULAR FUND,
    paper payable out of, 19.
PARTIES,
    joint and several, 28–30.
    joint, 104, 105.
    mediate and immediate, 221, 222.
PARTNERS,
    promise by, 29.
    indorsement by, 63, 64.
    death of partner indorser, 64, 65, 105, 123.
    dissolution of partnership not by death, 65.
PAYEE,
    must be existing, 13.
    may be ascertainable by evidence ab extra, 13.
    fictitious payee, 13, 14.
    payment to either of two persons, 14.
    capacity of, 199.
PAYMENT,
    in money, 14.
    on or before a certain time, 18.
    certainty of time of, 19–25.
    paper taken in conditional, 220.
    when it extinguishes all liability, 242.
    of unnegotiable paper, 242.
    presumptions of, 242, 243.
    surrender of paper, 244.
    should be made at the right time, 245.
        to the right person, 246.
        by the right person, 246–248.
    who is meant by the right person, 246–248.

PENCIL,
    signature in, 25.
POST-OFFICE,
    notice of dishonor through, 124-127, 135.
    several post-offices in same town, 135, 136.
    no post-office, 137.
PRE-EXISTING DEBT,
    as a valuable consideration, 214-219.
PRESENTMENT AND DEMAND,
    presentment for acceptance, 57-60. (*See* ACCEPTANCE.)
    distinction between presentment and demand, 81, 82.
    presentment, what, 81.
    why presentment required, 82.
    equivalent acts, 82, 83.
    presence of paper in bank, 83.
    demand and equivalents, 84.
    place of, 84-89.
    paper payable at place named, 84, 85.
    drawer may designate place, 85.
    paper payable generally, 85.
    place of business, 85-87.
    place of residence, 86, 87.
    removal, 87, 88.
    date as evidence of place, 88, 89.
    bank with branches, 89.
    time of presentment, 89-100.
    in case of presentment for acceptance, 89-92.
    bills payable after date, 89, 90.
    bills payable at or after sight, 90, 91.
    indorsement after maturity, 91, 92.
    presentment for payment, 92, 93.
    at maturity, 92.
    where grace is excluded, 92, 93.
    with grace, 93.
    how grace is reckoned, 93.
    instalment notes, 93, 94.
    obstacle to presentment, 94.
    what constitutes an obstacle, 94.
    inevitable accident, 94, 95.
    existence of war, 95, 96.
    epidemic, 96.
    death of maker, 96, 97.
    time of day of making presentment, 97-100.
    early closing, 99.
    presentment, by whom, 100-103.
    by holder or his agent, 100.

PRESENTMENT AND DEMAND, — *continued.*
    by one not entitled to receive payment, 100, 101.
    death of holder, 101.
    foreign bills often have double presentment, 102.
    action of notary in case of foreign bill, 102.
    notary's deputy, 102, 103.
    absence of notary, 103.
    presentment, to whom, 103–105.
    to maker or acceptor, or to his agent, 103.
    death of maker or acceptor, 103.
    bankruptcy of maker or acceptor, 103, 104.
    maker as 'agent,' 104.
    two or more makers or acceptors, 104, 105.
    joint parties, 104, 105.
    partners, 105.
    death of one of the joint parties, 105.
    several makers or acceptors, 105.
    conflict of laws as to presentment, 253, 254.
PRESUMPTION,
    of payment, 242, 243.
    from fraud, duress, or illegality, 222–224.
PROMISE,
    need of, for promissory note, 10–12.
    word 'promise' not required, 11.
    equivalents of 'promise,' 11, 12.
    to accept, 43, 44.
PROMISSORY NOTE,
    defined, 6.
PROMISE TO ACCEPT,
    called 'virtual acceptance,' 43.
    a contract of the common law, 43.
    not of the law merchant, 43, 44.
    nature of, 44.
    before and after the bill, 44.
    should identify the bill, 44.
    who may act upon, 44.
    consideration, 44, 45.
PROTEST,
    by notary, 102, 103.
    by deputy, 102, 103.
    absence of notary, 103.
    in case of foreign bill, 106–108.
    how manifested, 106.
    no form of words prescribed, 106.
    what facts should appear, 106, 107.
    certificate of protest as the evidence of dishonor, 107, 108.

PROTEST,—*continued.*
    States of the Union foreign to each other, 108.
    protest of inland bills and promissory notes, 108–110.
    not necessary, 108.
    permitted by statute, 108, 109.
    certificate as evidence, 109.
    when to be made, 109.
    'noting,' 109, 110.
    conflict of laws as to protest, 253.
PUTTING UPON INQUIRY, 208–210.

Q.

QUASI-ACCEPTANCE, 39–45.

R.

REASONABLE GROUND,
    for drawing bill, 49–51.
REASONABLE TIME, 24.
'RELEASE' AND COMPOSITION, 232–234.
REMOVAL,
    as excuse of presentment, 87, 88, 150, 151.

S.

SET-OFF,
    as an equity, 228.
SIGNATURE,
    may be in pencil, 25.
    by mark, 25.
    in cipher or the like. 25.
    omission of, 26.
    of maker, 27.
    may be anywhere on the paper, 27.
    out of usual place, 27.
    joint and several, 28–30.
    of agent, 30–32.
    anomalous signature of stranger, 33–35.
    admission of drawer's, 197–199.
    acknowledging signature, 200.
STATES,
    foreign to each other, 108.
STATUTE,
    paper void by, 204, 205.
STATUTE OF FRAUDS,
    oral acceptance, 38, 39.
    as to contract of guarantor or surety, 164, 165.

STRANGER,
    notice of dishonor by, 119, 120.
SUNDAY.
            (*See* NOTICE OF DISHONOR.)
SURETYSHIP.
            (*See* GUARANTY AND SURETYSHIP.)
SURRENDER OF PAPER,
    on payment, 244.
SUSPICION,
    of defence, turning away, 210.

T.

TELLER OF BANK,
    power of, to certify cheques, 45.
TIME OF PAYMENT,
    certainty of, 19-25.
TREASURER,
    signing as, 32.
TRUSTEES,
    exempting themselves from liability, 31, 32.

U.

UNNEGOTIABLE PAPER,
    payment of, 242.

V.

VALID CONSIDERATION, 214.
VALUABLE CONSIDERATION,
    term explained, 213-219.
'VIRTUAL ACCEPTANCE,' 42-45.

W.

WAIVER.
        (*See* EXCUSE OF NOTICE; EXCUSE OF PRESENTMENT.)
WAR,
    as excuse of presentment, 95, 96.
WARRANTY,
    by indorsement, 77-79.
    by acceptance, 197-199.
WORDS.
            (*See* DEFINITIONS; MONEY.)
WRITING,
    bills, notes, and cheques must be written, 10.
    law-merchant, not statute, so requires, 10.
    no particular writing material required, 10.
    in pencil proper, 10.

THE STUDENTS' SERIES.

ELEMENTARY LAW TREATISES

BY ABLE WRITERS,

including the most important topics of law.

The volumes of the Students' Series are in use as Text-Books in leading Law Schools throughout the United States.

In planning this series of law books for students, you have rendered a very great service, not only to the students themselves, but also to the profession. There has been no greater obstacle to all efforts for a higher standard of legal education than the lack of such books. — Prof. WILLIAM G. HAMMOND, Law Department, Iowa State University.

If these unpretending volumes, so full of instruction, are estimated at their true value, their sale and circulation will not be confined to the legal profession alone. — HON. JOHN CROWELL, LL.D., President of Ohio State and Union Law College.

The plan needs only development to render it popular, and the volumes now out are a worthy execution of it. . . . Either volume would serve the purposes of a mature lawyer, desiring to refresh his memory of the general principles of the subject. — N. Y. TIMES.

VOLUMES READY.

BIGELOW ON TORTS.
BIGELOW ON EQUITY.
HEARD ON CRIMINAL PLEADING.
HEARD ON CIVIL PLEADING.
COOLEY ON CONSTITUTIONAL LAW.
LANGDELL'S SUMMARY OF CONTRACTS.
CURTIS ON UNITED STATES COURTS.
MAY ON CRIMINAL LAW.
STIMSON'S LAW GLOSSARY.
ROBINSON'S ELEMENTARY LAW.
EWELL'S MEDICAL JURISPRUDENCE.
STEPHEN'S DIGEST OF EVIDENCE.
ROBINSON ON FORENSIC ORATORY.
BIGELOW ON BILLS, NOTES, AND CHECKS
BRYANT ON CODE PLEADING.

Volumes on Agency, Contracts, Corporations, Insurance, Sales, and Wills are in preparation.

PRICE OF EACH VOLUME. — CLOTH, $2.50 *net*; LAW SHEEP, $3.00 *net* Postage 10 cents per volume additional.

I. BIGELOW ON TORTS.

The style is attractive, the definitions concise and accurate, and the size of the volume so moderate as to be equally attractive both to the practitioner and the student. — *From Hon. John Crowell, President of Ohio State and Union Law College, Cleveland.*

ELEMENTS OF THE LAW OF TORTS FOR THE USE OF STUDENTS. — By MELVILLE M. BIGELOW, PH.D., author of "A Treatise on the Law of Estoppel," "A Treatise on the Law of Fraud," and Editor of "Leading Cases in the Law of Torts," etc. Fifth edition, revised and enlarged Cloth, $2.50 *net*; law sheep, $3.00 *net*.

Among the best books for the use of students, this popular text-book deservedly takes a high rank. It is in use in law schools all over the country: for example, in Boston University; University of Michigan; Northwestern University, Chicago; University of Texas; Washington and Lee University; also in Canada at the Osgoode Hall Law School, Toronto; and a few years since was adopted as a text-book in the famous University of Cambridge, England. *Probably no other students' book is so widely used.* The new fourth edition embraces many late cases, and a new chapter on Malicious Interference with Contracts. The whole book has been carefully revised, and many passages rewritten.

It seems to me admirably adapted to the purpose for which it is written. Mr. Bigelow is very happy in his statement of legal principles, and nowhere so much so, I think, as in this book. — *Hon. Thomas M. Cooley.*

I have looked through this volume with particular interest, from my own experience in teaching the same topic; and I have no hesitation in saying that it is much better fitted for the student than any work on Torts we have had before. — *Prof. William G. Hammond.*

Mr. Bigelow, in his clear and succinct statement of the duties of individuals toward each other as members of society, has made a valuable contribution to your Law Students' Series. — *Hon. Morrison R. Waite, Chief Justice of the United States.*

Its methodical arrangement of the classes of Torts, its clear style, and its simple manner of treatment, render it specially useful to beginners in the study of law. — *James R. Black, Central Law School of Indiana.*

It is the product of real thought and diligent labor; and the thought and labor have been too skilfully applied not to result in a substantial addition to legal literature. — *Boston Daily Advertiser.*

II. BIGELOW ON EQUITY.

The arrangement and treatment of the subject are admirable. — *From Samuel D. Davis, Professor of Law, Richmond College, Virginia.*

ELEMENTS OF EQUITY FOR THE USE OF STUDENTS. — By MELVILLE M. BIGELOW, Author of "Law of Estoppel," "Law of Fraud," etc. 12mo. Cloth, $2.50 *net*; law sheep, $3.00 *net*.

A clear and compact treatise, well fitted to be a manual of a student of law. — *Hon. John Bascom, University of Wisconsin.*

I have examined Bigelow on Equity. It is to be commended for its clearness and conciseness of statement. I regard the first chapter as a model. The doctrines of Tacking, Subrogation, and Marshalling, found in Chapters 14, 19, and 20, are more easily comprehended than in any other work on those subjects that I have seen. — *Hon J. H. Carpenter, Dean of Law Faculty, University of Wisconsin.*

III. HEARD ON CRIMINAL PLEADING.

It deserves an important position among the text-books in every Law School in the country. — *From William C. Robinson, Professor of Criminal Law, etc., Yale College.*

THE PRINCIPLES OF CRIMINAL PLEADING. — By FRANKLIN FISKE HEARD. 12mo. Cloth, $2.50 *net*; law sheep, $3.00 *net*.

The style in which the author writes is admirably adapted to the object to be accomplished, — it is clear and precise, and the whole matter is kept within the bounds of a manual. — *N. Y. Tribune.*

An interesting manual, thoroughly supported by legal authorities. — *Hon. John Bascom, University of Wisconsin.*

IV. HEARD ON CIVIL PLEADING.

An admirable companion volume to his "Principles of Criminal Pleading," — full, clear, concise. — *From Lemuel Moss, Indiana University, Bloomington.*

THE PRINCIPLES OF PLEADING IN CIVIL ACTIONS. — By FRANKLIN FISKE HEARD, Author of "The Principles of Criminal Pleading." 12mo. Cloth, $2.50 *net*; law sheep, $3.00 *net*.

He has taken the leading and established rules, and illustrated them by ample citations from ancient and modern learning. Whoever shall make himself thoroughly acquainted with those rules as here laid out and enforced, cannot fail of being a good pleader. — *Boston Courier.*

Under whatever system of statutory procedure a law student may design to practise, he will find it equally necessary to become familiar with the principles of common law pleading. Mr Heard's work is a plain and clear guide to these, and its silence in regard to many of the formal and adventitious technicalities of the older English system will commend it to American readers. — *Hon. Simeon E. Baldwin, Law Department of Yale College.*

V. COOLEY ON CONSTITUTIONAL LAW.

No Lawyer can afford to be without it, and every voter ought to have it. — *From Hon. J. H. Carpenter, Dean of Law Faculty, University of Wisconsin.*

THE GENERAL PRINCIPLES OF CONSTITUTIONAL LAW IN THE UNITED STATES OF AMERICA. — By THOMAS M. COOLEY, Author of "A Treatise on Constitutional Limitations." Second edition, by Alexis C. Angell, of the Detroit Bar. 12mo. Cloth, $2.50 *net*; law sheep, $3.00 *net*.

The new edition contains large additions. In its preparation, the editor, while aiming to keep the book a manual, and not to make it a digest, has treated briefly all important points covered by the cases decided up to a very recent date. He made such changes in the text and notes as had been required by the many important decisions upon constitutional law rendered in the last ten years.

A masterly exposition of the Federal Constitution as actually interpreted by the courts. . . . This book, of moderate dimensions, should be placed in every student's hands. — *Hon. P. Bliss, Dean of Law Department, State University of Missouri.*

It is worthy of the reputation of the distinguished author. It is the best book on the subject to be placed in the hands of a student, and is a convenient book of reference for any one. — *Prof. Manning F. Force, LL.D., Cincinnati Law School.*

It ought unquestionably to be made the basis of a course of instruction in all our higher schools and colleges. — *Hon. John F. Dillon, Professor of Columbia Law School, New York.*

It is a work of great value, not only for students in institutions of learning, but as well for the lawyer, to whom it supplies at once a Treatise and a Digest of Constitutional Law. — *Henry Hitchcock, Dean of the St. Louis Law School.*

Clearly and compactly written, and the general arrangement well adapted for students' use. — *Hon. Simeon E. Baldwin, Law Department of Yale College.*

I have examined it with great care, comparing it closely with the old edition, and testing it in various points. As a result, it gives me pleasure to state that we shall use the book both in the courses in constitutional history and law in the collegiate department, and in one of the classes in the law school. The work of the editor of the new edition, Mr. Angell, has been done with the exactness and care which an intimate acquaintance with him, as a classmate at the University of Michigan, led me to expect in whatever he undertook. Judge Cooley is fortunate in having so excellent an editor for the revision. — *Letter from George W. Knight, Professor of International and Constitutional Law, Ohio State University.*

Your name alone as its author is a sufficient guarantee of its high character and general usefulness, not only for the use of the students of law schools and other institutions of learning, for which it was originally prepared, but also for members of the bar. The matters discussed are stated so concisely and clearly as to be of great benefit for ready reference. The edition sent me seems to have all the late cases cited and referred to; and Mr. Angell seems to have been very careful and successful in making the changes from the first edition, and adding additional notes. — *Hon. Albert H. Horton, Chief Justice of the Supreme Court of Kansas, to Judge Cooley.*

VI. LANGDELL'S SUMMARY OF CONTRACTS.

No man competent to judge can read a page of it without at once recognizing the hand of a great master. Every line is compact of ingenious and original thought. — *American Law Review.*

A SUMMARY OF THE LAW OF CONTRACTS. — By C. C. LANGDELL, Dane Professor of Law in Harvard University. Second edition. 12mo. Cloth, $2.50 *net*; law sheep, $3.00 *net*.

VII. CURTIS ON UNITED STATES COURTS.

A work of the highest standard on the subject treated. — *Boston Post.*

CURTIS ON THE UNITED STATES COURTS. — Jurisdiction, Practice, and Peculiar Jurisprudence of the Courts of the United States. By BENJAMIN R. CURTIS, LL.D. Edited by GEORGE TICKNOR CURTIS and BENJAMIN R. CURTIS. 12mo. Cloth, $2.50 net; law sheep, $3.00 net.

These lectures were delivered by the late Judge Curtis to a class of students in the Harvard Law School, in the academic year 1872-73.

Cannot fail to be of great service to the student in the prosecution of his legal studies. *Chicago Legal News.*

It is by far the best epitome of that extensive subject, and the clearness of the style and orderly arrangement of the learned author will especially recommend it to students. *Hon. Edmund H. Bennett, Dean of School of Law, Boston University.*

There is not to-day in existence so admirable a treatise on United States courts and their jurisdiction as this little book. — *Milwaukee Republican.*

VIII. MAY'S CRIMINAL LAW.

I have carefully examined and read through May's Criminal Law. This work is certainly one of distinguished merit. Its definitions and statements of principles are clear and concise. Its discussions of doubtful or controverted points are calm and scholarly. The cases to which it refers embrace the most recent English and American decisions, and therefore, both as a *vade mecum* for the criminal lawyer and as a text-book for the student, it must at once take a high position in the literature of that branch of jurisprudence. — *From William C. Robinson, Professor of Criminal Law, etc., Yale College.*

THE LAW OF CRIMES. — By J. WILDER MAY, Chief Justice of the Municipal Court of the City of Boston. Second edition, edited by JOSEPH HENRY BEALE, JR., Assistant Professor of Law in Harvard University. 12mo. Cloth, $2.50 net; law sheep, $3.00 net.

This new edition of Judge May's deservedly popular work contains large additions. The editor states in the preface that the original plan included no discussion of the subjects of Criminal Pleading and Practice, but it was found that it would be better adapted to the use of students if these subjects were briefly considered, and this has accordingly been done. Much has also been added to the first chapter, which contains the general principles underlying the criminal law.

It is to be especially commended for its clear and concise definitions, as also for its citations of leading cases directly upon the matter under discussion. — *From J. H. Carpenter, Dean of Law Faculty, University of Wisconsin.*

It is not a mere synopsis, but an interesting discussion, quite full enough to give the student a true view of the subject, and minute enough to be a useful handbook to the practitioner. — *New York Law Journal.*

IX. STIMSON'S LAW GLOSSARY.

It is a valuable addition to the Students' Series, and I shall cordially recommend it as a first dictionary to our students. — Hon. Edmund H. Bennett, *Dean of School of Law, Boston University.*

GLOSSARY OF TECHNICAL TERMS, PHRASES, AND MAXIMS OF THE COMMON LAW. — By FREDERIC JESUP STIMSON. 12mo. Cloth, $2.50 *net*; law sheep, $3.00 *net*.

A *concise* Law Dictionary, giving in common English an explanation of the words and phrases, English as well as Saxon, Latin, or French, which are of common technical use in the law.

The information crowded by Mr. Stimson in his duodecimo volume of a little more than three hundred pages, is very great; his explanations are given with remarkable brevity, and legal technicalities are avoided so completely as to make the work a valuable and welcome supplement to the common English Dictionaries. — *Boston Daily Advertiser.*

X. ROBINSON'S ELEMENTARY LAW.

The book is convenient to the instructor who will use it as a text to be amplified in his lectures, and valuable to the student who will consult the references. — Prof. M. F. Force, LL.D., *Cincinnati Law School.*

ELEMENTARY LAW. — By WILLIAM C. ROBINSON, LL.D., Professor of Elementary Law in Yale College. 12mo. Cloth, $2.50 *net*; law sheep, $3.00 *net*.

It contains a statement of the principles, rules, and definitions of American Common Law, both civil and criminal, arranged in logical order, with references to treatises in which such definitions, rules, and principles are more extensively discussed.

This volume is used largely in law schools, and the author has a special knowledge of the requirements of the student, being a leading instructor at the Law School of Yale College. The student who intelligently studies this work may store his mind with lucid and concise statements of the leading topics of law; and, having been grounded in this primary information, a course of reading is laid down, including the best text-books together with the special portions of the works which relate to the subjects in question. It may also be used with great benefit as a review book for examinations. The purpose of this most useful elementary work cannot better be explained than by here reprinting, from page 33, Section 61, relating to Transfer of Estates: —

SECTION 61. OF THE OWNERSHIP AND TRANSFER OF ESTATES.

An estate may belong to one person or to several persons collectively. It may also be transmitted from one person to another, or lesser estates may be carved out of it by the owner and be granted to others. The relation between co-owners or successive owners of the same estate, or between persons one of whom derives his estate from the other, is known as *privity of estate.*

Read 2 Bl. Comm., pp. 107, 179, 200, 201.
    1 Wash. R. P., B. i, Ch. xiii, Sec. 1, § 1.
    2 Wash. R. P., B. ii, Ch. i. Sec. 1, § 16.
    1 Greenl. Ev., §§ 189, 523.

The principles are admirably stated. — *Albany Law Journal.*

It would be a benefit to every law student to put this volume into his hand, and make it his *vade mecum* throughout the whole of his professional studies. — *Boston Advertiser.*

It might worthily be adopted as a text-book for every senior class in a male or female college, and will be found an invaluable accession to every public and private library. — *New York World.*

XI. EWELL'S MEDICAL JURISPRUDENCE.

It is excellently done. I wish it might be read by every student of law as well as by every student of medicine. — *Prof. Henry Wade Rogers, University of Michigan.*

A MANUAL OF MEDICAL JURISPRUDENCE FOR THE USE OF STUDENTS AT LAW AND OF MEDICINE. — By MARSHALL D. EWELL, M.D., LL.D., of the Union College of Law, Chicago. 12mo. Cloth, $2.50 *net;* law sheep, $3.00 *net.*

Mr. Ewell has endeavored to produce a work which, *within a moderate compass,* states all the leading facts and principles of the science concisely and yet clearly. In it will be found *the substance of all the principles stated in the more voluminous and expensive works.*

XII. STEPHEN'S DIGEST OF EVIDENCE.

Short as it is, I believe it will be found to contain practically the whole law of the subject. — *The author.*

A DIGEST OF THE LAW OF EVIDENCE. — By Sir JAMES FITZJAMES STEPHEN, K.C.S.I., a Judge of the High Court of Justice, Queen's Bench Division. From the Fourth English Edition. With Notes and Additional Illustrations to the Present Time, chiefly from American Cases, including those of JOHN WILDER MAY, late Chief Justice of the Municipal Court of the City of Boston, author of "The Law of Insurance," etc. 12mo. 251 pages. Cloth, $2.50 *net;* law sheep, $3.00 *net.*

A full and exact reprint of the Fourth (latest) English Edition, revised by the author, with references to American cases. Many editions of the work have been published in America, but the present will be found to be the most useful, as it includes the very valuable notes prepared by the late John Wilder May, author of "The Law of Crimes," etc., together with a selection of cases and references supplementing his important editorial work.

XIII. ROBINSON'S FORENSIC ORATORY.

This is a book which no student of law can afford to pass by without a thorough study of it. It is also a work which no practising lawyer who understands the trial of causes and is not already an acknowledged leader in the courts, can afford not to read and read again.— *American Law Review.*

FORENSIC ORATORY: A MANUAL FOR ADVOCATES. — By William C. Robinson, Professor of Elementary Law in Yale College, author of "The Law of Patents for Useful Inventions," "Elementary Law," etc. 12mo. Cloth, $2.50 *net*; law sheep, $3.00 *net*.

A new and suggestive work on the Duties and Functions of the Advocate. The chapters on the Presentation of Ideas by the Production of Evidence in Court, the Qualification and Training of Witnesses, and on Direct, Cross, and Re-Direct Examination, commend the book especially to the bar as well as to students.

XIV. BIGELOW'S BILLS, NOTES, AND CHEQUES.

ELEMENTS OF THE LAW OF BILLS, NOTES, AND CHEQUES — By Melville M. Bigelow, Ph.D., author of "Element of the Law of Torts," etc. 12mo. Cloth, $2.50 *net*; law sheep, $3.00 *net*.

Mr. Bigelow's reputation as a clear, logical, and strong student and instructor in the law is established by his standard treatises no less than by the masterly "Elements of Torts," so well known to and extensively used by teachers and students of law. To the preparation of the "Bills and Notes" he has given much time, labor, and research. No better book on the elements of the subject has been offered to the student or practitioner. It is a discussion of the *Elements of the Law of Bills and Notes,* not an elementary treatise in the sense of touching on the simpler questions only. The groundwork of the law, complex as well as simple, is discussed fully, clearly, and exhaustively. Cases that are really *leading cases* are referred to in sufficient number to illustrate and support the points of law stated.

I believe it to be decidedly the best student's book upon the subject that has yet appeared. — *Prof. F. R. Mechem, Law Department, Michigan State University.*

I regard it as an admirable Treatise. — *Prof. N. Green, Cumberland University, Lebanon, Tenn.*

I am very glad to have found it eminently satisfactory. It is the best work of its class that I have seen. It exhibits the very desirable mean between too little and too much, which so many elementary text writers fail to attain. — *Prof. W. M. Lile, Law Department, University of Virginia.*

I know of no book that I would put in the hands of a student before Bigelow. — *Prof. D. D. Banta, Indiana University Law School, Bloomington, Ind.*

Mr. Bigelow's book is a convenient manual of the law of bills and notes, and his explanations of the unwritten customs of banks and notaries in this country give it an added value. — *Prof. Simeon E. Baldwin, Law Department, Yale University, New Haven, Conn.*

To accompany the foregoing work:

CASES ON THE LAW OF BILLS, NOTES, AND CHEQUES. — Edited by MELVILLE M. BIGELOW. To accompany "The Elements of the Law of Bills, Notes, and Cheques." Crown 8vo. Cloth, $3.00 *net*.

Recognizing the necessity of the close study of cases, and the difficulty experienced by the greater number of students in getting control of the volumes of reports, for more than a passing examination, if at all, Mr. Bigelow has collected eighty or ninety cases which he deems most useful for the purpose of analytical study of the subject, and embodied them in this book.

The most *instructive* cases, those most clearly reasoned and most plainly decided, have been chosen, because they were *clear* and *instructive*. Neither have the most ancient or always the most recent been taken, for either of those reasons, but those best calculated to teach the student how and why the point of law under consideration was settled.

XV. BRYANT ON CODE PLEADING.

The science of Code Pleading being a development of the last fifty years, and getting its shape and form gradually from the decisions of the courts as well as from the enactments of the law-making bodies, it is only within a few years that text writers have treated it in any satisfactory way.

THE LAW OF PLEADING UNDER THE CODES OF CIVIL PROCEDURE. — With an Introduction briefly explaining the Common Law and Equity Systems of Pleading, and an Analytical Index, in which is given the Code Provisions as to Pleading in each of the States which have adopted the Reformed Procedure. — By Hon. EDWIN E. BRYANT, Dean of Law Department of State University of Wisconsin, and late Assistant Attorney-General of the United States. 12mo. Cloth, $2.50 *net*; law sheep, $3.00 *net*.

The present work has been prepared to bring within easy reach, in condensed and clear form, the true elements of the subject; to give the student sufficient knowledge of the old Common Law Pleading for a foundation for the less formal, but not necessarily less exact pleading under the Code, and to put in orderly array the principles of this branch of the law, which have too frequently been considered, by students at least, as of little importance; to cite and indicate for more careful and particular reading those cases deciding the important points, and give a comparative table of the different State Codes on the more important subjects.

XVI. ABBOTT'S LAW OF WILLS.

ELEMENTS OF THE LAW OF WILLS. — By NATHAN ABBOTT, Professor of Wills, etc., at Northwestern University, Chicago. 12mo. Cloth, $2.50 *net*; law sheep, $3.00 *net*. (*In preparation.*)

LITTLE, BROWN, & CO., Publishers,
254 WASHINGTON STREET, BOSTON.

www.ingramcontent.com/pod-product-compliance
Lightning Source LLC
Chambersburg PA
CBHW030258240426
43673CB00040B/991